MAGNUM

OPUS

MAGNUM OPUS

THE CYCLE PLAYS

OF EUGENE O'NEILL

Zander Brietzke

Yale

UNIVERSITY PRESS

New Haven & London

Published with assistance from the Kingsley Trust Association
Publication Fund established by the Scroll and Key Society of
Yale College, and from the foundation established in memory of
Philip Hamilton McMillan of the Class of 1894, Yale College.

Yale University Press books may be purchased in quantity for
educational, business, or promotional use. For information, please e-mail
sales.press@yale.edu (U.S. office) or sales@yaleup.co.uk (U.K. office).

Set in type by Newgen North America.
Printed in the United States of America.

Library of Congress Control Number: 2020943126
ISBN 978-0-300-24847-0 (hardcover : alk. paper)

An earlier version of Chapter 6 appeared in the *Eugene O'Neill Review* (Vol. 40,
no. 1, 2019) as "Sara Melody: Stripped Stark Naked in the Cycle," by Zander
Brietzke. Copyright © 2019 The Pennsylvania State University, University Park,
PA. This article is used by permission of the Pennsylvania State University Press.

A catalogue record for this book is available from the British Library.

This paper meets the requirements of ANSI/NISO
z39.48-1992 (Permanence of Paper).
10 9 8 7 6 5 4 3 2 1

With admiration for the groundbreaking research of Martha Gilman Bower,

in memory of my Irish mama, Hazel Riley,

and for Carol, the One

For what shall it profit a man, if he shall gain

the whole world, and lose his own soul?

—*Mark 8:36 (KJV)*

CONTENTS

CONTENTS

PREFACE

I heard a very interesting paper by Martha Gilman Bower about *More Stately Mansions* at a Eugene O'Neill conference in Tours, France, in 2003. Confusion surrounded the three versions of the play that existed. Bower discussed how she had discovered O'Neill's original typescript in the 1980s at the Beinecke Rare Book and Manuscript Library at Yale University, and she enumerated the significant problems she encountered before and after Oxford University Press published her unexpurgated version of the play. The new happy ending, she announced, was that Yale University Press had just contracted her to edit both *A Touch of the Poet* and *More Stately Mansions* in a combined softcover volume. I eventually published her account of these events in my inaugural issue as editor of the *Eugene O'Neill Review* in 2004.

Much of what I thought I knew about *More Stately Mansions* turned out to be wrong. Although I did know that it was one of the Cycle plays— O'Neill's history of America through the lives of a single family—I had never contemplated the significant differences between Bower's version of the play and the previously published edition that was only about a third as long, or the 1967 Broadway production script that was even shorter. O'Neill, I had read in all his biographies, wanted to destroy the play with the rest of his unfinished Cycle plays. His decision was good enough for me at that time. *The Aesthetics of Failure* (McFarland, 2001), my previous monograph on O'Neill, had discounted the play as unworthy of serious study.

I could certainly not name the other plays of the proposed Cycle. The number ranged from as few as four to as many as eleven different plays. I knew *A Touch of the Poet*, but I had not read any of the other nine plays. Had O'Neill burned them all? What was left? I could not keep track of all the various and variant titles. Many of them sounded the same. O'Neill did not start at the beginning of his family saga and write chronologically to the end. The story started somewhere in the middle, then moved forward in time, and then receded well before the original starting point for the rest of the plays. And, to make matters worse, O'Neill frequently switched titles between one play and another, making it very difficult to discern what play he was working on at a given time. Trying to figure out the intricacies of the whole thing seemed too big a mystery. The game was not worth the candle.

Ten years later, Felicia Hardison Londré invited me to write an essay on O'Neill's late plays for her book *Modern American Drama: Playwriting in the 1940s* (Bloomsbury, 2018). In search of a focal point for that article, something that might come across as both fresh and familiar, I considered intimate relationships and seized upon the female characters, including Sara Melody in *A Touch of the Poet*. I liked her dramatic split between passionate love for Simon Harford and greedy desire to climb economically and socially in the United States. Marriage becomes her means to make it, but she still loves her husband completely, if possessively, at the same time.

Sara's story just gets started in *A Touch of the Poet*. *More Stately Mansions* is the sequel and picks up where the first play ends. Piqued by my initial interest in Sara as an unusually complex female character, I began to see her as the hero of the two plays. Moreover, I began to see the Cycle as only these two plays and Sara as the central figure. Research at the Beinecke convinced me that the two extant plays with Sara could represent the rest of the planned Cycle as one epic event. The Eugene O'Neill Society hosted a conference in Galway, Ireland, fictional birthplace of Sara

Melody, in 2017 and gave me an opportunity to introduce her as the protagonist of the Cycle.

Behind my portrait of Sara in the Cycle lurks the specter of my mother. She died as I finished the essay on women in the late O'Neill plays, and I have no doubt that this book attempts both to recreate her life and to mourn her passing. O'Neill clearly projected his childhood into *More Stately Mansions* with the mother-son relationship between Deborah and Simon. Ironically, I have paid short shrift to that bond in this study. That I did not pursue it is either a case of truth hitting too close to home, or simply a feeling of having been there and done that. That I transformed my mother into Sara rather than Deborah, into who she might have been instead of who she was, is a bit of dramatic license and wish fulfillment on my part. I have tried to project an image of Sara as a woman with a flattering array of attractive qualities as well as some significant flaws.

Beyond a personal psychodrama, the present cultural moment seems right for an epic work to critique rampant greed and capitalism run amuck. O'Neill suggests that Sara knows the very simple solution to the severe situation in which she leads her family. He leaves it to the reader to figure it out as well. I have tried to write a book with a possible production in mind. Drawing on my training as an actor and a director and a scholar, *Magnum Opus: The Cycle Plays of Eugene O'Neill* invites an audience to ponder its role in these turbulent times.

ACKNOWLEDGMENTS

I am grateful for the unflagging support, criticism, and encouragement of the Eugene O'Neill Society throughout the development of this project. In particular, Dave King pored over the first draft and generously shared his lively questions, comments, considerable expertise, and unmatched copyediting skills. Beth Wynstra, a welcome ray of sunshine on academia, urged me through multiple drafts of the introductory chapter and did not let me settle for less than I could do. Dan and Carolyn McGovern of the Eugene O'Neill Foundation in Danville, California, patiently endured my talk and talk about the book and forced me out of my bad habit to bury the lead. Rob Dowling, the current president of the O'Neill Society, endorsed my book proposal and weathered both the first and third drafts of the manuscript with good cheer, critical insights, and unwavering optimism. The new editor of the *Eugene O'Neill Review*, Alex Pettit, took hold of the second draft and strengthened and streamlined the argument. He elegantly guided a revision of Chapter 6, "Stripped Stark Naked," for publication as an article in the fall 2019 issue of the journal. Patrick Midgley, the new secretary of the Society, took time away from his dissertation to review the third draft. In addition to his positive feedback, he included nine pages of notes in his report for me to consider at a time when I could no longer see the manuscript with fresh eyes.

Library staffs at the Stephen A. Schwarzman Building of the New York Public Library, the Billy Rose Theatre Division of the New York Public Library for the Performing Arts, and the Museum of the City of New York provided excellent assistance for my research. In a pinch, Ryder Thornton sent me images from his personal collection that I would not have been able to procure otherwise. Without my asking, Joel Pfister emailed a relevant excerpt from his book *Surveyors of Customs* that anticipated my argument. I owe special thanks to Melissa Barton, Curator, Prose and Drama, Yale Collection of American Literature, and the entire staff at the Beinecke Rare Book and Manuscript Library in New Haven, Connecticut. I spent a highly productive week examining the Cycle materials among the Eugene O'Neill Papers at Yale in late November 2017. The discoveries that I made there would not have been possible without the polite efficiency and helpfulness of everyone, from clerk to security officer, at the Beinecke. Finally, I am thankful for my wife, Carol, who supports all of my projects, financially and spiritually, from first thought to last dot.

MAGNUM
OPUS

INTRODUCTION

EIGHT HUNDRED MILLION NOTES

AND BUT TWO PLAYS DONE

In act 4 of *More Stately Mansions,* Sara Melody Harford stares at architectural drawings for an enormous Irish-castle-in-Spain that she hopes to build in New England. Construction would be a sign of her material success and also revenge against the Yankee elite who despised her parents as poor and lowly immigrants. Possessed by these twin goals, she dreams aloud:

> Stables full of thoroughbred hunters and fast trotters! Me the great lady, full of airs and graces, riding in my carriage with coachman and footman, through the castle park, or out past the lodge down the road to the city, with the crowds on the street staring, their hearts eaten with envy, and the shopkeepers bowing and scraping, and me gazing down my nose at them, and at the whole pack of the meek, weak, timid, poor poverty-stricken beggars of life! No one will ever dare sneer at my origin then, or my poverty! By the Eternal God, I'll spit in their faces and laugh when they thank me kindly for the favor! No! I don't mean it! God forgive me, what makes me say such evil, spiteful things? They're not in my dream at all! All I want is a safe home for our love—and peace![1]

Sara catches what she says and tries to take it back, but she cannot let go completely her pride and ambition. Her marriage to the man whose parents destroyed her father complicates and confuses her motives: she loves Simon Harford but vows to get even with his rich family in the name of Cornelius Melody. The balance between love for the one and hatred for the others spawns an epic struggle. Love wins in the end but with a wicked twist.

Eugene O'Neill (1888–1953) conceived this play in the 1930s as just one part of his most ambitious drama, longer than the nine acts of *Strange Interlude* or the trilogy of *Mourning Becomes Electra,* the story of America through seven generations of a family from the colonial period to the present day. He called the series of plays required to tell the whole story his Cycle because each one circulated the essential theme: the corrosive effects of greed and materialism upon the individual and nation. The initial plan called for four plays, each focused on one of four brothers in the second half of the 1800s. Quickly, though, O'Neill decided to involve their parents and added a fifth play to show how they met, and then a sixth play to dramatize their marriage and introduce their sons as small boys. Then, he added a seventh play that began at the turn of the twentieth century and ran almost to the time in which O'Neill wrote. Having gone as far forward as he could go, he next went back in history to feature the grandmother of the boys as a young woman. Finally, he added a ninth play that went even further back to depict the three great aunts of the four boys. O'Neill considered abandoning these last two plays due to their excessive length, but changed his mind and decided in 1940, between drafts of *Long Day's Journey Into Night,* to divide and rewrite them as four separate plays. The final tally for the Cycle reached eleven.

Of that number, he completed only *A Touch of the Poet* and *More Stately Mansions,* the two plays on which he spent the most time and the only ones for which he composed multiple drafts. Still, these two plays, plays 5 and 6 of the eleven-play Cycle, represent the core of the entire project (see "The Eleven-Play Lineup" in the back matter of this book). They fit seamlessly together and allude to the family's past and project its future as they convincingly express the biblical theme: "For what shall it profit a man, if he shall gain the whole world, and lose his own soul?"[2] Sara, the mother of the four sons, and the only character to play a major role in both dramas, emerges as the protagonist, whose ambition, gender, ethnicity, and complexity present a unique slant on the hollowness of the American Dream. Depicting the years 1828–1842, *A Touch of the Poet* and *More Stately Mansions* cap O'Neill's critique of materialism that started with *Desire Under the Elms* (1924), *Marco Millions* (1924), and *The Great God Brown* (1925) and complement, but do not anticipate, *The Iceman Cometh* (1940), *Long Day's Journey Into Night* (1941), and *A Moon for the Misbegotten* (1943) at the end of his career.

The two Cycle dramas, considered together as a single event, differ thematically and stylistically from O'Neill's final plays and deserve separate consideration. *A Touch of the Poet* adheres to the tenets of realism, but *More Stately Mansions* draws upon theatrical devices from earlier periods of O'Neill's career to visualize the swell of avarice and possessiveness among the characters. Extravagant monologues, thought asides to the audience, grand gestures, and physical transformations manifest as symptoms of spiritual decay. After years drag by in the family saga, the principal characters ultimately purge the sickness from their systems and theatrical style reverts once again to that of *A Touch of the Poet*. Swings in theatrical style between the two plays actually express structural unity. In a flash, though, the final image reveals that the survivor, Sara, has received not a cure for her affliction, but only a momentary stay: the epilogue forecasts another future outbreak of greed.

In an epic that resembles more a novel than a drama in terms of length, the Cycle tried to leave nothing for a potential performance to add. O'Neill's antitheatrical prejudice, however, created a theoretical problem that only a theatrical production could solve. The illusion of depth that O'Neill wanted to create required the simultaneous staging of thoughts and feelings in conflict within and between characters. The only way for O'Neill to express the teeming world of action, however, was to write word after word in a linear sequence that belied the very simultaneity of experience that he sought to represent. For that, he needed theater . . . but not in his lifetime.

Neither *A Touch of the Poet* nor *More Stately Mansions* received a stage production prior to O'Neill's death in 1953. The Theatre Guild, O'Neill's regular producer in New York, announced plans to stage several of the other Cycle plays and eventually leaked the titles of all eleven to the *New York Times*. But O'Neill did not deliver a single script. He felt that he needed to finish several plays before releasing even one for performance. O'Neill intended each play of the entire Cycle to stand independently but also form part of a link between one play and the next. Changes made on one play caused a chain reaction that required additional adjustments for other plays in the sequence. He could never get the whole thing to fit together.

The history plays of August Wilson (1945–2005) provide comparative insight into the problems O'Neill faced in terms of construction. Wilson wrote his own "cycle" of African-American history in the twentieth century by staging a separate play to represent each decade of the century. It is referred to as the Pittsburgh Cycle because all but one of the plays are set in the Hill District there. Wilson, like O'Neill, did not write chronologically, but started with *Jitney* (1970s) in 1979, then moved to *Ma Rainey's Black Bottom* (1920s) in 1981, *Joe Turner's Come and Gone* (1910s) in 1984, *Fences* (1950s) in 1987, and finally *Radio Golf* (1990s) in 2005.[3] Over almost 25 years, then, Wilson dramatized Black lives in ten separate plays, but he did not mandate connections between them. Rather, the plays weave a tapestry on the variations and even idiosyncrasies but essential dignity of individuals who had rarely received attention on any stage in this country. O'Neill, by contrast, tried to follow the descendants of a single family through the years. That he started in the middle and moved forward and backward in time meant that he had to adjust constantly plans for all the plays whenever he decided to change a single play. In the end, O'Neill could only make the two plays in the center cohere.

Andrew E. Lee articulated a point about *More Stately Mansions* that applies to O'Neill's entire Cycle project: "The real dilemma here seems to be the choice between assessing the play based on O'Neill's intentions and judging it based on the result of those intentions."[4] O'Neill paved the way of the Cycle with plenty of good intentions—and notes and comments and outlines and heady plans for this and that. His completed output, however, came to one normal-length play, *A Touch of the Poet*, and one extraordinarily long play, *More Stately Mansions*. O'Neill kept a work diary for twenty years, from 1924 until he stopped writing in 1943.[5] Each page of the four volumes allows space to make entries for a single date on five consecutive years (see Fig. 3 in Chapter 1). O'Neill used the diaries to monitor his output and record progress each day on a particular project. He also noted if he did no work, or if he were sick, and if the work went well or not. With respect to the Cycle plays, O'Neill's *Work Diary* shows definitively what engaged him at any time and shows what pleased him and what did not. It reveals what caught his attention and fired his imagination as well as what stymied him. He had trouble making some of the plays come out right; he was never pleased with the first drafts of "Greed of the Meek" or "And Give Me Death" and frequently noted that he felt "stuck" and/or "depressed" working on them.[6] By contrast, the entries on *A Touch of the Poet* and *More Stately Mansions* record steady progress toward eventual completion.

The sheer numbers present a convincing case for O'Neill's preoccupation with the two middle plays. He wrote the bulk of the Cycle in four and a half years between January 1935 and June 1939. He spent 225 days writing *A Touch of the Poet* and worked another 350 days on *More Stately Mansions*.[7] He only devoted a total of 445 days to the rest of the Cycle during that period. The combined efforts on the two central plays represented much more than half of his total number of working days.[8] That percentage actually went up after O'Neill turned his primary attention to *The Iceman Cometh* and *Long Day's Journey Into Night*. O'Neill spent sixty days total on notes for revising his Cycle in 1940, first in January and then again in October through December at the end of the year. In 1941, he worked a total of only fourteen days on the Cycle for the whole year. By contrast, he spent 150 days on the final draft of *A Touch of the Poet* in 1942, two-thirds of his total work time devoted to the Cycle during the final phase of his writing career.[9]

O'Neill completed four drafts of *A Touch of the Poet* between 1935 and 1942. He revised the last one when he realized that he would not write any more plays and coordinated it with the sequel, *More Stately Mansions*, which he completed in three consecutive drafts over just ten months that ended in January 1939. These two plays, together, comprise the extant Cycle. They *are* the Cycle. Even though they represent only a fraction of what O'Neill proposed, they are themselves massive in size and scope and combine to tell a complete story.

A Touch of the Poet focuses on the Melody family, Irish immigrants, and the patriarch's inability to adapt to life in America and his unwillingness to let go of his pride and humble himself among his new countrymen. The plot revolves around his daughter Sara's desire to rise in the world through marriage to a rich Yankee named Simon Harford, the titular character who does not even appear onstage in the final version of the play.[10] Their relationship is the subject of the sequel, *More Stately Mansions,* in which Sara, now married to Simon four years later, inherits the Harford estate and dreams of an even more grand domain to signal her success and triumph. Sara perseveres as an attractive character, though, in spite of O'Neill's intent to demonize her as "unscrupulous."[11] In my reading of the combined plays, Sara emerges as the hero, not Simon, despite what O'Neill might have originally conceived when he planned the plays as discrete units.

Sara seems remarkably similar to another heroic female character, Maggie, in Tennessee Williams's *Cat on a Hot Tin Roof.* The prototype for this character appeared first in Williams's short story "Three Players of a Summer Game" (1952), in which a wife completely emasculates her husband and seems not to care for him at all. In the course of writing the play, however, Williams's estimation of the character changed, and she developed nuance that refreshed the action. Maggie embodies the future as Sara does in *More Stately Mansions.* Born into poverty, both characters resort to devious tactics to secure a footing in the rock of the world. They marry wealth in order to climb. As Maggie says, "You can be young without money but you can't be old without it."[12] Simon, rich and privileged, always has a soft place to land; Sara does not have the same cushion. The same is true for Margaret and her marriage to Brick Pollitt. *Cat on a Hot Tin Roof* questions Maggie's love for her husband. Whether she does or does not love him influences an interpretation of what transpires.[13] The same question hovers over *A Touch of the Poet* and *More Stately Mansions* as well. Sara loves Simon and she also loves material success. These amalgamated desires drive the action. Much as the title *Cat on a Hot Tin Roof* represents a metaphor for the slippery nature of truth and refers to Margaret, *More Stately Mansions* alludes to the acquisitive instinct best embodied by Sara Melody Harford.

O'Neill authored a number of strong female characters throughout his career, but none can match Sara's dynamic force of will. In *Beyond the Horizon,* his first big success and winner of the Pulitzer Prize in 1920, a romantic dreamer longs to leave his family farm and see the wonders of the world, but the natural beauty of a sunset and the girl-next-door divert his focus and he gives up his lifetime dream in an instant to settle down and marry her, an impulsive yet fateful decision that ruins both of their lives. Similarly, the eponymous heroine of *"Anna Christie"* (Pulitzer Prize, 1922), a hardened prostitute, comes clean in the ocean air, but agrees to a dubious marriage contract just as she asserts her freedom. In *Desire Under the Elms,* Abbie Putnam schemes to take possession of the Cabot farm, but sacrifices her stake and her life, potentially, when she tries to prove her love for her husband's son (a deadly compound of Euripides' *Hippolytus* and *Medea*). O'Neill's third Pulitzer winner of the decade, *Strange Interlude* (1927), presented Nina Leeds as a woman who regretted her failure to consummate her love for her fiancé before he was killed in the First World War. Nina goes on to use men in various combinations to recreate her ideal, lost man. Her son, the very image and even namesake of the former lover, literally flies away with another woman at the end and leaves his mother alone once again to ponder the ways in which her preoccupation with the past stole her future. Finally, Lavinia Mannon, the protagonist of *Mourning Becomes Electra* (1931), O'Neill's remake of Aeschylus's *Oresteia,* desires to live freely from the sexual repression of New England Puritanism, but ultimately conforms to family obligations and clings to the dead.

The development of female characters traces O'Neill's growth as a playwright. Ruth Atkins, for starters, functions primarily as a blocking agent to Robert Mayo's happiness in *Beyond the Horizon.* She marries him because he is different from her and from anyone she knows, but she does not understand him and assumes that he will be a productive farmer and contented family man because that is what she wants.[14] In these respects, then, Ruth is very similar to Maud Steele in O'Neill's first full-length play, *Bread and Butter,* who loves John Brown, but expects him to forget about his dreams of becoming a serious artist once he marries her. His artistic sensibility appeals to her, so long as it does not interfere with him working hard in business to earn a good standard of living for them. In another early one-act, *Before Breakfast* (1916), modeled after Strindberg's *The Stronger,* a young woman harangues her offstage husband, who is shaving in the bathroom, about his inability or unwillingness to provide for her. Alfred slashes his throat at the end of her lengthy monologue. John Brown, too, kills himself at the end of *Bread and Butter.* Robert Mayo dies of tuberculosis at the end of *Beyond the Horizon,* but he takes responsibility for what happened to him and even begs Ruth not to blame herself. In a change that reflects O'Neill's progress as a playwright, Robert reasons that their marriage was a bad match from the beginning and that she should have married his brother instead of him.

The female characters in the four other plays, though, display much greater levels of agency and complexity than Ruth. O'Neill always took the side of the underdog in his plays, and he shows great sympathy for his female characters who must often toil under the reign of men who, at worst, exploit them, but even at best do not understand them or even once consider their needs. Anna Christopherson, for example, became a prostitute because her father abandoned her and did not recognize the signs of abuse from other family members. Anna gives voice to her hatred of all men in the third act in a monologue that presents her as an unwilling victim who had to submit to the sexual demands of men because she had no other options. Abbie, too, made her fateful decision in *Desire Under the Elms* to sacrifice her child because Eben would not listen to her. She transforms in the play, though, from a greedy opportunist to a woman with a moral conscience willing to accept responsibility for her actions. Nina Leeds also learns something about the world and herself in her passionate quest to recreate her dead lover, and ultimately forgives herself and seeks forgiveness. Lavinia, one of O'Neill's favorite characters, does not ask forgiveness from anyone for anything. She inters herself among the Mannons in their mansion rather than face public scrutiny. She struggled to break free of her family, but ultimately decides to preside over the dead as her fate.

Judith Barlow wrongly casts the "earthy Sara" in *A Touch of the Poet* and *More Stately Mansions* as a familiar figure and "nothing new in O'Neill's canon."[15] Sara possesses an assorted complex of qualities, virtues and vices, that go beyond mere greed or true love. She shares some of the anger of the former prostitute Anna in *"Anna Christie,"* but she does not present herself as a victim in the way that the earlier character does, although she, too, suffers from a deluded father and a seemingly weak mother. Sara bears guilt throughout events of the Cycle, but it does not spring from a single source as it does for Nina Leeds. Nina's guilt, stemming from the loss of her fiancé, propels all the action in *Strange Interlude*. Sara retains aspects of a tragic character, but she does not let notions of fate or destiny drag her down as Lavinia does in the modern remake of Aeschylus's trilogy.

Sara Melody is most similar to Abbie Putnam in *Desire Under the Elms,* who seems both to be greedy to possess her new home as hers alone and to love her new son-in-law passionately. Abbie, however, undergoes a transformation in the development of the play from gold digger, always redolent of desperation, to a woman willing to make any sacrifice to prove her worthiness. She moves from one state to the other. Sara possesses these traits as well, but rather than exhibit them in sequential fashion, first one and then the other, her greed for money and love for Simon play concurrently from beginning to end. She displays a mixture of warring attributes that humanizes her. Befitting a protagonist on par with Lavinia Mannon, Sara ultimately realizes that she must put a stop to certain behaviors in order to preserve the safety of her family, and her decisions force a change of events and a different outcome than would have been possible without her self-reckoning.

Despite the sprawl of the planned Cycle, O'Neill wrote the two extant plays in relatively short order. Publicity around the Nobel Prize slowed him down in November 1936, and illness landed him in Oakland's Merritt Hospital in late December. Diagnosed with appendicitis, he underwent the standard procedure after Christmas, but a postoperative infection nearly killed him: "Temp up to 102 — chill — caffeine, adrenalin, codeine, morphine, at[r]opine! — they give me the works! — Carlotta [O'Neill's wife] & nurses up all night — Dukes [his doctor] at 4 am — bad sinking spell with everyone worried but I feel too sick and ratty to give a damn whether I croak or not."[16] When he recovered, though, and especially after he moved almost a year later into his new home, Tao House, in Danville, California, he resumed work on his Cycle with a vengeance. In anticipation of the progress he hoped to make, he informed critic Barrett Clark that all the prospective plays were "well thought out and scenarioed with much detail. And eight hundred million notes — more or less!"[17] Carlotta Monterey O'Neill, whom O'Neill claimed was the only person in the world who could decipher his minuscule handwriting, finished typing what she called the first play of the Cycle, *A Touch of the Poet* (the second draft), on 30 April 1938. She began to type *More Stately Mansions,* what she called the second play of the Cycle, on 17 May.[18] O'Neill had only begun his first handwritten draft the previous month, and he had never asked Carlotta to type his other plays before he had finished at least a first draft. He must have been very confident about the new play—with a relatively good run of health, he wrote fast and furiously.

After finishing the third drafts of *More Stately Mansions* and *A Touch of the Poet* by May 1939, O'Neill turned to *The Iceman Cometh* and *Long Day's Journey Into Night*, a couple of memory plays from his youth, and essentially put the Cycle on the shelf. O'Neill claimed that he was tired of working on the Cycle and that he wanted to pursue some other projects that had been on his mind for a while. Most scholars and biographers, though, ascribe more complicated, psychological reasons for the abrupt break between the historical Cycle plays and the final plays. A group that includes Travis Bogard, Arthur and Barbara Gelb, Virginia Floyd, Normand Berlin, Donald Gallup, and Martha Gilman Bower, often at loggerheads with one another on other key points of interpretation, agree that the Cycle represented an important interlude in O'Neill's dramatic development and that it occupied him until he felt emotionally prepared to write the masterworks about his own family.[19] The Cycle plays can be seen in this view as rough drafts of the final plays, and the historical figures and characterizations in them as nothing more than the O'Neills or Tyrones dressed up in period costumes. This argument assumes that O'Neill wanted to write about his family honestly and that it took him his whole life to summon the courage to do so. It overlooks the fact that *The Iceman Cometh* directly abuts *More Stately Mansions* in O'Neill's chronology of composition and that, while drawn from O'Neill's experiences and acquaintances as a young man in New York, it is definitely not a family play.

Occam's razor generates the third and simplest and therefore best reason for O'Neill's shift away from the Cycle: he had nothing more to say on the subject after he finished a discrete unit of work. Despite bouts of illness, including the debilitating and degenerative tremor that would ultimately defeat him, and despite depression brought on by the gloom of world war, O'Neill managed to complete six plays in six years at Tao House (1938–1943)—tremendous achievements, especially given the variety of experience and the expertise of construction displayed first in *A Touch of the Poet* and then in *More Stately Mansions, The Iceman Cometh, Long Day's Journey Into Night,* the one-act *Hughie,* and *A Moon for the Misbegotten.* This formidable string of great works compares favorably to the output of any other playwright except Shakespeare. O'Neill wrote these plays against the great odds of deteriorating health and the usual trajectory of a literary career. How many artists create their finest works after accepting what amounts to a lifetime achievement award?[20]

While *A Touch of the Poet* only hints at the themes of greed and possessiveness that O'Neill elaborates more fully in *More Stately Mansions,* there is no question about the former play's completeness or integrity. The Royal Dramatic Theatre of Sweden staged the premiere production in 1957, and Yale University Press published the play later that same year. It has been produced many times on its own since then, although it suffers apart from the context of the sequel. *More Stately Mansions* reveals much more clearly than *A Touch of the Poet* the direction for the Cycle that O'Neill had in mind. But, while O'Neill thought about producing and publishing *A Touch of the Poet* at the end of his career, he never considered doing the same for *More Stately Mansions.* O'Neill labeled the play "unfinished" and left instructions to destroy the script in the case of his death. The O'Neills "inadvertently" included the play in a large box of materials sent to the Eugene O'Neill Collection at Yale in 1951.[21] The original typescript, with many, many revisions in the playwright's hand, resides in the Yale Collection of American Literature at the Beinecke Rare Book and Manuscript Library. Martha Gilman Bower, who has studied the original typescript more than anyone else, argued against O'Neill and claimed that it was finished and lacked only a few changes that the dramatist likely would have made in the rehearsal process; Stephen A. Black, an O'Neill biographer, took the middle ground to declare the play "not-quite-finished."[22] This study sides unequivocally with Bower and regards O'Neill's disclaimer as contrary to what his *Work Diary* and Carlotta's personal diary suggest. They sent the typescript to Yale on purpose.

In full, *More Stately Mansions* remains the longest play that O'Neill ever wrote and would require ten to twelve hours to perform. Shortened abridgements, though not by O'Neill, appeared onstage and in print long before the public realized the existence of the much longer original. The Royal Dramatic Theatre of Sweden received permission from O'Neill's widow, literary executrix of her husband's estate, to cut the manuscript to fit the demands of a theatrical audience with the proviso that they use not one word that was not O'Neill's. Donald Gallup, curator of the Yale

Collection of American Literature at the Beinecke Library for over thirty years, developed a close friendship with Carlotta and got rights from her to produce a "reading" version of the play based on the Swedish production script. Having first been cut and translated from English to Swedish, the play was now subjected to the reverse process: Gallup, with the help of a Swedish dictionary, made a new translation/adaptation, moving back from Swedish to English. This version, published in 1964, served as the basis for a further adaptation of the play in 1967 when José Quintero, the leading director of O'Neill at that time, staged an even shorter version in Los Angeles and on Broadway with Colleen Dewhurst, Arthur Hill, and, in her return to the United States, Ingrid Bergman as Deborah. Almost twenty years passed before Martha Gilman Bower, conducting research at Yale for her doctoral dissertation on the Cycle plays, discovered that both the published version of the play and the Broadway production script differed significantly from the original typescript. Bower published the complete version of the play in 1988, the centenary of O'Neill's birth. The play has never been produced in its entirety using her edition.

O'Neill destroyed a great deal of Cycle material, but also preserved enough for scholars to speculate about the shape of the entire endeavor. The original typescript of *More Stately Mansions* fills six folders of a total of about sixty devoted to the Cycle plays in four boxes of the Eugene O'Neill Papers at Yale. What remains of the "eight hundred million notes" that O'Neill alleged to have written can be found there in the form of general notes and outlines for drafts and revisions, technical specifications and ideas for dramatic techniques, drawings for set designs and ground plans, scenarios, a few dramatic scenes, historical dates, and the title pages for several plays. Carlotta encouraged Gallup to transcribe the Cycle papers, and a Guggenheim Fellowship made it possible in 1968. In addition to establishing a timeline for when O'Neill wrote what, Gallup collated the disparate materials pertaining to the Cycle and made them available to readers and scholars for the first time. This is in itself a significant contribution because O'Neill's handwriting, though neat, is incredibly small and virtually illegible to the naked and untrained eye. Unfortunately, Gallup did not immediately publish his research and eventually lost interest in the project after Carlotta's death in 1970. Almost thirty years passed before *Eugene O'Neill and His Eleven-Play Cycle* (Yale University Press, 1998) appeared in print.

In the meantime, Travis Bogard surveyed the playwright's entire career with *Contour in Time: The Plays of Eugene O'Neill* (Oxford University Press, 1972) and firmly established his reputation as the preeminent O'Neill scholar. At that time, the Cycle papers were strictly off-limits at Yale; only Gallup had seen them, and Bogard published little about the project. Gallup more than likely shared his unpublished transcriptions of the papers with Bogard for the revised edition of *Contour in Time* in 1988. Curiously, although Bogard undoubtedly had gained access to the typescript of *More Stately Mansions* at that time, the twenty-five new pages in the revised version refer only to Cycle plays *other* than *A Touch of the Poet* and *More Stately Mansions*. Bogard limited analysis of those two plays to what he had written for the prior edition, which meant that all references to the latter play were to the severely shortened version edited by Gallup, the only version available in 1972, and not to the full typescript of the play at the Beinecke. What seems even more curious is that Library of America published a three-volume set of O'Neill's complete plays in 1988, including the uncut version of *More Stately Mansions,* edited by Bogard.

As it turns out, Library of America managed to wangle Bower's just-published version from Oxford University Press. On page 994 of the third volume of *Complete Plays,* in the final sentence of a long paragraph in the "Note on the Texts" section, Bogard cites the source for the play that spans pages 283–559 in the volume: "A new edition, *More Stately Mansions: The Unexpurgated Edition,* edited by Bower, presents the text of the entire typescript; that edition is printed here." The story of how that text came into being and the full implications of Bower's edition are the subjects of Chapter 3 below. Here, it is important to note that her edition of *More Stately Mansions,* despite appearing in *Complete Plays,* edited by Bogard in 1988, is most assuredly *not* the edition to which Bogard refers in the revised version of *Contour in Time.* Instead, the citations in both the 1972 edition and the revised 1988 version refer to the much shorter version of the play published in 1964 and edited by Gallup. That text represents less than a third of the original typescript.

Years later, Bower recalled that Library of America contacted her because Bogard was struggling to decipher O'Neill's handwriting.[23] Bogard was almost seventy years old at the time. It made perfect sense for Gallup, a fellow World War II veteran, to share his research with Bogard in anticipation of the O'Neill centenary. But Gallup never transcribed the original typescript of *More Stately Mansions.* Having previously translated the short-ened Swedish version into English for the 1964 edition, Gallup did noth-ing further with the play when he transcribed the rest of the Cycle papers later in that decade. In the first edition of *Contour in Time,* Bogard thanked Gallup before anyone else in his Introduction and said that the curator had gone beyond his normal duties to read portions of the manuscript and correct any errors that he saw. In the revised version of his book, Bogard thanked Gallup in a second place, "A Note on the Revised Edition," "for permitting me to write a fuller account than was earlier possible."[24] Ten years later, Bogard returned the favor and endorsed the publication of *Eugene O'Neill and His Eleven-Play Cycle* at Yale.[25]

Though an invaluable resource and reference for an O'Neill scholar, Gallup's book fails as a chronicle of what O'Neill accomplished with his Cycle. Both Gallup and Bogard, for that matter, focus more on what O'Neill *thought* about doing as opposed to what he actually *completed.* Bogard covers all the Cycle plays that O'Neill started to write, but the shortened version of *More Stately Mansions* to which he refers in his book represents much less than what O'Neill wrote. Similarly, the last sixty-four pages of Gallup's 263-page book concern the period of time after O'Neill had turned his attention away from the Cycle and directed most of his energies to *The Iceman Cometh, Long Day's Journey Into Night, Hughie,* the final draft of *A Touch of the Poet, A Moon for the Misbegotten,* and a host of other ideas for plays. O'Neill wrote three drafts of *More Stately Mansions* in 279 consecutive days from April 1938 to 20 January 1939, but Gallup cov-ers that period in only two pages, numbers 196 and 197.

Magnum Opus: The Cycle Plays of Eugene O'Neill untangles many myths about the project, advances a female character as hero in a new inter-pretation, and proposes a new production concept as an epic event. I do not consider the Cycle as a failure and lament what might have been if O'Neill had written all eleven plays. Nor do I cast the Cycle as an ambi-tious interlude upon which O'Neill toiled until he was ready to write *The Iceman Cometh* and *Long Day's Journey Into Night.* O'Neill spent most of his time on only two plays in the entire Cycle, and he crafted a large and com-plete narrative from them with a beginning, middle, and end. He did not necessarily know what he accomplished with these two works. He certainly planned to do more. But he stopped in 1939 when he had done enough.

With world war imminent, O'Neill convinced himself that he did not give a damn about the Cycle and that it was no longer relevant in the violent and self-destructive modern world of abundance. I believe that he was wrong. The two plays as one said it all about the acquisitive instinct before Nazi aggression became fully apparent. The history of the world since then has only further shown humanity's devotion to destruction. O'Neill's answers, love and sacrifice, blink hope in our dark world.

O'Neill's comic satire, *Marco Millions,* pilloried the American business-man as more interested in monetary profits than human relations. The princess dies in that play for want of Marco's love and an honest look in his eyes. Sara Melody Harford assumes the male prerogative of Marco in the Cycle plays, and she must decide between love and money. Sara, who must choose between pursuing her own dreams and protecting those of others about whom she cares the most, falls victim to her greedy compul-sions. Her persistent struggles ennoble the action, though, and remind an audience of the primacy of love and the need for compassion and under-standing and forgiveness for continual human failure to meet love's huge demands. Sara stands among Anna and Abbie, Nina and Lavinia, or even Mary Tyrone and Josie Hogan, as a leading female character in O'Neill's lineup, but she is not of them. More than any other female character in the O'Neill canon, Sara possesses the guts to make the world hers, and she wields that power to the brink of self-destruction and then almost sal-vation. Her battle to resolve irreconcilable desires posits a simple moral equation about the difficulty of living in the world. She knows the differ-ence between right and wrong, but she cannot always do the right thing. In a tragic battle of mighty opposites, Sara accumulates wealth and status in society to secure her freedom and independence, but her possessions enslave her and nearly destroy her family.

Instead of trying to build the Cycle from its many fragments, *Magnum Opus* examines the center of the Cycle and evaluates not so much how O'Neill started with the project, but how he finished. Staged together, back to back, *A Touch of the Poet* and *More Stately Mansions* could be an event that exhausts the subject of American materialism and offers solutions for the greedy times in which we live today. Sara's trajectory invites an audi-ence to follow the arc of her development. It would be hard to come away from this epic without taking to heart the same questions that Sara faces in the two plays: What is enough to survive and be content? How much is enough? And, most important, when is enough enough? O'Neill repeatedly poses these questions in the two Cycle plays and asks his audience to consider its position in a capitalist economy.

Chapter 1, "From Spithead to Tao House," charts the progression of the Cycle from its nascency in the 1920s until O'Neill allegedly destroyed most of it in the days before his death in Boston. Laying down a baseline of what he did and when for subsequent chapters, the initial one describes a narrative that is not as straightforward as it might seem because of the vastness of O'Neill's project and the specific ways in which he worked. Despite all his notes about the Cycle, he constructed no comprehensive plan and it expanded like civic planning gone terribly wrong in a small town. He did not start at the beginning and move forward in time. To the contrary, he started somewhere in the middle, and the Cycle expanded forward and backward in time as O'Neill progressed.

His interest always dwelled in the middle of the Cycle—not according to what he said, necessarily, but definitely according to what he did. As he continued to add plays to the Cycle and move further and further back in time, he shifted the names of characters and plays and even the overall title from one play to another. Simon Harford's mother, for example, is called "Abigail" in the typescript of *More Stately Mansions,* but O'Neill ultimately decided to change her name to "Deborah" and also penciled in the correction with a corresponding name change in *A Touch of the Poet.* That play was originally called "The Hair of the Dog" (Nora Melody encourages her alcoholic husband to imbibe the hair of the dog after his first entrance); the Cycle as a whole was called "A Touch of the Poet"; and the seventh play, always the last, was called "Twilight of Possessors Self-Dispossessed." O'Neill rotated these titles to their final positions at the end of summer 1937. The most confusing transposition of all also occurred at this time when O'Neill expanded the Cycle to include nine plays. He had already drafted the eighth play, "Greed of the Meek," but then decided to switch its title with the new play that preceded it in time, "And Give Me Death."

After establishing what O'Neill actually wrote, the next three chapters build a case for the extant plays as the core of the Cycle. Chapter 2, "Løvborg's Lost Manuscript," debunks several myths about its alleged destruction. When, for example, Carlotta O'Neill dramatized the burning of her husband's work in an interview with the *New York Times* in 1956, she already had one of the plays that had supposedly been destroyed, *More Stately Mansions,* in her possession. Travis Bogard contended that the Cycle plays would have contributed to world drama on a par with Shakespeare had O'Neill only finished them, but he overlooked what O'Neill accomplished with the completion of *A Touch of the Poet* and *More Stately Mansions.* "The Remainder in the Middle," Chapter 3, focuses on the second and more controversial of the two dramas. In the 1964 edition, the subtitle ran as follows: "Shortened from the author's partly revised script by Karl Ragnar Gierow and edited by Donald Gallup." Referring to the original typescript at Yale, supported by O'Neill's *Work Diary* and Carlotta's personal diary, evidence will show that O'Neill fully revised *More Stately Mansions,* as Bower concluded. Although O'Neill labeled the play "unfinished," even the playwright's word should not be regarded as definitive in lieu of what the typescript reveals and the circumstances of its survival. O'Neill tore up plenty of scripts in his lifetime—why didn't he destroy this one instead of running the risk of having someone fail to do it for him? What author at any time in history would take such a chance? The fourth chapter, "Sara Melody and the American Dream," puts the two plays together and argues that so doing moves Sara to the apex of the triangle that also comprises her husband, Simon, and her mother-in-law, Deborah. Sara becomes the protagonist in a story of an Irish immigrant's rise in the world, the conflict that continually tugs at her regarding her love for Simon, and her desire to avenge her father's humiliation at the hands of the Harfords.

Chapter 5, "Climbing the Harford Family Tree," demonstrates how *A Touch of the Poet* references the past and the four Cycle plays that O'Neill did not finish, going back in time to before the American Revolution. *More Stately Mansions* forecasts the future of the Cycle with its representations of the Harford sons: Ethan, Wolfe, Jonathan, and Honey. In the final five plays that O'Neill ultimately abandoned, beginning with *The Calms of Capricorn,* each son meets an inglorious fate (one son twice).

"Stripped Stark Naked," Chapter 6, cites similarities between adjoining plays, *More Stately Mansions* and *The Iceman Cometh,* to demonstrate quite different perspectives upon life. O'Neill did not so much refine and perfect the ideas of the Cycle after he pushed on to his next play, but rather he completed what he needed to say with *More Stately Mansions. The Iceman*

Cometh reworked some of the same phrases and recurring images to say something altogether different with totally new and different themes. Sara Melody aspires to build an impossibly ornate castle to replace her run-down cabin by the lake, but it is no pipe dream. If Hickey's sage advice to the drunks at Hope's hotel is to sink contentedly to the bottom rung of social life, Sara will have none of that as she moves into the Harford mansion and plots more square feet to come. More obstinately, Sara refuses to accept Simon's belittling attitudes and directives in order to learn new things and change at play's end.

Chapter 7, "Beyond the Threshold," interprets the length of *More Stately Mansions* as an attempt to avoid theatrical production. Ironically, though, O'Neill's wordiness actually invites a theatrical reinterpretation of his play, with bold gestures in terms of movement and design to replace the inordinate amounts of text. The final chapter, "The *Glencairn* Template," nods at O'Neill's cycle of one-act sea plays early in his career, as well as to the fine film version by John Ford in 1940, *The Long Voyage Home*, to suggest ways that such a production might be done. The process begins with recognition of Bower's unexpurgated edition as the basis for a new adaptation, promotes theatricality to alleviate the textual burden and provide visual relief and stimulation, and advocates for judicious yet substantial edits to shorten the playing time. The action unfolds around Sara in successive scenes and reaches a climax in Simon's office during the penultimate scene in act 4. The final scene, with an added splice from the epilogue, provides space for Sara to decide whether to destroy her rival, save her husband, or damn all of them.

Posthumous productions of O'Neill's other late plays sparked renewed interest in the playwright. *The Iceman Cometh* premiered in 1946, but the play did not get its due until José Quintero directed an off-Broadway production downtown at Circle in the Square a decade later. The success of that revival in 1956 made a star out of Jason Robards and rewarded Quintero and his producing partner, Theodore Mann, with the rights from Carlotta O'Neill to stage the American premiere of *Long Day's Journey Into Night* later that same year, also with Robards as Tyrone, Jr. In the wake of those successes, Robert Brustein included O'Neill as one of eight playwrights in *The Theatre of Revolt* (1964), and the lone American representative. Ibsen, Strindberg, and Chekhov, Nobel winners Shaw and Pirandello, and Brecht and Artaud/Genet (Brustein quixotically considered the two Frenchmen jointly) rounded out the international list. Brustein defined his criteria for selection in his Introduction: "I believe these eight dramatists to be the finest, most enduring writers in the field; and I was determined not to include any playwright who would not be read fifty years hence."[26] *Long Day's Journey Into Night* became the fastest-selling publication in the history of Yale University Press when it first appeared in 1956. A new "Critical Edition" of the play in 2014 marked the sixty-first printing of the title. The Yale University Press website claims that as of April 2020 the play's "continuing status as a classic has kept it among the Press's most perennially successful books."[27] A touring production from London's Old Vic, with Jeremy Irons and Lesley Manville, was staged at the Brooklyn Academy of Music in spring 2018. In April of that same year, a new production of *The Iceman Cometh,* directed by George C. Wolfe and starring Denzel Washington, opened on Broadway. It has been more than fifty years since *The Theatre of Revolt* first appeared in print and O'Neill is not only still read today, but also frequently performed in major productions.

But what about *More Stately Mansions?* Unfortunately, Brustein concluded his laudatory chapter on O'Neill with a disparaging footnote: "I have neglected to discuss *More Stately Mansions* because the play is sadly marred and incomplete. Its tedious soliloquies, mother-wife confusions, and Poet-Businessman conflicts suggest that it is a regression, a throwback to an earlier stage of O'Neill's development. O'Neill made notes for completely revising the play in 1941, and, failing this, left instructions for it to be destroyed at his death; it would have been no loss if his instructions had been heeded."[28]

In a scant few lines, Brustein synthesized the major attacks against the play that this study must rebut. The first edition of *The Theatre of Revolt* came out in the same year in which Gierow and Gallup published *More Stately Mansions.* It is entirely likely that Brustein had very little time to evaluate O'Neill's drama before having to meet his own publishing deadline. It is even more likely that the placement of the footnote at the very end of the O'Neill section became a function, even a necessity, of the publishing process. At such a late date, that was the only place even a limited commentary could go. Still, when publishers reprinted yet another version of his now-classic study in 1991, three years after Bower published her edition of *More Stately Mansions,* Brustein gave no indication that he was aware of O'Neill's completed play and made no comment about it. He still described *A Touch of the Poet* as a "minor masterpiece" and summed up O'Neill with strong praise: "In power and insight, O'Neill remains unsurpassed among American dramatists, and, of course, it is doubtful if, without him, there would have been an American drama at all."[29] Yet, the same damning footnote about *More Stately Mansions* persisted at the bottom of the page.

O'Neill wrote *More Stately Mansions* immediately prior to *The Iceman Cometh* and at the height of his dramatic powers, yet Brustein regarded the play as a "regression." He undoubtedly derived his criticism from the point of view of Simon as the protagonist and a stand-in for the playwright trying to resolve tensions and anxieties about the women in his life—resentments against his mother, but also against Carlotta as his wife-mother. Brustein suggests what Louis Sheaffer later stated emphatically: that Simon was essentially the playwright's own persona and that the play was more about the playwright's relationship with his own mother than about the fictional triangle of Simon, Deborah, and Sara.[30] In this light, *More Stately Mansions* provides little more than a warm-up for the main event of *Long Day's Journey Into Night,* in which Edmund (O'Neill) begs for his mother's love, but Mary (Ella O'Neill) pulls away and even suggests that it might have been better if he had not been born. To be sure, Deborah Harford is more ruthless and vindictive toward her son than Mary is toward Edmund, but the issues are the same and compel fascination. On the one hand, according to Brustein, O'Neill crudely employs theatrical devices reminiscent of his worst excesses from the 1920s, especially the thought asides from *Strange Interlude* and explorations of duality as expressed in *The Great God Brown.* On the other hand, the intimate relationships between mother and son in *More Stately Mansions* scribble only a rough outline of the nuanced portrait in *Long Day's Journey Into Night.*

But what if Sara, not Simon, were the center of *More Stately Mansions?* And what if it were paired with a "minor masterpiece," *A Touch of the Poet,* to form an epic event over two nights of performance in which Sara rises in the world from a poor, Irish immigrant in a rundown New England tavern to a bejeweled lady in a Bullfinch mansion? What about her grandiose plans for an even more grandiose estate tacked up on her wall? And what if this drama were situated in the greedy times of the first populist president, Andrew Jackson, a reviled outsider from Tennessee who rebelled against the Yankee elite, to resonate with the populist rhetoric of another outsider's regime almost 200 years later? What if Sara sold her soul to gain her riches, but the strain of doing so nearly destroyed her? And what if her adventures in trade were nothing more than a kind of prostitution, but less honest because sex clients at least come away from a transaction with something? What if Sara knew in the course of her transgressions that she made mistakes and recognized that she was hurting the ones she loved as well as herself? And what if, in the end, she had the chance to take what she wanted with strength on her side, but she paused, reflected, and then relented and gave way to her rival? What if we saw in her submission an act of victory over the self and a cure for greed and possessiveness? What would we think when, in the very final moments of such a long epic, she could not resist condemning her sons to the same greedy grab that had nearly killed her husband? Would we not see the flip-floppy, acquisitive compulsion and emotional volatility that tweet the story of America 24/7 in social media? Might this then be a drama for our time?

CHAPTER ONE

FROM SPITHEAD TO TAO HOUSE

O'Neill labored exclusively on his Cycle, usually spelled with a capital C, from January 1935 to June 1939, but the roots of the project went back as far as 1927 and extended to the end of his writing days in 1943. His first notes for what ultimately served as the last play of the Cycle coincided with his decision in 1927 to abandon his second wife, Agnes Boulton, and their two children at Spithead, his home in Bermuda, for the glamorous Carlotta Monterey in New York. After a three-year interlude overseas that wound up at a rundown chateau near Tours, France, the new Mr. and Mrs. Eugene O'Neill returned to the States for the triumphant production of *Mourning Becomes Electra* in 1931. They bought land in Sea Island, Georgia, and built a Spanish-style compound, Casa Genotta (a combination of Gene and Carlotta), on the Atlantic shore, where O'Neill wrote *Ah, Wilderness!* (1933) and *Days Without End* (1934). After that, he began the Cycle in earnest, but by the end of summer in 1936 he had endured his limit of southern heat and escaped to what he thought was a better climate for his work in Seattle, Washington.

Constant rain had no more salutary effect on the playwright than constant sun, though, and the couple shortly ventured down the West Coast to

San Francisco in search of another new home. They purchased 158 acres in what O'Neill called the Corduroy Hills of Danville, California, and moved into Tao House at the end of 1937. In almost total seclusion, far removed from the Show Shop of Broadway, O'Neill worked nearly every day for over a year on the Cycle, but then stopped abruptly to write *The Iceman Cometh* and *Long Day's Journey Into Night* back to back. Sagging health and increasing isolation due to the loss of domestic help to the war effort forced the O'Neills to sell their favorite home early in 1944. O'Neill packed his prized Cycle scripts with him when he backtracked to hotels first in San Francisco and next in New York for the premiere of *The Iceman Cometh* in 1946, and then to a little house above the ocean at Marblehead Neck, Massachusetts, and finally, in 1951, to the Shelton Hotel in Boston. Ensconced there, O'Neill and Carlotta burned his unfinished Cycle plays, according to his biographers, in advance of his imminent death on 27 November 1953.

As much as O'Neill moved around, the Cycle, too, was always a complicated mess of moving parts (see "Chronology of the Cycle"). In December 1934 O'Neill juggled work on two seemingly unrelated plays. He had been wrestling with one about a greedy female industrialist, "The Career of Bessie Bowen," under a variety of titles since Bermuda. Originally, it was to have been the third part of a trilogy, "Myth Plays for the God-Forsaken," that included *Dynamo* and *Days Without End*, both of which had failed on Broadway. O'Neill set the other project, *The Calms of Capricorn*, almost entirely aboard a clipper ship in the year 1858. O'Neill had floated this idea for several years as well, and it most likely derived from *Mourning Becomes Electra*, a retelling of Aeschylus's *Oresteia* in the immediate aftermath of the American Civil War. O'Neill planned the clipper-ship play as the first of a series of plays, and the word "cycle" first appears in his *Work Diary* on 1 January 1935, to which he appends: "grand idea for this Opus Magnus [sic] if can ever do it—wonderful characters." Despite that show of interest, O'Neill continued with "Bessie" throughout the month, outlined it for the fifth time and wrote dialogue for four days, but then confided: "This damned play won't come right—not big enough opportunity to interest me—should be part of something, not itself."[1] That something else proved to be the Cycle that started with *The Calms of Capricorn* and three more interconnected plays about the four sons of an Irish immigrant mother and a well-to-do Yankee businessman.

Designed for speed to transport tea to the West from the Far East, the clipper ship dominated the seas for a relatively short time in the mid-nineteenth century before the opening of the Suez Canal in 1869 cut the route short and no longer necessitated ships going around the southern tip of Africa. Although clippers, sleek vessels with massive sails, were faster than steamships, reliance upon wind for power made them less reliable, and they were also much less suitable to travel along the canal. These ships enjoyed a twenty-five-year reign on the seas, but the clippers occupied a far more important and lasting role in O'Neill's creative imagination (Fig. 1). For O'Neill, the clipper ship represented the quest to catch God in nature and leave behind the petty squabbles of human affairs. The open sea beckoned as an escape from the narrow constrictions of sexually repressed New England. The objective of the clipper ship was not to advance the tea trade, but to follow the trade winds to remote islands in the Caribbean where the laws of civilized society no longer applied and relations between people relaxed into a more natural state.

The difference between sailing a boat and piloting a steamship was the difference between human skill and technological assistance that rendered those skills useless. Triumphs of design and technology of the time, clippers needed a captain and crew who could navigate both the ship and the seas. Steamships required less expertise but ultimately replaced the clippers. Steam put the sailors below deck, designated them for the stokehole, and robbed them of their sense of wonder and autonomy.

In the middle of *Mourning Becomes Electra*, O'Neill staged a crucial act on the stern section of the *Flying Trades*, Captain Adam Brant's clipper ship docked at a wharf in Boston. The other twelve acts take place at the Mannon home in Massachusetts, described by Christine Mannon as a "whited sepulcher."[2] Each part of the play, "Homecoming," "The Hunted," and "The Haunted," begins outside the stately façade, and successive acts explore the corruption that lies within. Various Mannon portraits on the walls show generations of the dead. Even the living characters are described as having not entirely living flesh. They made their fortune through shipbuilding, but trade corrupted them. Family secrets and betrayals leeched from sexual lusts and indiscretions. Christine, the Clytemnestra character, turns to lover Adam Brant not because of the loss of a child, but because her husband had sexually repulsed her for years. Adam cut a romantic

FIGURE 1. Eugene O'Neill and his dog, Blemie, at his Park Avenue apartment in New York during rehearsals for *Mourning Becomes Electra*, 1931. The model of the clipper ship in the background foretells what is to come. (Courtesy of Eugene O'Neill Papers, Yale Collection of American Literature, Beinecke Rare Book and Manuscript Library.)

figure with a "Byronic appearance," and he represents a chance for Christine to escape the frigid morality of the Mannons.[3] No corresponding scene exists in the *Oresteia*. In the modern revenge play with so much death and dying, the act aboard the clipper ship shines as a moment in which escape from the land seems possible and love flickers briefly before the Mannon progeny sneak in to snuff the dream.

Just as the progression in other parts of the play moves from exterior to interior scenes, the act aboard the *Flying Trades* begins on deck and progresses to Brant's cabin below deck after he welcomes Christine. O'Neill manages this scene change by specifying that an exterior wall of the ship's hull be removed in a transition to reveal the interior scene below deck.[4] O'Neill first tried this technique on "land" with his farmhouse in *Desire Under the Elms,* in which exterior walls were removed during specific scenes to reveal the kitchen, upstairs bedrooms, and parlor downstairs.[5] A few years later, he specified a similar technique of displaying scenes of neighboring Fife and Light households in *Dynamo.* When he planned *The Calms of Capricorn* aboard the clipper *Dream of the West*, he exploited the same technique again to reveal interior sections of the ship or to show only its exterior with walls in place. And for the other plays of the Cycle, all of which take place on land, he imagined versions of the *Desire/Dynamo* technique to show different rooms of a structure without requiring a completely new setting. The design concept for these plays resembled a child's dollhouse or scale model. O'Neill commissioned a number of scale models of clipper ships from model maker Donald Pace in 1934 prior to the start of the Cycle, when he was still considering *The Calms of Capricorn* as a single play. O'Neill's letters to Pace questioned the precision and accuracy of the models and demonstrated that O'Neill had done a good bit of research on the history of the vessels.[6]

O'Neill displayed the model ships at Casa Genotta and later brought them with him to Tao House in California. They inspired the entire Cycle project. In the act aboard ship in *Mourning Becomes Electra*, an early exchange between Brant and the Chantyman discloses a nostalgia and romantic longing that possibly reflect the playwright's state of mind. Set in the aftermath of the Civil War, the play marks the time in which the clippers began to wane. The Chantyman is out of work. He hopes to find a sailing vessel that still needs his particular skill: he can sing tunes that coordinate and motivate group labor. The rise of new technology, he realizes, threatens to end his and Brant's careers. He tells the younger man: "[S]team is comin' in, the sea is full o' smoky teakettles, the old days is dyin', an' where'll you an' me be then?"[7]

Such romanticism harks back to an earlier O'Neill play, *The Hairy Ape* (1921), in which an old Irishman, Paddy, waxes nostalgic in a paean to life above board on clipper ships:

> Oh, to be back in the fine days of my youth, ochone! Oh, there was fine beautiful ships them days—clippers wid tall masts touching the sky—fine strong men in them—men that was sons of the sea as if 'twas the mother that bore them. [. . .] Oh to be scudding south again wid the power of the Trade Wind driving her on steady through the nights and the days! Full sail on her! Nights and days! Nights when the foam of the wake would be flaming with fire, when the sky'd be blazing and winking wid stars. [. . .] 'Twas them days men belonged to ships, not now. 'Twas them days a ship was part of the sea, and a man was part of a ship, and the sea joined all together and made it one.[8]

The old days are not the new days. Paddy reminisces to his mates in the boiler room while they take a break from shoveling coal into the blazing furnaces of a twentieth-century steam-powered ocean liner.

Paddy verifies in this early O'Neill play on modern life what the Chantyman fears later in *Mourning Becomes Electra*: the modern steamship destroys the rugged individualism of a romantic life at sea. Clearly, the reader might do well to suspect that the romantic tale from a drunken Irishman is not to be believed as whole truth, but the destination, in this case, is just as important as the romantic journey. Paddy talks in general about the joys of sailing south, but Adam Brant has a particular spot in mind for his Caribbean cruise. He and Christine seek an island getaway that transcends the materialism of New England. He evokes a similar experience to Paddy's as he recalls the Blessed Isles: "The warm earth in the moonlight, the trade winds rustling the coco palms, the surf on the barrier reef singing a croon in your ears like a lullaby! Aye! There's peace, and forgetfulness for us there—if we can ever find those islands now!"[9] In an early scene, Brant emphasizes the importance of the Blessed Isles as an opportunity to rehabilitate one's sense of humanity: "You can forget there all men's dirty dreams of greed and power."[10]

Brant's love of clipper ships leads him to consider them in gendered terms as "beautiful, pale women," in opposition to what he finds repellent and dirty about men on land.[11] As the prostitute Anna in *"Anna Christie"* finds that the fog at sea cleans her as if she had taken a long bath, Brant sails in order to get clean. Orin, the Orestes figure from the Greek tragedy, responds to the Blessed Isles as a redemptive locale in opposition to the violent and bloody combat that he experienced during the war. In light of having read Melville's *Typee,* Orin figures his mother as an island: "The breaking of the waves was your voice. The sky was the same color as your eyes. The warm sand was like your skin. The whole island was you."[12] Orin and Lavinia later travel to those same islands and Lavinia enjoys sexual freedom for the first time in her life "without knowledge of sin."[13] She returns to New England eager to retain what she has learned from her trip and incorporate new knowledge into her prospective marriage: "We'll make an island for ourselves on land, and we'll have children and love them and teach them to love life so that they can never be possessed by hate and death!"[14] Tragically, she cannot sustain this freedom or peace at home.

Only a few weeks after finishing *Mourning Becomes Electra,* while living in a Long Island rental house and awaiting rehearsals to begin, O'Neill recorded in his *Work Diary* an "idea for Clipper Ship-around-Horn Play."[15] The destination of travel for *The Calms of Capricorn* deviated from the freedom-inspired climate of the Blessed Isles to the Golden West of California. Clipper ships could bring tea from China fresh to consumers, but they could also transport fortune hunters to the site of the Gold Rush as fast as possible. The *Flying Cloud* set the record in 1854 for the fastest time to California from New York by making the trip in eighty-nine days. By sea was a much faster mode of travel than by land, even though the overall distance was much farther than the overland haul via the Oregon Trail. Prior to the establishment of the transcontinental railroad, the route by sea, which might take a shortcut across the Isthmus of Panama to the Pacific Ocean (in anticipation of the Panama Canal which opened, finally, in 1914), or the longer but safer journey all the way around the southern tip of South America, proved to be a more attractive option than the shortest distance on land between two points.

The clipper ship took a similar turn in *Desire Under the Elms.* Set in 1850, the play concerns two elder sons of Ephraim Cabot who work the land in rocky New England but long to give up their hard labor for the prospect of gold and easy money in the West. Stage directions in an early scene describe a poster of a clipper ship emblazoned with "California" on the kitchen wall.[16] Simeon and Peter's half-brother, Eben, promises to give them money for secure passage on a ship to California if only they will relinquish their stake in the land and bequeath it to him. They do, and the rest of the play is a three-way battle for possession and ownership of the farm between Eben, Ephraim, and Abbie, Ephraim's new wife.

The *Dream of the West,* the clipper in *The Calms of Capricorn,* the first of the four original Cycle plays, sails the same route as the ship in *Desire Under the Elms,* in an attempt to break the speed record of the *Flying Cloud.* It fails. Lack of wind dooms its timely progress (an ironic echo of Agamemnon's voyage to Troy), first in the South Atlantic and then near the finish outside San Francisco's Golden Gate. O'Neill wrote summaries and general ideas for all four of the prospective plays between 21 and 25 January 1935. Each play foregrounded one of the brothers. *The Calms of Capricorn* included all four of them but featured Ethan as the overly ambitious First Mate in the year 1858. "The Earth Is the Limit" was set in California (1858–1860) and chronicled the profligate gambling of Wolfe Tone Harford and his eventual suicide. The third play, "Nothing Is Lost but Honor" (1862–1870), took place mostly in Washington, D.C., and followed the crooked path of the youngest brother, Owen Roe, nicknamed Honey, who aspired to be president, but settled for a seat in the Senate, and ultimately resigned from that position in a corrupt deal that allowed the fourth brother, Jonathan, to triumph in the last play. Set in New York, "The Man on Iron Horseback" (1876–1893) dealt with Jonathan's construction of the transcontinental railroad and the brutality he inflicted upon everyone in its path. Overall, the prospective plays dramatized the rise of industrialism and the rape of the country due to lust for greed and power.

Almost immediately after O'Neill finished with the outlines and summaries of the four plays about the brothers, he decided that he needed to expand the Cycle to include their parents. On 27 January 1935 he added a fifth play to the Cycle dealing with the marriage of Sara Melody and Simon Harford. O'Neill soon discovered that he would need two plays to cover their story, and the Cycle quickly ballooned to six plays. With Simon perhaps in mind, he named the entire Cycle "A Touch of the Poet," and thus drew upon a phrase that he had first coined for the dreamer Robert

Mayo in *Beyond the Horizon* to suggest the split nature of identity. O'Neill initially titled the play dealing with the courtship of Sara and Simon "The Hair of the Dog" and wrote the scenario for it in February, followed by the scenario for the sequel with its triangular relationship between Sara, Simon, and Simon's mother (named Abigail, but changed later to Deborah). O'Neill wrote the scenario for what was originally called "Oh, Sour-Apple Tree" in March and April and then changed the title to *More Stately Mansions*. The advance in titles from the tone-deaf first effort to the evocative and musical final version, from a poem by Oliver Wendell Holmes, reflected the overall concern of the Cycle with greed and materialism.[17]

The Cycle stood at six plays at this point and O'Neill returned to *The Calms of Capricorn*, which now represented the third play in the Cycle, to write its scenario in May and early June 1935. For O'Neill, the scenario was a specific step in his writing process. Ever since he had been a student in Professor George Pierce Baker's English 47 playwriting workshop at Harvard in 1914, O'Neill imposed a disciplined regimen on the development of his plays. He started with an idea for a play that he would jot in a notebook. He would follow that with an outline to include the setting(s), act divisions, character descriptions, and plot outlines. The scenario represented a third level in development that amounted almost to a first draft (Fig. 2). Donald Gallup eventually transcribed and published the scenario of *The Calms of Capricorn* in 1981. Stage directions mix with dialogue to create a lengthy narrative text in paragraph form of about 25,000 words. The play that Gallup simultaneously published from the scenario is more a reformation of text from narration to dialogue than an original interpolation. These remarkable documents show an aspect of O'Neill's technique and an important stage in his writing process, as well as an advanced level of commitment and interest with regards to a particular project. Revealingly, O'Neill next turned to the other three plays after *The Calms of Capricorn* and outlined them further between 22 June and 27 August, but elected not to write scenarios for them at that time.

Back in January, O'Neill commented to Carlotta that he thought he might be able to incorporate material from his "Bessie" play, the one that he dropped in favor of *The Calms of Capricorn*, into the Cycle as the final play, the seventh, that would bring the history of the Harfords up to almost the present day in which he was writing. O'Neill had recorded an

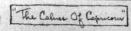

FIGURE 2. The opening scene from the scenario of *The Calms of Capricorn.*
O'Neill claimed that his third wife, Carlotta Monterey O'Neill, who typed
his manuscripts beginning with *Mourning Becomes Electra,* was the only person
who could decipher his minuscule handwriting. (Courtesy of Eugene O'Neill
Papers, Yale Collection of American Literature, Beinecke Rare Book and
Manuscript Library. Copyright © Yale University. All rights reserved.)

idea for a forerunner of "Bessie" called "Billionaire" in a notebook back in 1927 that resonated with the big theme of the Cycle: "[V]ast symbolic play of the effect upon man's soul of industrialism—a man rises from a mechanic, becomes a billionaire—from a man with simple ambitions for success for the sake of wife and family and his standing in community, after his lucky investment with fellow mechanic, money suddenly pours in and bewildered, swamps and corrupts him and his family. It fascinates him by its power."[18] A throng at the man's gates chants, "Billion in gold cannot be mad," but the mechanic still shoots himself to end the play.[19]

O'Neill never developed this play any further, but the next idea for a play, which Virginia Floyd describes in *Eugene O'Neill at Work* takes its title from the crowd in "Billionaire." In this retelling, a young girl named Bessie asserts control of an automobile company in the first part of the twentieth century and rises to prominence. Intended as one of the three "Myth Plays for the God-Forsaken," "It Cannot Be Mad?" echoed "Billionaire" and purported to fill the void of God's absence with the love of money. The first play in the trilogy, *Dynamo*, depicted the pursuit of science as a substitute for God; the second installment, *Days Without End*, offered human love and forgiveness as a replacement for God. Although O'Neill never finished the trilogy, word of his ambitious plans leaked to the press and branded him as the "Wagner of Playwrights."[20] Even the four operas of the *Ring* cycle, however, would pale in size and scope to O'Neill's nascent Cycle.

O'Neill tinkered with various titles for "It Cannot Be Mad?" from 1927 to 1935 without ever finishing the play. In 1932 he called it "The Life of Bessie Bowen," then emended it to "The Career of Bessie Bowen," and then changed his protagonist's surname to Bowlan emended to Bolan at the end of 1934. Prior to those slight variations, though, he called the play "On to Betelgeuse" in 1929, when he was living with Carlotta on the French Riviera near Monte Carlo. He put it aside to write *Mourning Becomes Electra* and oversee its successful production in New York. His subsequent move to Sea Island, Georgia, slow progress on *Days Without End*, and the rapid writing that produced his comedy *Ah, Wilderness!*, prevented him from giving his undivided attention to "Betelgeuse." Instead, O'Neill referenced it in the play that he struggled mightily to complete. In the second scene of act 3 of *Days Without End*, John Loving's alter ego, named Loving, asserts: "We know we are all the slaves of meaningless chance—electricity or something, which whirls us — on to Hercules!"[21] Hercules refers to Betel-geuse, a bright star in the Orion constellation. "On to Hercules!" exclaims John in a second reference: "Let us face that! Once we have accepted it without evasion, we can begin to create new goals for ourselves, ends for our days!" In response to such optimism, Loving calls John a "romantic idealist" and utters the phrase "On to Hercules!" for the third time.[22] He distorts John's intended meaning to suggest a sort of Faustian quest, not for knowledge, but for the accumulation of power and wealth that accepts no bounds. Reach for the stars and accept no limitations, he advises.

Set in 1932 and subtitled "A Modern Miracle Play," *Days Without End* marked the last time that O'Neill completed a play about contemporary life and times. Debate about the pursuit of money and a critique of capital-ism made perfect sense at a time when economic depression in the United States was fully underway. The projected plot revolved around John's search for the proper ending for his new novel. (The playwright, O'Neill, took two years to discover the conclusion for *Days Without End*.) Impor-tantly, though, John does not seem to depend upon the novel's success to make an adequate living during a precarious time. John may not even be a novelist by trade. The play opens in the New York office of "Eliot & Com-pany," although the precise nature of what that company does remains mysterious. The named partner, Eliot, appears in the first scene and seems to endorse the idea that his relatively new employee, John, aspires to write a new novel. That he seems to be doing so on company time further begs the question about the nature of the company's business. John, too, appar-ently assumed this job because he needed to earn money after flailing for a number of years as a writer. Nevertheless, as the play unfolds there are subtle allusions to financial distress, particularly voiced by the woman with whom John indulged in a brief affair, and dialogue suggests that many of John's contemporaries do not enjoy the same privilege of gainful employ-ment and a forgiving employer that he does. If "It Cannot Be Mad?"/ "The Career of Bessie Bowen" / "On to Betelgeuse" suggests an endless stream of profits and commercial conquests, *Days Without End* reports that there must be some other response, perhaps a spiritual reawakening, in the face of uncertain times and economic collapse.

At the end of August and beginning of September 1935, O'Neill wrote notes for the seventh and final play, now renamed "Twilight of Possessors

Self-Dispossessed" (close to what he would ultimately title the entire Cycle), that brought the Cycle into the twentieth century and up to the present day (1900–1932), the same year in which he had set *Days Without End.* Since this new play included much of the "Bessie Bowen" material that O'Neill had been working on for years, he felt that he did not need to add anything further to it at this point. Thus, after only eight months of work on his Cycle, O'Neill seemed to have sketched out a plan of seven plays that stretched over a century of American history through the lives of one family from 1828 to 1932. It remained unclear at this point how O'Neill intended to adapt the "Bessie Bowen" material to fit with the Harford clan. Thematically, he had tied the saga together with the pursuit of wealth, but the challenge remained for O'Neill to work out the details of the "marriage." It would be almost two years before O'Neill looked at "Twilight of Possessors Self-Dispossessed" again, at which time he decided to make the youngest son of Sara and Simon, Honey, the political scoundrel of "Nothing Is Lost but Honor," speak the last lines of the Cycle.

The character of Deborah, Simon's mother, fascinated O'Neill. When he had been developing the scenario a few months earlier for *More Stately Mansions,* about the parents of the four Harford boys, he had noted in his *Work Diary* that the play actually seemed to be evolving around her.[23] So, now, O'Neill made a fateful decision to add yet another play to his Cycle that traced Deborah's marriage as a young girl to Henry Harford. Having already extended the Cycle almost up to the present day of 1932, the only direction for the Cycle to expand was further back in history.

In early November 1935, O'Neill finished the scenario for "Greed of the Meek," now the first play in an eight-play Cycle that ranged from 1806 to 1932. For almost the entirety of the next year, 1936, he alternated work on drafts of the first two plays, starting with the second, "The Hair of the Dog." Work went quickly and O'Neill finished the first draft of the play on 18 March. He proceeded immediately to "Greed of the Meek," but struggled when he reached the fourth act. By mid-June, he toyed with the idea of adding yet another play to the Cycle, the ninth, called "And Give Me Death," which would go back prior to the American Revolution on the Harford family farm. He did not make a definitive decision to add the play at this time, but remained stuck with "Greed of the Meek." Returning to "The Hair of the Dog," he finished a second draft of that play on 21 August. He revised "Greed of the Meek" next, but still did not like the end and lamented that the play was as long as *Strange Interlude*. The following day, 18 September, O'Neill decided to "throw away this damned play for time being and call it finished, pending revision and condensation." Sometime that summer, too, O'Neill decided to sell Casa Genotta and leave Georgia. Professor Sophus Winther of the University of Washington, whose book *Eugene O'Neill: A Critical Study* had greatly pleased the playwright, visited O'Neill that summer and invited the O'Neills to Seattle. O'Neill, in somewhat of a surprise to Carlotta, thought that a change of scenery would do him good and agreed to pack up and head to the Northwest.

O'Neill had a habit of making abrupt moves. His usual pattern was to love a new home in the beginning and talk about it as if it were the perfect place that he would never leave. Two letters to Kenneth Macgowan, his close friend and former producing partner in his Greenwich Village days, provide a before-and-after picture of O'Neill's prospects in Georgia. On his forty-fifth birthday (16 October 1933), O'Neill chimed: "I hope sometime you'll get a chance to visit us here. Carlotta has designed a really beautiful home for us. She has a marvelous flair for that—and for keeping it running right. At last I know the meaning of home. And don't we both love it!"[24] Scarcely three years later, in another letter to Macgowan that O'Neill sent from Seattle, dated 15 November 1936, he mentioned his former home as if it had been an arduous ordeal: "Truth is, I'm worn out physically and badly need a complete rest. I worked on my damned cycle constantly for seven months without one day off—all through an extra scorching Georgia summer—and by the end of Sept. I was a wreck and about ready to feed the hookworms. Carlotta was also climate-sunk. So we've decided to sell the Sea Island mansion and give Dixie back to Tin Pan Alley."[25] (The music publishing industry in New York at that time, referred to as Tin Pan Alley, released 1,000 or more songs in the first several decades of the twentieth century that idealized the South as the land of belles and beaux, without mentioning its widespread poverty and racism. James Agee—who would write a cover story on O'Neill for *Time* magazine in 1946—and photographer Walker Evans had just received commissions to write an article for *Forbes* that would turn into their award-winning photojournalist book *Let Us Now Praise Famous Men*, on tenant farmers and economic deprivation in the South.)

35

Almost exactly a year after his letter to Macgowan, O'Neill further decried the South and its tobacco-road ethos in a letter to his lawyer in which he declared violent opposition to his son's wish to attend Duke University. In a humorous rant, O'Neill invoked Tin Pan Alley again on 12 November 1937:

> I haven't lived in the South for five years without learning a lot about the effect of the atmosphere in the Tin-Pan Alley, Fair Dixie—nor without hearing and seeing a great deal of Southern college students and grads. Sea Island in summer was infested with them. Their colleges have the very lowest cultural and ethical standards of any in this country. [. . .] Southern colleges, it must be remembered in justice to them, are run for Southerners to prepare them for Southern life. If, for example, Shane's ambition is to run a gasoline—and corn whiskey—filling station in the Carolina sticks, then Duke is surely the spot to instill the proper culture for it—or if he wants to raise tobacco or cotton. Duke should be the Alma Mater for all tobacco growers![26]

O'Neill lived at Casa Genotta a little over four years, longer than his stays at previous exotic outposts, including Peaked Hill Bar, an old life-saving station in Provincetown, Massachusetts, that eventually slipped into the Atlantic Ocean and washed away; Brook Farm, an estate in Ridge-field, Connecticut; Spithead in Bermuda; and his first house with Carlotta, Château du Plessis in France. Without mentioning his upcoming move, O'Neill updated Lawrence Langner of the Theatre Guild on the progress of the Cycle on 12 August 1936 and hinted that a production any time soon would be impossible. It had been almost two years since the Guild had produced *Days Without End*. The starting point for the Cycle had originally been the eldest son in *The Calms of Capricorn*, but O'Neill had since shifted to the parents and "The Hair of the Dog." That play was almost done, O'Neill reported to Langner, but the new first play, "Greed of the Meek," was only in first draft. O'Neill suggested, too, that the beginning point might soon recede again in the near future in the form of a ninth play as yet undetermined and nowhere near written. To further explain the situation in which he found himself with his work, O'Neill advised his friend and producer: "Try a Cycle sometime, I advise you—that is, I would advise you to, if I hated you! A lady bearing quintuplets is having a debonair, carefree time of it by comparison."[27] O'Neill never delivered his octuplets to the Guild, but now envisioned a ninth play. At the end of September, he spent a week drafting the first act of *More Stately Mansions,* the third play in the Cycle, but could not continue further due to illness. He left Georgia on 4 October 1936 and headed to New York to see his doctor, who prescribed rest as treatment and charged O'Neill not to think anymore about plays.

He wrote almost nothing for the next eight months as he moved about the country by train in search of a new home. On 30 October 1936 he left New York on the *Twentieth Century Limited* for Chicago and then continued on the Great Northern's *Empire Builder* to Seattle, where he and Carlotta rented a house overlooking Puget Sound. In its coverage of the Nobel Prize award, the *New York Times* reported: "Eugene O'Neill has come to the Pacific Northwest to rest. He has come also to gather material on the settlement of the Oregon country in the Eighteen Sixties and the Eighteen Seventies when the first transcontinental railroad was being pushed across the Rocky Mountain Divide."[28] He did not stay there long. Weary of all the rain, the O'Neills left Seattle on 14 December and checked into the Fairmont Hotel in San Francisco, but O'Neill became ill again at the end of the month and did not check out of Merritt Hospital in Oakland until March, soon after which the couple rented a house in the East Bay in Berkeley. In late April 1937, they finally located an ideal spot for their new home in Danville. They purchased the property on 24 May and then rented a house for six months in nearby Lafayette to allow for construction. Throughout the summer, O'Neill made notes for revisions of the first play in his Cycle, "Greed of the Meek," as well as the last, the "Bessie Bowen" material, now called "Twilight of Possessors Self-Dispossessed," but did not incorporate these ideas into any drafts. He did, however, use drafting tools to construct an elaborate Harford family tree on 10–11 July that included seven generations (see Fig. 8 in Chapter 5).

A month later, on 9 August 1937, O'Neill switched some of his established titles and came up with a new scheme. By this time, too, he had definitely decided to add a ninth play to the Cycle. In a move that confused all future scholars, he transposed the titles of the first two plays, called the third play what he had previously titled the whole Cycle, and gave what was now the ninth and final play the title for what had once been the first play about the courtship between Sara and Simon. The play that had been first on O'Neill's mind in 1927 was now the last in the Cycle. In a few strokes, the new arrangement now looked like this:

1st Play: "Greed of the Meek" (formerly "And Give Me Death")
2nd Play: "And Give Me Death" (formerly "Greed of the Meek")
3rd Play: *A Touch of the Poet* (formerly "The Hair of the Dog")
4th Play: *More Stately Mansions*
5th Play: *The Calms of Capricorn*
6th Play: "The Earth Is the Limit"
7th Play: "Nothing Is Lost but Honor"
8th Play: "The Man on Iron Horseback"
9th Play: "The Hair of the Dog" (formerly "Twilight of Possessors Self-Dispossessed")

O'Neill had initially called the entire Cycle "A Touch of the Poet," but changed it to "Lament for Possessors Self-Dispossessed" and thus advanced the themes of greed and materialism over questions of identity. While still living in Lafayette, O'Neill returned to his first serious stint of writing in a long while and finished a first draft of the new "Greed of the Meek" by the end of 1937. It was now the first play in a nine-play Cycle that went back in time all the way to 1755. Unfortunately, though, this play also ran twice the length of a normal play. Still, the first three plays of the Cycle now existed in draft form, O'Neill had set a title for the last play, and the overall title of the Cycle reflected the drift of the whole project.

In a September letter to Barrett Clark, O'Neill had announced that he was ready to work on his Cycle again with new ideas and fresh enthusiasm. He was looking forward to moving into the new house, Tao House, with eager anticipation and invited his old friend to visit: "We have a beautiful site in the hills of San Ramon Valley with one of the most beautiful views I've ever seen. This is final home and harbor for me. I love California. Moreover, the climate is one I know I can work and keep healthy in. Coastal Georgia was no place for me."[29] In another letter to Macgowan, O'Neill bragged that the new home would be Carlotta's "masterpiece."[30] The couple moved into Tao House at the end of December and O'Neill intended to get down to business right away. Health problems beset his plans, however, with an attack of neuritis and then the need to extract four teeth followed by four more the next month. A month of steady rain, a record for the region, did not help, and must have reminded him of Seattle. Once both problems lifted, however, O'Neill launched into the most intense and productive period of his entire career.

O'Neill resumed the first draft of *More Stately Mansions* that he had started before he left Georgia on 1 April 1938 and finished it on 8 September. He recorded in his *Work Diary* on that date that this play, too, was as long as *Strange Interlude* (longer actually), but that he did not think that he could cut it. He immediately started a second draft of the play and finished it on 1 January 1939. O'Neill next revised the third act of the typescript prepared by Carlotta and completed a third draft of the play on 19 January. From late January to mid-May 1939, O'Neill wrote the third draft of *A Touch of the Poet*. He then started to write a prologue for *The Calms of Capricorn* on 24 May, but did not like it and destroyed it on 5 June. He recorded that same day in his *Work Diary* that he was "fed up and stale on Cycle after 4 and a half years of doing nothing else." He wrote Richard Dana Skinner in June with a current update of the Cycle: "The score is four down and five to go. However, of the four, two—the first and second—are still in first draft and, for reasons too complicated for a letter, it is better not to try and finish them until I have gone on much farther with the whole thing." In the very same letter, though, O'Neill suggested that he might not go much farther at all: "But I would like a vacation from the Cycle and I may try writing a single play which is quite outside its orbit. Have quite a few ideas I like."[31] The single play turned out to be four of O'Neill's greatest plays, *The Iceman Cometh*, followed by *Long Day's Journey Into Night*, the brilliant one-act *Hughie*, in which a deceased character is brought to life through the memories and recollections of another character, and *A Moon for the Misbegotten*, a remembrance of his dead brother. Once he turned away from the Cycle, he never completed any substantive new work on it again, but settled with a final and finished fourth draft of *A Touch of the Poet* in 1942.

One page in O'Neill's *Work Diary* nearly summarizes the main run of the Cycle from 1934 to 1938 (Fig. 3). Before he got started with the four brothers, O'Neill labored on the "Bessie" play in Georgia that harkened all the way back to ideas for "Billionaire" and "It Cannot Be Mad?" in Bermuda. A year later, 1935, O'Neill was working on the first draft of "The Hair of the Dog" (*A Touch of the Poet*). He moved to the West Coast in October 1936 and by the end of the year he was looking for a new house in the Bay

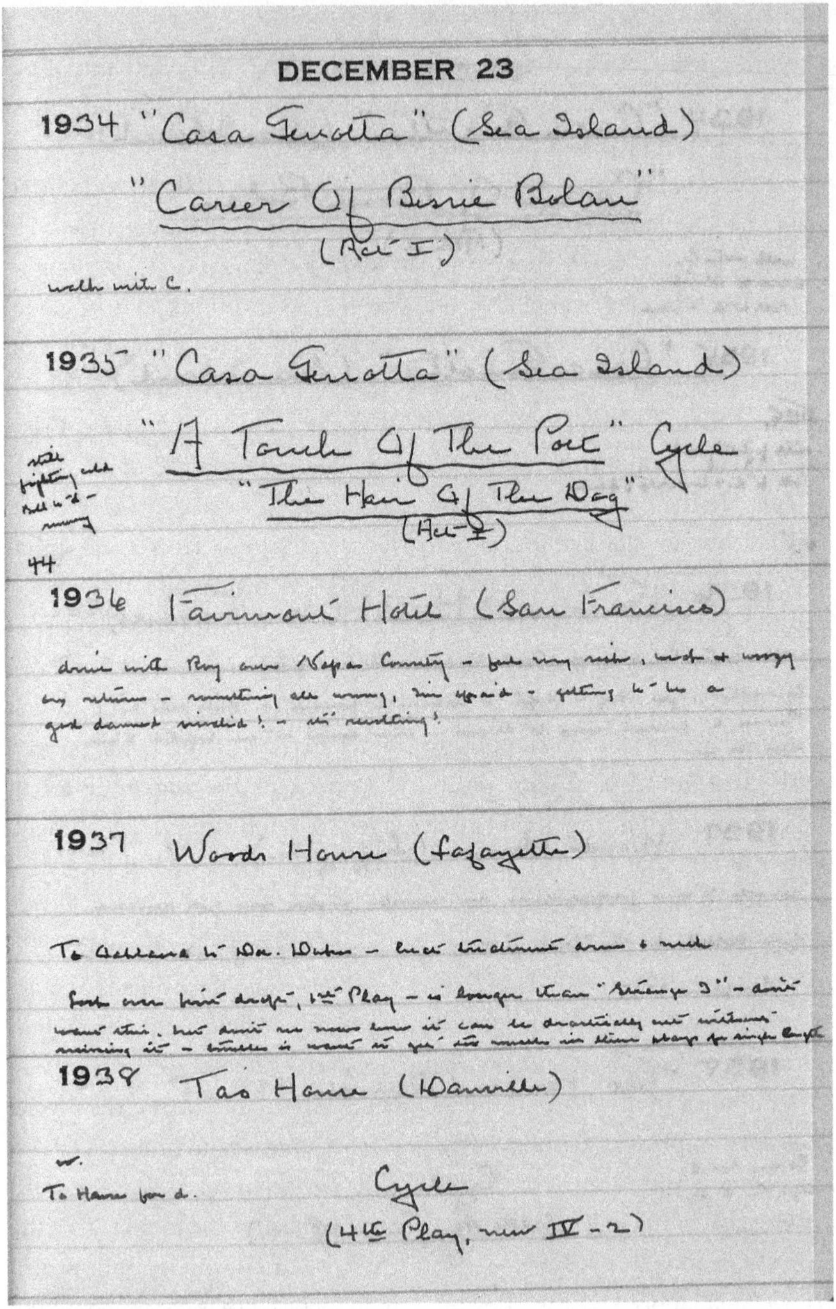

DECEMBER 23

1934 "Casa Genotta" (Sea Island)

"Career Of Bessie Bolan"
(Act I)

walk with C.

1935 "Casa Genotta" (Sea Island)

"A Touch Of The Poet" Cycle

"The Hair Of The Dog"
(Act I)

44

1936 Fairmont Hotel (San Francisco)

drive with Roy over Napa County — but very sick, weak & unhappy by return — something all wrong, am afraid — getting to be a god damned invalid! — am revolting!

1937 Woods House (Lafayette)

To Oakland to Dr. Dukes — liver treatment arm & neck

look over first draft, 1st Play — is longer than "Strange I" — don't want this, but don't see now how it can be drastically cut without maiming it — trouble is want to get its meaning in this play for single length

1938 Tao House (Danville)

w.

To Home for d.

Cycle
(4th Play, now IV - 2)

FIGURE 3. These dates, from the third of four volumes of O'Neill's *Work Diary*, December 23, 1934–1938, show the progression of the project during the years in which O'Neill worked exclusively on the Cycle. (Courtesy of Eugene O'Neill Papers, Yale Collection of American Literature, Beinecke Rare Book and Manuscript Library. Copyright © Yale University. All rights reserved.)

Area around San Francisco. His notation says that he felt ill as Roy Stram, the husband of Carlotta's daughter, drove him to Napa County: "getting to be a god damned invalid!—it's revolting!" he concludes. This malady turned out to be appendicitis and landed him in an Oakland hospital. By 23 December 1937 O'Neill was working again, though the entry begins with a visit to Oakland for another appointment with his doctor and friend Charles Dukes to treat his arms and neck for a nerve ailment. The rest of the entry reads: "Look over first draft, 1st Play [the new version of 'Greed of the Meek']—is longer than 'Strange I' [*Strange Interlude*]—don't want this but don't see now how it can be drastically cut without ruining it— trouble is [I] want to get too much in these plays for single length." One year later at Tao House O'Neill was writing the last scene (4.2) of *More Stately Mansions*.

Hitler and Nazi aggression validated O'Neill's later insistence about where the United States had gone wrong despite its vast opportunities, but his dramatic representations of history in the Cycle paled in comparison to present realities. O'Neill no longer saw the point of the Cycle's existence and confided as much in a letter to his friend George Jean Nathan on 15 June 1940: "I cannot believe the Cycle matters a damn, or could mean anything to any future I can foresee. And if I become finally convinced it is not in me to go on with it, I shall destroy all I have done so far, the completed plays and everything else down to the last note. If it cannot exist as the unique whole I conceived, then I don't want it to exist at all."[32] O'Neill added in a letter to his daughter, Oona, the next month, "With so much tragic drama happening in the world, it is hard to take the theatre seriously."[33] Nine months later, on 28 April 1941, in a letter to his eldest son, Eugene, Jr., O'Neill sounded more optimistic: "The Cycle, although on the shelf, is still very much alive. I constantly make notes of fresh angles I get on individual plays, or on the nine as a whole, and these will be a big help when I return to it."[34]

O'Neill must have forgotten that he had already expanded his Cycle to eleven plays. In October 1940, he reread the first drafts of "Greed of the Meek" and "And Give Me Death" and decided that they were too long and required drastic cuts. On 24 October he decided to split the two plays into four, bringing the grand total to eleven, and made outlines until 13 November 1940 of all four new plays: "Give Me Liberty and—," "The

Rebellion of the Humble," "Greed of the Meek," and "And Give Me Death." Through the end of that year and into the next, O'Neill continued to make notes about these plays and the Cycle as a whole, but did not incorporate any substantive new ideas into actual drafts of any individual play. He did work sporadically, yet persistently, as his health allowed, to finish the fourth and final draft of *A Touch of the Poet*. He concluded in his *Work Diary* on 13 November 1942 that he had "made it a better play, both in itself & as part of cycle—a triumph, I feel, considering sickness & war strain—still has minor faults—needs some cutting and condensing, but that can wait a while."

Further cuts never came. O'Neill stopped making entries in his *Work Diary* on 4 May 1943, and that effectively marked the end of his writing career. His debilitating tremor prevented him from holding a pencil, the only method he had ever employed to write his plays; Carlotta was ill, too; neither was young any longer, and the departure of house staff in service of the war effort left them stranded alone on top of the hill. They could no longer find cooks or servants or handymen to hire. Tao House, it turned out, was not to be the final harbor after all.

O'Neill voiced his need to get out from under home ownership similar to how Sara and Simon shouldered the burdens of acquisitiveness and possessiveness in *More Stately Mansions*. O'Neill explained to Eugene, Jr., in a letter dated 28 January 1944: "A home loses its charm when you begin to feel it owns you, and not you, it—when you have to live from day to day in continuing dependence on other people." After they were able to sell the house in February, a much-relieved O'Neill rationalized the experience to George Jean Nathan: "It had become a case of the place owning us, and it was crushing both of us. Carlotta, particularly, since most of the burden fell on her. We had loved it but we were getting to hate it because we were slaves to it—always living in daily uncertainty and insecurity."[35] In April he wrote Robert Edmond Jones: "We had become slaves to the damned place and it had worn us to a frazzle."[36] Then, in words that could have been spoken by Sara Melody Harford in the epilogue, after she and Simon have lost their money and their mansion and returned to the Thoreauvian cabin-by-the-lake where the story began, O'Neill elaborated to his friend:

> We don't own anything now except the books in storage—no house, no furniture, no automobiles or tractor, no fields to be cultivated, no chickens

to be tended, no roads to be mended or orchards to be pruned, no lawn to be watered or flowers to be reared, no hedge to be trimmed, no meals to be cooked or dishes to be washed! We got rid of everything—and at a fine price, no sacrifice, that's the best part of it. So although neither of us has recovered from the strain yet, we do feel free.[37]

The O'Neills returned to New York in 1945 in advance of the Theatre Guild production of *The Iceman Cometh,* the only one of O'Neill's final plays to be staged in New York during his lifetime. "After twelve years in the wilderness known as California," Kyle Crichton reported, "O'Neill had returned to civilization."[38] He received something of a hero's welcome from old friends, enjoyed the rehearsals of *Iceman* to an unusual degree for him, garnered a lot of attention from the press, and granted private interviews to his old friend George Jean Nathan for the *American Mercury,* S. J. Woolf for the *New York Times Magazine,* and James Agee for *Time.*

The public had read about the Cycle plays, but knew nothing of *The Iceman Cometh, Long Day's Journey Into Night,* and *A Moon for the Misbegotten* when O'Neill held his first press conference in years in fall 1946. No surprise, then, that one reporter, thinking that *The Iceman Cometh* was the fifth play in the Cycle, questioned the playwright about its theme. O'Neill, who did not like big gatherings and shied from public events, and who typically responded laconically, became downright loquacious with his explanation:

I'm going on the theory that the United States, instead of being the most successful country in the world, is the greatest failure [. . .]. It's the greatest failure because it was given everything, more than any other country. Through moving as rapidly as it has, it hasn't acquired any real roots. Its main idea is that everlasting game of trying to possess your own soul by the possession of something outside of it, thereby losing your own soul and the thing outside of it, too. America is the prime example of this because it happened so quickly and with such immense resources. This was really said in the Bible much better. We are the greatest example of "For what shall it profit a man if he shall gain the whole world, and lose his own soul?" We had so much and could have gone either way.[39]

Instead of saying anything about *The Iceman Cometh,* O'Neill stated the grand theme of the Cycle. In fact, *Iceman,* with its emphasis upon the need for pipe dreams, represented something quite different from, and in opposition to, what O'Neill said about the collective loss of a nation's soul. The reporter was understandably confused and conflated the late autobiographical play with the historical play that immediately preceded it in composition. No one stepped up to straighten him out. *The Iceman Cometh* opened to mixed reviews at the Martin Beck Theatre (now the Al Hirschfeld Theatre) on West 45th Street on 9 October 1946 and ran 136 performances before closing on 15 March 1947. Over the years since then, however, its posthumous success, along with that of the other Tao House plays, especially *Long Day's Journey Into Night*, eclipsed knowledge and appreciation of the earlier and unproduced Cycle. O'Neill, in keeping with his pledge to Nathan, later claimed that he had destroyed nearly all of it.

O'Neill granted his last interview to Hamilton Basso in the first months of 1948 for a three-part profile in the *New Yorker*. Regarding the Cycle, Basso seemed to elicit a sense of closure from the playwright. Only the third play (Basso did not recognize the late addition of two more plays on the front end), *A Touch of the Poet*, survived. O'Neill, according to Basso, took care of the rest: "He has destroyed the manuscript of everything else in the cycle—three completed plays, three that were practically completed, and two on which he had done considerable work."[40] Basso's math accounts for all nine plays of the Cycle (O'Neill never disclosed plans for expansion to eleven plays) and ties up loose ends. O'Neill's tremor had prevented him from doing any writing in five years. Yet, in the very last lines of the interview, the playwright expressed optimism that he would soon be back to work. "I want to get going again," O'Neill said. "Once I get over this thing—these shakes I have—I feel I can keep rolling right along."[41]

O'Neill did not get going again, except to move again with Carlotta, this time to the Ritz-Carlton Hotel in Boston, where he hoped to find a cure for his debilitating disease. His tremor only got worse and his overall health continued to deteriorate. The O'Neills moved into their final house, a cottage overlooking the turbulent Atlantic Ocean at Marblehead Neck, in the fall of 1948 and remained there until a temporary and tempestuous separation of the couple resulted in a final reconciliation and move to the Shelton Hotel in Boston. Once there, in May 1951, O'Neill almost never left the suite on the fourth floor. He died in his bed on 27 November 1953 of pneumonia at age sixty-five. Carlotta ordered an autopsy to determine what had killed her husband, and though the results showed no clear evidence of Parkinson's disease, the official cause of death listed "Parkinsonian Disease" along with bronchopneumonia. She buried her husband according to his wishes, with only his nurse in attendance, in an inconspicuous plot of Forest Hills Cemetery in Boston. Almost fifty years later, doctors performed a second autopsy using slides of O'Neill's preserved brain tissue and diagnosed "a rare neurodegenerative disease: late onset spinal cerebellar atrophy."[42]

Less than three years after her husband's death, Carlotta, whom O'Neill had designated as his sole literary executrix, granted Yale University Press rights to publish *Long Day's Journey Into Night*. Soon after that, she allowed the Royal Dramatic Theatre of Sweden to produce the play. O'Neill had stipulated that this most personal play not be published until twenty-five years after his death and that it never be performed. Carlotta intended to burnish her husband's reputation and accomplished this by making sure that heretofore unknown plays from the Tao House years received polished, first-rate productions. On the basis of José Quintero's very successful Circle in the Square revival of *The Iceman Cometh*, Carlotta picked the young director to stage the American premiere of *Long Day's Journey Into Night* at the Helen Hayes Theatre on 7 November 1956. In advance of that opening, on 4 November, an interview with Carlotta by Seymour Peck appeared in the *New York Times* in which she spoke at length about that play, but also about life with her husband and many of his other plays. In particular, she described a more poignant and far more dramatic end to the Cycle plays than the version recounted by Basso in his article from 1948.

Both Basso and Carlotta agreed that *A Touch of the Poet* had been finished, but Carlotta reduced the number of plays that had been destroyed from eight to six. Still, she added a memorable story in which she played a dramatic part to justify the destruction of such valuable literary property. Peck quoted a vivid conversation between Carlotta and her husband that must have occurred at least four years earlier at the Shelton Hotel. Near death at that time, O'Neill insisted that something might happen to Carlotta as well—she might get run over or something—but that no one should be allowed to finish his plays. To prevent that possibility, they committed to decisive and drastic action: "We tore them up, bit by bit, together. I helped him because his hands—he had this terrific tremor, he could tear just a few pages at a time. It was awful, it was like tearing up children." Arthur and Barbara Gelb, based on their conversations with Carlotta, added a few more dramatic touches to the scene in *O'Neill*. In their version, Carlotta said: "We tore up all the manuscripts together, bit by bit. It took hours. After a pile of torn pages had collected, I'd set a match to them. It was awful. It was like tearing up children."[43]

Louis Sheaffer repeats the same quote about children in his Pulitzer Prize–winning biography of 1973, and he also records that Carlotta set the manuscripts aflame. She "flung them into a fire" in Robert M. Dowling's masterful biography of 2014, after which "he lost any will to live." *By Women Possessed: A Life of Eugene O'Neill* (2016), the Gelbs' third and final O'Neill volume, repeats the allusion to children, but further reduces the number of manuscripts to four. Just as in their first volume, however, and in agreement with Dowling's assessment, they equate the end of the Cycle with O'Neill's impending death: "With the destruction of the Cycle, O'Neill gave up his last feeble pretense of a grip [changed from 'hold' in the 1973 revised edition of *O'Neill*] on life." The Gelbs, Sheaffer, and Dowling, despite subtle differences in their accounts of the Cycle, provide a dramatic ending and retrospective shape to O'Neill's life.[44] About her husband, Carlotta observed, too, that he was "always a tidy man."[45] The further examination that follows will ruffle the pages of this convenient narrative and show that O'Neill may have put the Cycle aside at a certain point, but he did not destroy it. In fact, as it turns out, he finished far more than he knew.

CHAPTER TWO

LØVBORG'S LOST MANUSCRIPT

Carlotta's bit about tearing up children and burning the Cycle scripts in the Shelton Hotel cleverly alludes to the climactic scene of Ibsen's *Hedda Gabler*. In act 3 of the play, the brilliant and wild Eilert Løvborg returns to the Tesman residence after losing his precious manuscript to declare that his life is over. Hedda had encouraged her unrequited, erstwhile lover to attend a bachelor party and wow his audience with readings from his new book about the future. Unfortunately, Løvborg got drunk, lost control, and dropped it along the way. Unable to admit what happened to his present companion, Thea Elvsted, Løvborg tells her along with Hedda that he "tore the manuscript into a thousand pieces." Pressed by them for further explanation, he launches into a melodramatic account: "I've torn my own life into bits. [. . .] And scattered them into the fjord." Devastated, Mrs. Elvsted departs, but not before she levels a charge: "this thing you've done with the book—for the rest of my life it will seem to me as if you'd killed a little child." Løvborg affirms her accusation: "It was like murdering a child."[1]

After Thea leaves, Løvborg confesses what he did during the night's debauch. Hedda does not disclose, however, that she now possesses the lost

47

manuscript. She convinced her husband, George, who picked it up after it fell from Eilert's grasp, to leave it in her care. Devastated that Løvborg failed to return to her a hero with "vine leaves in his hair," that she could not inspire him to victory in front of his peers, and jealous, too, that he seemed still to favor Thea over her, Hedda now instructs Løvborg to make a sacrificial gesture of suicide. She even gives him one of her father's pistols to finish the job and implores him to do it beautifully. If Løvborg had responded differently, if he had deferred to Hedda rather than to Thea when he lied about the night's events, if he had not agreed with Thea that the manuscript was their child, if he had figured it as his and Hedda's, maybe then Hedda would have told him that she had the manuscript and returned it to him. Instead, he leaves, and Hedda retrieves the stack of pages, opens the stove door, and begins to feed the pages to the fire as she delivers the curtain line: "Now I'm burning—I'm burning the child."[2]

In a letter to a Norwegian journalist dated 13 May 1938, O'Neill interrupted work on *More Stately Mansions* to recall seeing ten successive performances of *Hedda Gabler* in 1907 with the great Alla Nazimova in the title role. Ibsen, O'Neill acknowledged, "gave me my first example of a modern theatre where truth might live."[3] Ibsen, as much as Strindberg, really, deeply influenced O'Neill's development as a playwright, though O'Neill's most Ibsen-like play, *Servitude*, is worse than his Strindbergian *Welded*. Parodies of Ibsen fare a bit better in O'Neill's rare comedies, *Now I Ask You* and *Ah, Wilderness!* Richard Miller, the young protagonist in the latter play, reads all the modern literature of the day (the play is set in 1906) and quotes Ibsen, Kipling, Wilde, Dowson, and Swinburne whenever he can fit them into a sentence. Quite often he does not fully understand what he says when he invokes them. His distraught mother seems convinced that he cavorts with a fancy woman named Hedda Gabler.

Forward to the Shelton Hotel, Carlotta Monterey O'Neill, a former Broadway actress, assumes the part of Hedda to O'Neill's Løvborg. His Cycle manuscripts are their children; there is no third party such as Thea Elvsted, but the dying artist and his unfinished work stir dramatic intensity. In *By Women Possessed*, the Gelbs repeat the same dialogue from the first edition of their biography in which O'Neill announces, "Nobody must be allowed to finish my plays."[4] That is virtually verbatim the statement that Carlotta delivered to the press in 1956. The Ibsen scene conveys a devastating sense of loss of what George Tesman, an expert in Løvborg's academic field of study, confirms as a singular work. Hedda burned it in the stove and deprived the world of a unique and original effort of genius. After that, Løvborg could find no reason to live. Likewise, the scene that Carlotta dramatizes in the Shelton Hotel portrays the destruction of manuscripts that O'Neill agonized over for years, but could not bring to fruition and finally abandoned. After that, O'Neill, like Løvborg, had no reason to live.

Carlotta, much like the fictional Hedda Gabler in the play that bears her name, is no villain in the real-life story of the Cycle (Fig. 4). Judge

FIGURE 4. Carlotta Monterey O'Neill (1888–1970) at the taping of *The Iceman Cometh,* directed by Sidney Lumet, in 1960. Robert Redford as Don Parritt stands far left. Actors Myron McCormick (Larry Slade) and Jason Robards (Hickey) stand right. After the death of her husband, Carlotta dedicated the rest of her life to the resurrection and preservation of his legacy. (Courtesy of Eugene O'Neill Papers, Yale Collection of American Literature, Beinecke Rare Book and Manuscript Library.)

Brack figures as the true villain of the Ibsen play, in which Hedda functions as another of his many victims. Brack manipulates Hedda, her husband, George Tesman, and Løvborg from beginning to end, and only Hedda's sudden suicide takes him by surprise in the fourth act. Earlier, at the end of the third act, Hedda's decision to burn Løvborg's manuscript stems from a complicated set of motives: jealousy, for one, but also rage and malice, as well as an overwhelming sense of frustration and impotence. She wants to rival Judge Brack and experience power over another human being for the first time in her life. Hedda kneels before the stove and contemplates a decisive act that represents both her last chance and the end of the line.

Carlotta O'Neill, as fascinating and multifaceted a woman as Hedda Gabler is as a dramatic character, borrowed imagery from the Ibsen heroine in order to restore the vine leaves to her husband's head. She orchestrated an amazing sequence of posthumous productions of O'Neill's plays, but created the illusion of great loss of the Cycle without reference to an actual script. Just as Løvborg lost his manuscript and never got to read it to his audience, no one read or saw any of O'Neill's Cycle plays during his lifetime. There is much talk in the Ibsen play about Løvborg's genius and his brilliant new book, but no verification of its contents. And, given the "future" as its subject, Ibsen would have been hard pressed to deliver a recitation. The ideas in Løvborg's book remain necessarily abstract, but watching his manuscript go up in flames, page by page, as the curtain falls in the pivotal third act is concretely theatrical and emotionally moving. In the same way, the metaphor of tearing up children in the Shelton Hotel describes a dramatic scene of almost unspeakable loss without disclosing any names of the dead.

The drama of it all deeply impacted one young reader, Nicholas Gage, as he turned the almost 1,000 pages of the Gelb biography in 1962. He was a student at Boston University at the time and an editor at the student newspaper, and he recalled a very interesting anecdote about his response to the biography in his 1989 memoir, *A Place for Us*. Gage had no money at that time and could not afford the $12.50 price of *O'Neill*. A drama fan, he recalled how he read the book over the course of several days standing up in the aisles of the university bookstore. As he neared the end of the book, he encountered the disturbing scene in the O'Neills' hotel suite on page 938. Gage described it as "one of the most terrible acts of destruction in America's literary history."[5] He realized that the Shelton Hotel was now Shelton Hall, a dormitory on the Boston University campus, and decided to write a story about what had happened there in Suite 401 ten years earlier. Like the good journalist that he was and the fine investigative reporter that he was to become, Gage visited the scene, but discovered that there was no fireplace in the room.[6] Building records confirmed that there had never been a fireplace and the national press picked it up after Gage published his story in the *BU News*. The dean of Boston drama critics, Elliot Norton, "wondered if O'Neill's widow had perhaps lied to the Gelbs and still had the precious missing plays in her possession."[7] Norton's idle speculation turned out to be almost perfectly accurate.

At the time, though, Gage solved the mystery regarding the means and mode of destruction. He was able to track down former members of the hotel staff, now employees of the university, who confirmed that Carlotta had taken the manuscripts to the basement, where a maintenance man helped her incinerate them in the furnace. So, the scene of destruction shifted and the drama changed a little. Rather than playing Hedda Gabler on the fourth floor, Carlotta reprised her role as Mildred in *The Hairy Ape* and descended to the stokehole of the Shelton Hotel to burn the manuscripts. While this revised version of the end detracted from the romance of the dying artist, the facts of destruction remained unchallenged. Carlotta and O'Neill may not have torn the manuscripts to bits in their hotel suite, but they destroyed them nevertheless, and biographers and scholars have subsequently repeated the same lines ever since.

In addition to Arthur and Barbara Gelb, Louis Sheaffer, and Robert M. Dowling, Stephen A. Black declared in *Beyond Mourning and Tragedy* that O'Neill "destroyed all the drafts and scenarios from the Cycle that he could find." In *Staging Depth: Eugene O'Neill and the Politics of Psychological Discourse*, Joel Pfister documents the end of the Cycle in 1952 with his introductory chronology: "The remaining cycle plays (except for *A Touch of the Poet* and *More Stately Mansions* in draft), including many, but not all, of his outlines, notes, and scenarios, are destroyed by Eugene and Carlotta." And, finally, in the chronology for the Library of America's three-volume set of O'Neill's complete plays, Travis Bogard wrote for the 1952 entry: "Destroys drafts and scenarios of unfinished cycle plays."[8]

Bogard wrote expansively and eloquently in the 1970s about the fate of the Cycle plays in a passage that verifies Gage's reaction to the burning of the manuscripts. In *Contour in Time* (1972), Bogard opined:

> That Eugene O'Neill could not complete the historical cycle as it was designed is one of the greatest losses the drama in any time has sustained. Goethe's comment on Marlowe's *Dr. Faustus,* "How greatly it was planned," has more relevance to *A Tale of Possessors Self-Dispossessed.* It was a work of astonishing scope and scale. Theresa Helburn rightly called it a *comédie humaine.* Nothing in the drama, except Shakespeare's two cycles on British history, could have been set beside it. The two plays that have survived reveal something of the power of life that beat in it, but they show only vestiges of what its full plan realized would have provided: a prophetic epitome of the course of American destiny.[9]

This passage next appeared in the revised version of Bogard's book that Oxford University Press published in 1988 to coincide with the O'Neill centenary. This nationwide event featured productions, panels, and publications throughout the year to celebrate the playwright's career. Ten years later, Bogard's summation of the Cycle continued to disseminate. Donald Gallup copied Bogard's evaluation above in full on page 5 of his Introduction to *Eugene O'Neill and His Eleven-Play Cycle* (1998) and chose the same lengthy quotation for the epigraph of his chapter excerpted from his book that same year in *The Cambridge Companion to Eugene O'Neill.* First published in 1972, repeated in 1988, and amplified further by Gallup at the end of the next decade, the authoritative words of Travis Bogard embellished and then perpetuated a myth about the Cycle plays that the scene from *Hedda Gabler* enacted.

Hedda burned Løvborg's manuscript in Ibsen's play, but when the smoke that shrouds O'Neill's Cycle clears, the two plays that O'Neill finished still remain. Bogard's hyperbole about the project, as grandiose as O'Neill's reference to his "Opus Magnus," considers O'Neill's notes and scenarios and plans for plays and speculates about what he might have done. His oft-repeated summary overstates, misstates, and equivocates in ways that cast the Cycle as a tragic failure.

To imply that the Cycle would have ascended to great literary heights had O'Neill only finished goes down the rabbit hole of comic subjunctive expressed by Chekhov's Uncle Vanya: "I could have been another

Schopenhauer, another Dostoevsky."[10] O'Neill, in Bogard's formulation, could have risen to Shakespearean heights if only he had finished the Cycle. But there is no better example in modern drama than Georg Büchner's *Woyzeck,* written in 1836–1837 but not discovered and performed until 1913, of an unfinished drama that ultimately achieved great-play status. Büchner died of typhus at the age of twenty-three before he could complete the play, but critics regard it as a classic forerunner of modern theater and drama. With its episodic scenes that anticipate Brecht, its sympathies with the working class, its stylistic variations from naturalism to expressionism, its panoply of characters, its use of sound and music (Alban Berg based his opera *Wozzeck* on the play), themes of social justice and individual agency and responsibility, all condensed in a short form that nonetheless suggests expansive possibilities in terms of both interpretation and production, *Woyzeck* presents almost a case study in modernism. Richard Gilman includes Büchner among the usual suspects—Ibsen, Strindberg, Chekhov, Pirandello, Brecht, Beckett, and Peter Handke—in *The Making of Modern Drama.* The incompleteness of *Woyzeck* invites interpreters to finish the play as they see fit. Whether O'Neill finished his Cycle or not, critics can still make an informed judgment about the significance of his accomplishment based on what remains.

Bogard stretches to compare O'Neill's Cycle with Marlowe's *Dr. Faustus* and Shakespeare's history plays, but goes to absurd lengths when he alludes to the *comédie humaine* of Balzac in the nineteenth century, a collection of ninety-something novels and stories completed in about a twenty-year time period. By comparison, O'Neill's project of eleven plays seems puny. Bogard attributes the Balzac reference to Theresa Helburn, the theatrical producer and cofounder of the Theatre Guild, the organization that produced all of O'Neill's plays after 1928, beginning with *Marco Millions* and *Strange Interlude* and ending with *A Moon for the Misbegotten* in 1947 (which closed out of town and never reached New York). How would Helburn know to compare O'Neill to Balzac? O'Neill never released any of the Cycle plays for production and there is no evidence that Helburn ever read any of the drafts. O'Neill wrote to her on 7 April 1936, after he had been working on the Cycle for over a year, and warned her not to expect any plays from him anytime soon. "Don't begin to plan for the production of the Cycle," O'Neill wrote, "except in a very general way, until you receive finished plays from me to plan on."[11] O'Neill never sent a finished play to the Guild, Helburn, or anyone else.

Contrary to Bogard's description of the project as "greatly planned," O'Neill improvised the development of the Cycle and made spontaneous decisions rather than adhering to a master outline. His letter early in the writing process (3 July 1935) to Robert Sisk, the public relations man for the Theatre Guild at the time, belies the dead ends and no ends at all that O'Neill encountered as the project unfolded and developed:

> It's a cycle of seven plays portraying the history of the interrelationships of a family over a period of approximately a century. The first play begins in 1829 [O'Neill later changed the date to 1828 to accord with the Battle of Talavera], the last ends in 1932. Five generations of the family appear in the cycle. Two of the plays take place in New England [*A Touch of the Poet, More Stately Mansions*], one almost entirely on a clipper ship [*The Calms of Capricorn*], one on the [West] Coast ["The Earth Is the Limit"], one around Washington principally ["Nothing Is Lost but Honor"], one in New York ["The Man on Iron Horseback"], one in the Middle West ["The Hair of the Dog"].[12]

After working on the Cycle for scarcely six months, O'Neill had almost doubled its initial size from the original conception of four plays about four brothers in the second half of the industrialized nineteenth century. The two plays about their parents and grandparents showed how the Irish Melody and the American Harford families came together and added two generations of history to the core of the Cycle. O'Neill tacked the "Bessie Bowen" material, ultimately renamed "The Hair of the Dog," onto the end of the Cycle to bring the time period up to the present day and add two more generations of family descendants. As the Cycle expanded further in subsequent years, to first eight, then nine and finally eleven, O'Neill had to adjust the starting point for the Cycle continually as the time period receded to 1755. He discovered that he had to juggle two temporal schemes simultaneously. Working backward and forward in time, O'Neill complained that he could never find a proper starting point for the Cycle, yet what he committed to write speaks volumes for what actually caught and held the playwright's imagination. He did not write the plays chronologically, the action of one play flowing into the next, except for the two plays that he completed, *A Touch of the Poet* and *More Stately Mansions,* the exact center of the eleven-play Cycle. In these two plays, unified by their contrasting styles, the action flows seamlessly from one to the other and the themes of the first play develop fully and in surprising ways in the second.

A Touch of the Poet foretells a drama of aspiration and split identity among the Melodys; *More Stately Mansions* evokes O'Neill's main themes of greed and possessiveness. These titles resonate poetically with some of his best works, including *Beyond the Horizon, Desire Under the Elms, Strange Interlude, Mourning Becomes Electra, The Iceman Cometh, Long Day's Journey Into Night,* and *A Moon for the Misbegotten.* Although the starting point for the Cycle was the four brothers, O'Neill never drafted any of the four plays about them. The musicality of *The Calms of Capricorn,* for which O'Neill wrote a full scenario, alludes to the tragic condition that precipitates Ethan Harford's suicide. The other titles concerning the brothers, including "The Earth Is the Limit," "Nothing Is Lost but Honor," and "The Man on Iron Horseback," ring hollow and seem almost interchangeable. The same is true for the four plays on the other end of the Cycle. While "Give Me Liberty and—," "The Rebellion of the Humble," "Greed of the Meek," and "And Give Me Death" certainly refer to revolutionary times and rhetoric, they also remain mutually indistinguishable. Variant titles for these plays—"The Poor in Spirit," "The Pride of the Meek," "The Rights of Man," and "The Patience of the Meek"—as well as "Oh, Sour-Apple Tree" for *More Stately Mansions,* contain no elements of poetry in either sound or sense. These working titles seem similar to ones that Virginia Floyd chronicles in *Eugene O'Neill at Work* for late plays that O'Neill never developed much beyond notes: "Blind Alley Guy," "Malatesta Seeks Surcease," "The Last Conquest," "The Thirteenth Apostle," and "Time Grandfather Was Dead." The vast difference between the poetic titles of the completed plays and the prosaic names for the unfinished bunch says much about the time and energy that O'Neill devoted to the respective groups. The poetic aspects of a title, or lack thereof, did not necessarily guarantee quality or success, but they did signify O'Neill's level of commitment to a particular play in line with his progressive steps of development from idea to outline to scenario and finally to successive drafts.

In terms of the one and the many, the part and the whole, the design of the Cycle posed a severe challenge for O'Neill. Each play was supposed to stand on its own (O'Neill recognized the need to do this for the sake of a ticket-buying public) and dramatize the fate of one family member, yet inextricably link to the whole series of plays. *A Touch of the Poet,* it turned out, seemed to feature Con Melody, the grandfather of the four Harford sons, as the protagonist. In the sequel, the boys' father, Simon Harford, appears to be the central character as he battles for supremacy among his wife, Sara, the boys' mother, and his mother, Deborah, their grand-mother. Both individually and collectively, however, all of these plays were intended to advance the theme of the corruption of the soul through pos-sessiveness, greed, and materialism. The combination of focusing on a single character in each individual play and developing a complete action within it that would simultaneously function as a link to a successive play, even as the starting point for each play moved back in time, raised too many obstacles for O'Neill to overcome.

The burden of connecting one play to the next continued to weigh on O'Neill as the Cycle dragged on and he added plays to its inventory. In separate letters to critic and friend George Jean Nathan and scholar/ writer/editor Richard Dana Skinner in May and June 1939, just before he set aside his Cycle and took up *The Iceman Cometh,* O'Neill voiced concern with the technical obstacles of the Cycle challenge. To Nathan, he did not give any indication that he was less than resolute with a desire to go for-ward until the job was complete:

> I've been working steadily, without yet taking the rest I'd promised myself.
> Going back over the third play [*A Touch of the Poet*] lately to make some
> changes that will hook it up more closely with the fourth [*More Stately Man-
> sions*]. That's the devil of this job, the amount of time spent on such revision.
> It's a sort of special, additional task for a playwright. No one who confined
> himself to writing single plays could ever imagine how much extra thought
> and labor are involved. Sometimes, I feel sick about it, the constant driving
> on while seeming, in the light of final completion, to be making no progress.
> Still and all, I do keep pretty damned interested, for it is an arousing chal-
> lenge, and the stuff is there, if I have the stuff to make it mine.[13]

Only a month later, O'Neill vented similar frustrations to Skinner, yet he did not bounce back with the same resiliency as he expressed to Na-than: "A devilish job, this Cycle! It involves problems of adjustment be-tween parts and whole for which there is no precedent in playwrighting [sic]. And how this element, which I only dimly foresaw, or I might never have attempted the thing, devours time and labor! Rewriting and then rewriting some more! I work and work and time passes while, in relation to the whole work, I seem to stand still."[14]

Actress Ingrid Bergman recalled an anecdote with a compelling visual image for the organizational problem that O'Neill dealt with in his Cycle. In 1941, Bergman starred in a production of *"Anna Christie"* in San Francisco. Carlotta admired her performance and invited the actress to lunch at Tao House a couple of days later. Bergman was thrilled by the opportunity to meet the famous playwright and did not hesitate to follow him upstairs to his office when he beckoned. She recalled that O'Neill laid out all nine plays of the Cycle for her to see and explained that he had written 150 years of American history through the lives of a single family through several generations. He gave her the impression that he was working on all nine plays at the same time. What he was really trying to do, though, with the display of scripts was to convince Bergman to join the proposed company of Cycle actors. O'Neill explained that he wanted a small cadre of performers to act in all the plays over a four-year period. Having received glowing notices of Bergman's performance from his wife, O'Neill recruited her for his prospective company and enticed her with potential roles for her to play. He tried to fool the actress to an extent. The number of plays had already swollen from nine to eleven in his mind, but O'Neill had only written four plays at this point, and two of those, "Greed of the Meek" and "And Give Me Death," were handwritten first drafts in need of almost complete revision. For purposes of demonstration (and to better woo the actress), O'Neill must have arranged his copious notes and outlines and drawings of the other five titles into neat piles that resembled manuscripts. Still, Bergman resisted his offer at that time. She was a movie star and had no intention of devoting four years of her career to the theater as part of an ensemble. A quarter of a century later, though, she created the part of Deborah Harford in Los Angeles and on Broadway in the 1967 American premiere of *More Stately Mansions*.[15]

The logistics and intricacies of tying the plays together were not the only or even the chief problems for the completion of the Cycle. The dramaturgical plan had gone awry as O'Neill contemplated Harford family history and departed from his original focus on a single family. When he expanded the Cycle beyond seven plays, O'Neill left the Irish Melodys behind and first followed Deborah Deane and her marriage to Henry Harford, and then the entire clan of Yankee Harfords, especially Henry's aunts, whom O'Neill dubbed the three Blessed Sisters. Enamored with Deborah, O'Neill considered changing the title of *More Stately Mansions* to "Brahma or Nothing," a reference to the Hindu god of creation and the Eastern values and beliefs to which Deborah aspires. O'Neill's decision to favor Deborah and the Harford ancestry distracted him from his main theme and led to a dead end.

In his profile of O'Neill in 1946, George Jean Nathan insisted that the playwright recognized his error: "O'Neill's dissatisfaction with the work as far as it had gone proceeded from his conviction that it should deal with one family and not two, as it presently did. And also that, in the form he had written it, it began at the wrong point and over-told the story."[16] The final iteration of the Cycle, an eleven-play opus, would neither have solved the problem that O'Neill identified in the interview with Nathan, nor have changed the starting point of the Cycle. Donald Gallup agreed with Nathan's assessment that the plan for the Cycle was flawed and theorized that O'Neill's interest in the Blessed Sisters led him astray from his focus on one family. Gallup concluded: "It seems probable that the major reconstruction of his plans for the first four plays [up to *A Touch of the Poet* in the eleven-play arrangement] that would have been required in order to correct this fault became an additional, final reason why O'Neill, his energies at a low point because of ill health and depression at the state of the world, failed to do any further major new work on the Cycle during the last years of his life."[17]

As he kept searching for the point to begin the Cycle and as he started further and further back in time, O'Neill overlooked the possibility that he had already finished a complete story. With its evocative and literary title and four full drafts between 1935 and 1942, *A Touch of the Poet* introduces the Melody clan as the true starting point of the Cycle, and *More Stately Mansions* completes the tale of Sara's rise in the world from a poor Irish immigrant to a lady in America. Despite the epic size of that story, O'Neill must have thought that an even bigger Cycle would also have been a better one.

The winner of three Pulitzers and the Nobel Prize always aspired to write drama, in words that Bogard described the Cycle, "of astonishing scope and scale." As far back as 1928, after the success of the nine-act *Strange Interlude* (his most lucrative play, especially including book sales, during his lifetime), O'Neill described his next play, *Dynamo,* as part of a larger project, "Myth Plays for the God-Forsaken":

> It is really the first play of a trilogy that will dig at the roots of the sickness of today as I feel it—the death of the old God and the failure of Science and Materialism to give any satisfying new One for the surviving primitive religious instinct to find a meaning for life in, and to comfort its fears of death with. It seems to me anyone trying to do big work nowadays must have this big subject behind all the little subjects of his plays or novels, or he is simply scribbling around on the surface of things and has no more real status than a parlor entertainer.[18]

Although O'Neill never completed this trilogy, he did write *Mourning Becomes Electra.* And, the play that he could not finish to complete the above trilogy, "It Cannot Be Mad?," a critique of materialism, morphed into variations of "Bessie Bowen" and ultimately served as the final play in the seven-, nine-, and eleven-play iterations of the Cycle, with the final title "The Hair of the Dog." In the same letter to Nathan, O'Neill also mentioned another large-scale project that he had been considering for some time:

> I want to give about three years to it—either one long stretch or, more probably, that amount of working time over a longer period with intervals of doing a play in between times. This G.O. [Grand Opus] is to be neither play nor novel although there will be many plays in it and it will have greater scope than any novel I know of. Its form will be altogether its own and my own—a lineal descendant of *Interlude,* in a way, but beside it *Interlude* will seem like a mere shallow episode! Does this sound ambitious? Well, my idea of it as it is growing in me certainly is aiming at stars and I only hope to God I have the stuff in me to do it right—for then it will be One of the Ones and no damn doubt about it![19]

In their collection of letters from O'Neill to Nathan, *"As Ever, Gene,"* Nancy and Arthur Roberts identified the above passage as the playwright's first reference to his Cycle plays.[20] O'Neill did not introduce the Cycle until almost seven years later, in 1935. But, given the hints of a big, sweeping project with a novel form and the need to devote years to the work, and even calling it a "Grand Opus," similar to the "Opus Magnus" moniker that O'Neill stuck on the Cycle, as well as the veil of secrecy that still covered the Cycle material at Yale as late as the 1980s, the Roberts's mistake in 1987 is completely understandable. The Grand Opus referred to "The Sea-Mother's Son," an autobiographical project that Virginia Floyd also dates from 1928. O'Neill bragged in a letter to Benjamin De Casseres in 1928 that this drama, subtitled "The Story of the Birth of a Soul," would "have ten or more *Interludes* in it."[21]

The successes of *Strange Interlude* and *Mourning Becomes Electra*, followed by the failure on Broadway of *Days Without End* ("Sometimes Mr. O'Neill tells his story as though he had never written a play before," critic Brooks Atkinson commented), surely motivated O'Neill to surpass all his previous efforts with the Cycle.[22] But as the Cycle expanded and increased in size, the possibility of realizing any of those plays in production receded. A series of dispatches from the Theatre Guild, announced by the *New York Times,* revealed the dissonance between the bustling theater scene in the city and the solitary retreats in Georgia and California at which O'Neill privately toiled. The Guild expected to produce O'Neill's plays as an integral part of its repertory over a number of years and generated publicity in anticipation of major theatrical events of "an astonishing scope and scale."

The Theatre Guild first announced the four-year O'Neill plan in September 1935, when the Cycle stood at seven plays. It would produce the first play the following season (1936–1937), and two plays each season thereafter "until it is all over in 1940. This is official, if remote." The next year (11 August 1936), the Guild confirmed: "a special company will be employed for the plays, with each drama to be self-sufficient and complete." This bit of news came in lieu of an actual production advertisement. O'Neill had finished two plays, the brief insisted, but "the author doesn't want them on until he has completed at least half of the cycle of which they are a part." O'Neill had added an eighth play to the group, too, and this caused a further delay in production plans. In May 1937, the *Times* reported the playwright's change in tone regarding possible productions. "Consider me for the nonce as one retired from the racket," rang the lead sentence. He had wired from San Francisco to say that no part of his eight-play cycle would be performed in the next season. Over three years later, in July 1940, in an announcement ostensibly about *The Iceman*

Cometh, the *Times* added that O'Neill wouldn't finish the Cycle for another two years and that he had completed only five of the plays thus far. In September 1940, the Guild published through the *Times* the titles of the now nine-play cycle and the overall title for the work: "A Tale of Possessors Self-Dispossessed." The paragraph concluded: "No production plans by the Guild were revealed."[23] The very next month, O'Neill decided to add two more plays to the Cycle and raise the count to eleven. Six months later he recorded in his *Work Diary:* "have not told anyone yet of expansion of idea to 11 plays—seems too ridiculous—idea was first 5 plays, then 7, then 8, then 9, now 11!—will never live to do it—but what price anything but a dream these days!"[24] O'Neill, by this time, held only a hopeless hope for the completion of his ambitious project.

Stunted plans and aborted productions beg the question: How many manuscripts did the O'Neills burn at the Shelton Hotel in 1952? Recall that Hamilton Basso reported in his 1948 *New Yorker* profile that eight plays had been destroyed. Carlotta, in 1956, stated that they had torn six to pieces and burned them. That's the number the Gelbs used in the first edition of *O'Neill* in 1962. More than fifty years later, in 2016, the Gelbs reduced the number to four in *By Women Possessed.* At a glance, that number accords with an inventory of the Cycle as it stood when O'Neill halted progress on it in June 1939 (contrary to the published report in the *New York Times* listed above, O'Neill did not complete five plays). At that time, the Cycle consisted of nine plays and O'Neill had written drafts of the first four—"Greed of the Meek," "And Give Me Death," *A Touch of the Poet,* and *More Stately Mansions*—plus the scenario for *The Calms of Capricorn* (probably the fifth play mentioned in the *Times* article). Just before O'Neill and Carlotta moved out of Tao House and back to an apartment in San Francisco, O'Neill burned the first drafts of "Greed of the Meek" and "And Give Me Death" on 21 February 1944. O'Neill recorded the date in his *Work Diary* and saved the title pages of the original drafts, which were included in papers that he later sent to Yale. In his mind the long drafts were perhaps no longer necessary to keep, perhaps even a hindrance going forward, as the new four-play scheme that he envisioned in 1940 had subsumed them to solve the problem of length. Although he outlined all four new plays at that time, including the new and much shorter versions of "Greed of the Meek" and "And Give Me Death," he did not write any new drafts.

The final inventory of the eleven-play Cycle shaped up in this form:

1st Play: "Give Me Liberty and—" (not written)

2nd Play: "The Rebellion of the Humble" (not written)

3rd Play: "Greed of the Meek" (new version not written)

4th Play: "And Give Me Death" (new version not written)

5th Play: *A Touch of the Poet* (published posthumously 1957)

6th Play: *More Stately Mansions* (published posthumously 1964, 1988)

7th Play: *The Calms of Capricorn* (scenario published posthumously 1981)

8th Play: "The Earth Is the Limit" (not written)

9th Play: "Nothing Is Lost but Honor" (not written)

10th Play "The Man on Iron Horseback" (not written)

11th Play: "The Hair of the Dog" (not written)

The Gelbs likely derived their final and reduced number of destroyed manuscripts, four, from Gallup's calculations in *Eugene O'Neill and His Eleven-Play Cycle.* He theorized that the O'Neills probably destroyed first drafts of *A Touch of the Poet* and *More Stately Mansions,* as well as outlines for the original versions of "Greed of the Meek" and "And Give Me Death," when they were conceived as part of the nine-play cycle.[25] While each of these documents might have proven beneficial to O'Neill scholars, the collective loss hardly compromises modern dramatic literature. It turns out, then, that "one of the greatest losses in America's literary history" did not take place in Suite 401 of the Shelton Hotel. Although Travis Bogard claimed that *A Touch of the Poet* and *More Stately Mansions* were the only two Cycle plays to survive, it would have been more accurate to say that they were the only two Cycle plays of the final eleven-play lineup to have been written.

Løvborg's manuscript may have been lost, burned in Hedda's stove, but O'Neill's Cycle plays, the only two that he completed, still exist. Two fictitious images merge to conflate lost work with what would count as, in Bogard's words, "one of the greatest losses the drama in any time has sustained." Oscar Wilde, another favorite writer of Dick Miller's in *Ah, Wilderness!,* one with whom the somber O'Neill would seem to share no affinity, made a joke of these sorts of mixed messages in *The Importance of Being Earnest.* Jack Worthing admits to a skeptical Lady Bracknell that he has lost both his parents. Appalled, Lady Bracknell accuses him of utmost carelessness! Lost, for Worthing, is a euphemism for dead, but Lady Bracknell applies a literal meaning to what she has heard. This misunderstanding, when applied to Bogard's rendering of the fate of O'Neill's Cycle, implies that the Cycle existed until it turned to ash in Carlotta's/Hedda's fireplace/stove.

Carelessness, though, is the charge that Løvborg levies against himself for losing his manuscript at the bachelor party bacchanal. He invents a story about tearing up his manuscript rather than admit that he lost it. He and Thea Elvsted conceived of the manuscript as their child. What could be worse than losing one's child? Not in the euphemistic or Worthing sense in which a loss means death, but in Bracknell's literal sense of misplacing and losing track of something precious. Worthing himself is a foundling in Wilde's comedy, misplaced in a handbag as a baby at London's Victoria Station. And what was found in Worthing's rightful place, but the hefty manuscript of a novel that his nurse had absentmindedly swapped for the baby in the perambulator! The manuscript represented the metaphorical child of Løvborg and Thea in *Hedda Gabler;* the discovery of the manuscript in the baby's perambulator makes the metaphor literal and very funny in Wilde's comedy. The drama at the Shelton Hotel between Carlotta and Eugene admitted no comedy. But if the Cycle did not ever exist as eight, six, or even four finished plays, how could it also represent a great loss for dramatic art?

Carlotta O'Neill brilliantly succeeded with her illusions of and allusions to scenes of destruction. She drew attention to her husband's work and described a fitting end to his story. Whereas Hedda's failed design for Løvborg's beautiful suicide precipitated her own death, Carlotta outlived O'Neill by seventeen years and dedicated the rest of her life to the restoration and preservation of his legacy. Her controversial decisions to publish and produce *Long Day's Journey Into Night* serve as only two perspicuous examples of her brilliant stewardship of the O'Neill estate. Her dramatic recollection of the death of the Cycle in that 1956 interview deflected inquiry about what really might have been lost at the Shelton Hotel. Instead, reporters, critics, and biographers, inflamed with the romantic myths of the tortured artist and his little torn children, focused on the manner of destruction and not the matter. A determined sleuth discovered that there was no fireplace at the Shelton Hotel and then questioned how the plays could have been burned. But no one ever questioned *what* was burned. The answer turned out to be only a couple of early drafts and outlines, but not any finished and completed manuscripts, and even that information did not come out until almost sixty years after O'Neill had put down the Cycle. Carlotta's performance beguiled an audience that was more than willing to suspend its disbelief.

The image of Eilert Løvborg's lost manuscript in Ibsen's *Hedda Gabler* subtly reappears in Bogard's final summation of O'Neill's Cycle project: "The two plays that have survived reveal something of the power of life that beat in it, but they show only vestiges of what its full plan realized would have provided: a prophetic epitome of the course of American destiny." Løvborg's great work purported to be the "prophetic epitome" that Bogard saw in O'Neill's Cycle. After his first entrance in act 2 of the Ibsen drama, Løvborg describes the two parts of his seminal grand opus matter-of-factly: "The first is about the forces shaping the civilization of the future. And the second part [. . .] suggests what lines of development it's likely to take."[26] The analogy between the analysis of the future by Løvborg, burned in Hedda's stove, and O'Neill's prophetic history, allegedly burned in the Shelton Hotel, props up the credibility of both as lost masterworks. But of the proposed eleven-play Cycle, O'Neill did not write the first four plays about Deborah and the Blessed Sisters. And he did not write the last five plays about the four brothers, either. He wrote two plays, *A Touch of the Poet* and *More Stately Mansions,* the heart of the whole thing, so conceived and revised to reveal a single action regarding the empty and futile pursuit of wealth and materialism in America.

Enter Donald Gallup as George Tesman at the end of *Hedda Gabler.* Tesman, in large part to expiate his complicit guilt in the demise of Løvborg, vows to piece together his rival's manuscript from the wads of notes divulged by Thea Elvsted. George will devote his life to the project and the two new companions decide to start work immediately, despite having just heard the news of Eilert's death. They rejoice at the prospect of bringing his work of genius back to life. Similarly, Donald Gallup attempted to resuscitate O'Neill's Cycle by processing and analyzing the vast array of "800 million" notes that survived O'Neill's supposed purge. Just as George Tesman promised to restore Løvborg's work, Gallup endeavored to show what O'Neill's work might have been. Gallup published the vastly shortened version of *More Stately Mansions* in 1964, followed by the scenario of *The Calms of Capricorn* in 1981, and finally his transcriptions of all the notes in his book at the end of the following decade. Like Tesman, Gallup marshaled the notes as best he could.

In the Introduction to *Eugene O'Neill at Work*, Virginia Floyd explains that the O'Neill collection at Yale had been off-limits to scholars and researchers until 1978, twenty-five years after the playwright's death. She received permission to edit and publish material from the collection beginning in March of that year, with the exception of notes and drafts pertaining to the Cycle. Carlotta O'Neill, according to Floyd, had given permission only to Donald Gallup, the curator of the collection, to prepare the Cycle materials for publication.[27] Floyd published her book in 1981, but, unfortunately, as noted previously, Gallup did not publish *Eugene O'Neill and His Eleven-Play Cycle* until 1998. Michael Manheim faced the same restrictions as Floyd in 1976 as he prepared *Eugene O'Neill's New Language of Kinship*. Gallup gave him permission to read the typescript copy of *More Stately Mansions* at Yale, but forbade him to take any notes or use any quotations that did not already exist in published form.[28] By the time Martha Gilman Bower began her research in 1983, Gallup had retired and the Beinecke had hired a new curator. At Bower's prodding, David Schoonover admitted that it was not in Carlotta's will that only Gallup should publish material on the Cycle. Bower gained access to the Cycle papers and ultimately made her discovery of the original typescript of *More Stately Mansions*.[29]

Unlike Løvborg's manuscript, *More Stately Mansions* is not lost and does not need to be recreated through notes. There has been something positively Wildean about the confusion, but a happy ending, however improbable, remains possible. As Worthing discovers that his first name really is Ernest and that he is the very person he has always pretended to be, the play O'Neill wrote had been at Yale all along. The shortened version of Gallup and Gierow possesses, in the words of Gwendolyn from *The Importance of Being Earnest*, about as much music as "John" or "Jack"—it "produces absolutely no vibrations" and is "more than usually plain."[30] A shortened adaptation is no substitute for what O'Neill wrote in full, and what he finished of the Cycle still exists.

Together, *A Touch of the Poet* and *More Stately Mansions* meet the standard of drama on an "astonishing scope and scale" as an epic battle covering a wide range of human experience and thought. The first play takes place entirely in a rundown New England tavern on a road outside Boston. The second starts in that same tavern, but then alternates among the Harford mansion, the garden outside the mansion, Simon and Sara's home, the cabin near the tavern where Simon and Sara first met, and the office of Simon's business. In terms of time, *A Touch of the Poet* takes place on a single day in 1828, 27 July, the anniversary of Con Melody's glorious victory over Napoleonic forces at Talavera in the service of the British army and the Duke of Wellington. The first play, realistic in style, always remained a normal length.

By contrast, *More Stately Mansions,* four acts as well but at least three times as long as *A Touch of the Poet*, contains stylistic variations and techniques that draw upon earlier plays (including *Desire Under the Elms, Strange Interlude,* and *Mourning Becomes Electra*), spans a decade rather than a single day, and shows the weight of time and spiritual corruption upon the principal characters as they accumulate wealth through years of financial fluctuations in the United States (1832–1842), a ten-year period in which great fortunes were won and lost. Unlike Bogard's pronouncement that the remains of the Cycle show only a vestige of what the entire version would have produced, the Cycle, composed of only two plays, prophesies the future with the children of Sara and Simon Harford in *More Stately Mansions,* and records the past of the Harford ancestry as reported by Deborah in *A Touch of the Poet.* These two plays fill 568 pages in the combined Yale University Press edition (2004), more than enough for O'Neill to tell the story of an American family.

CHAPTER THREE

THE REMAINDER IN THE MIDDLE

A Touch of the Poet, the single Cycle play that O'Neill definitively completed, for which he composed a fourth draft for that expressed purpose
in 1942, plants the seeds of corruption that will later sprout. The titular
character does not even appear in the final version of the play—O'Neill
turned Simon Harford into an offstage presence. The play very much sets
up the action for the much longer play that follows, *More Stately Mansions,*
in which Simon appears prominently. The self-contained action in the first
play focuses on the Melody family and the triangular relationship between
the parents, Cornelius (called Con) and Nora, and their daughter, Sara
Melody. With Con as the central figure, the play questions the ability to
forge and maintain identity, as well as the cost of doing so. Sara rebels
against her father's rule and threatens to go her own way. After the out-
of-town closing of *A Moon for the Misbegotten* in St. Louis in 1947, O'Neill,
sagging in health, declined to produce or even publish *A Touch of the Poet*
during his lifetime.

Although critics generally regard it as one of his better plays and rank
it just below the final Tao House plays, *A Touch of the Poet* did not receive

a full production until the Royal Dramatic Theatre of Sweden produced it in 1958, followed by the New York production with Eric Portman, Kim Stanley, and Helen Hayes. Since then, there have been only three Broadway productions, none of which received outstanding notices: five performances at the ANTA Playhouse (now the August Wilson, formerly Virginia Theatre) in 1967 with Denholm Elliott; José Quintero directed Jason Robards ten years later at the Helen Hayes Theatre (where he had directed, and Robards had starred in, *Long Day's Journey Into Night* twenty-one years earlier); and Gabriel Byrne played Melody for fifty performances at Studio 54 in a 2005 Roundabout Theatre revival directed by Douglas Hughes.

More Stately Mansions, in contrast to *A Touch of the Poet,* gives a much more accurate picture of the whole Cycle as it deals directly with the acquisitive instincts of Sara Melody and her quest to rise in the world after her marriage to Simon Harford, a ruthless businessman and mill owner. The general public and critics alike initially believed Carlotta's story that O'Neill wanted to destroy the play. As late as 2007, John Patrick Diggins wittily wrote in *Desire Under Democracy* that *More Stately Mansions* had somehow "escaped Carlotta's fireplace."[1] The manuscript, in fact, arrived at Yale University as part of the Eugene O'Neill Collection in 1951, though the adverbs "inadvertently" or "accidentally" usually modified how it was shipped.[2] After Carlotta "rediscovered" the play in the mid-1950s, she sanctioned Karl Ragnar Gierow and the Royal Dramatic Theatre of Sweden to perform a shortened version in 1962 and subsequently authorized Donald Gallup to produce a reading version in English of the Swedish adaptation in 1964. José Quintero further adapted that shortened version of O'Neill's original typescript for a Broadway production in 1967 and an avant-garde version, directed by the Belgian director Ivo van Hove, using the same shortened English version by Gierow and Gallup as the basis for the production script, was staged at the New York Theatre Workshop in 1997. In their article about the more recent production in the *Eugene O'Neill Review,* Arthur and Barbara Gelb made their feelings clear about the status of any production of the play: "Whatever the merits (or faults) of the published version of *More Stately Mansions,* it obviously can't be evaluated as 'a play by Eugene O'Neill,' nor can any stage production on which it is based. It's a play adapted by someone else from a draft manuscript by America's premiere dramatist—against his clearly stated wishes—and it is, at best, a curious hybrid for scholarly rumination."[3]

The author of this book ruminated in the preface of his first book on O'Neill that a mentor had urged him never to publish for fear of future regrets over what he had written. Sadly, the student did not heed the professor's advice and must now rue what he said about *More Stately Mansions* in 2001: "An extremely long draft of an unfinished play that O'Neill obviously intended to destroy along with his other incompleted work."[4] More than a sloppy grammarian ("incompleted"?), the author gullibly accepted the received opinion of the play and proceeded to double down on facets that made it seem less worthy of serious study than O'Neill's other plays and therefore easy to dismiss outright. Upon reflection, many things that the author said then seem downright wrong today. It no longer seems obvious that O'Neill intended to destroy the manuscript. "Unfinished," too, as in the case of Büchner's *Woyzeck*, does not mean that it is necessarily unfit for further and serious analysis and even production. The author of today believes that Martha Gilman Bower was right and that O'Neill did finish the play. The fact that *More Stately Mansions* still exists offers strong proof that O'Neill wanted to preserve it, and new facts call out for revised statements of formerly bold and foolish opinions.

O'Neill's own hand provides the most compelling evidence of his perceived intent to destroy the manuscript (Fig. 5). Either O'Neill or Carlotta laid an additional page within the typescript now at Yale that reads: "Unfinished work: This script to be destroyed in case of my death!" Since it was signed by O'Neill, there is no question about who made this declaration. What could be more unequivocal regarding intent than the playwright's own directive embedded within the manuscript? Quite a bit, I say now. O'Neill was famously unafraid of death. The man who wrote his own epitaph, "There's a lot to be said for being dead," held no illusions about the end of life.[5] He had no reason to hedge—"in case of my death"—he knew that he would die. Knowing that, why did he not destroy the manuscript, if he so desired, in advance? It would have made more sense for O'Neill to have written something to the effect, "Destroy this manuscript in case of an accident," or "in the event that I am incapacitated." The Gelbs credit O'Neill with that sort of line to his wife at the Shelton Hotel: "It isn't that I don't trust you, Carlotta," says O'Neill in dialogue, "but you might get

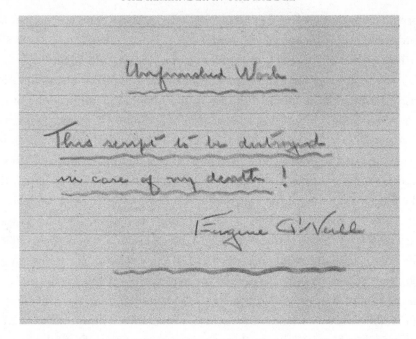

FIGURE 5. Clear instructions, written in O'Neill's hand, inserted among
the first pages of the typescript of *More Stately Mansions*. (Courtesy of Eugene
O'Neill Papers, Yale Collection of American Literature, Beinecke Rare Book
and Manuscript Library. Copyright © Yale University. All rights reserved.)

run over and I don't want anybody else working on these plays."[6] O'Neill's
note would only make sense if it were to safeguard against a surprise or
sudden event. In all other instances, O'Neill would have had plenty of time
to destroy the work, as he supposedly did with Carlotta at the Shelton.

Upon further review, too, for whom is such a note intended? And would
any recipient of this message execute the order to destroy the manuscript?
Is there a scenario in which an eager assistant at a Yale library, say, un-
packs the latest shipment of O'Neill materials, but tosses the manuscript
of *More Stately Mansions* per the author's request? Or, if it were left behind
in a desk drawer, for example, as Ingrid Bergman intimated in her remembrance, would someone find it later and burn it?[7] No, undoubtedly
not. In O'Neill's case, he appointed Carlotta as the sole executrix of his
estate and all literary property. Surely, O'Neill knew his wife well enough
to anticipate how she would respond to his orders. Although she allegedly
violated O'Neill's stated desire not to publish *Long Day's Journey Into Night*

for twenty-five years after his death and never to produce it onstage, Carlotta, beginning in 1956, rehabilitated his career by authorizing a series of publications and productions from among the hitherto unknown Tao House plays. O'Neill had to know that no one, known or unknown—but especially Carlotta, who loved him dearly—who encountered his signed authorization to destroy his work would carry out those same instructions, not in defiance of the man, but in deference, even reverence, to what his work, that which mattered most to him, represented.

The fact that O'Neill did not destroy *More Stately Mansions* when he had the chance suggests that he did not really want to destroy it at all. He disposed of literary material throughout his entire career, including Cycle stuff, but, for some reason, he did not incinerate the long play about the Harfords and the Melodys. He started getting rid of other parts of the Cycle after completing three drafts of *More Stately Mansions* and the third draft of *A Touch of the Poet*. In June 1939, he finished a prologue for *The Calms of Capricorn*, the play that followed *More Stately Mansions* in the Cycle, but did not like it and destroyed it immediately. He disposed of the earlier drafts of *A Touch of the Poet* in 1942 after he finished a fourth and final draft. After he and Carlotta sold Tao House in the early months of 1944, O'Neill burned the first and only drafts of "Greed of the Meek" and "And Give Me Death." While the length of these two drafts always bothered him, *More Stately Mansions*, of comparable length if not longer, never bothered him as much.

Over a year later, O'Neill corresponded with a budding playwright who, in frustration, had evidently torn up the play that he had been writing. O'Neill consoled the young man with the record of his own acts: "I've destroyed about ten or so myself, and this does not count my first publication (*Thirst* and other plays) which I wish had never been published, and about five in the *Complete Works* that I would gladly see in the ashcan."[8] Never reluctant to discard unworthy work, O'Neill certainly had opportunity to burn *More Stately Mansions* along with "Greed of the Meek" and "And Give Me Death," but he refrained and packed the play with him along with the other Tao House manuscripts when he moved first to San Francisco, then to New York, and finally to Boston. These manuscripts were his most important and valuable possessions, and O'Neill took good care of them and monitored their whereabouts at all times.

A poignant anecdote from Saxe Commins, O'Neill's editor at Random House and close personal friend, revealed the full value of the manuscripts. After the O'Neills returned to New York in late fall 1945, Commins saw O'Neill regularly and often dined with him. On one occasion, he witnessed a dispute between O'Neill and Carlotta of Strindbergian dimensions, à la *The Dance of Death*, stemming from O'Neill's realization that his trunk of manuscripts from California, including, according to Commins, all his plays and notes from the Cycle, had gone missing. The two men looked frantically throughout the suite at the Hotel Barclay for the missing manuscripts as Carlotta watched, but they found nothing and O'Neill became distraught. Carlotta falsely insinuated that O'Neill was becoming senile and did not always know what he was doing. A few days later, Commins reported, O'Neill quietly divulged that Carlotta had removed the manuscripts from the apartment as punishment for some crime against her that he had allegedly committed. Carlotta subsequently returned the manuscripts, the couple reconciled, and their life together continued.[9]

Given both Carlotta's and O'Neill's intense interest in the manuscripts, it seems highly unlikely that either of them "accidentally" or "inadvertently" sent the typescript of *More Stately Mansions* to Yale. By that time, they were both sick, suffering from the side effects of prescribed medications, and downsizing their cottage at Marblehead Neck in preparation for departing for their last stop, the Shelton Hotel in Boston. All of O'Neill's plays from the Cycle in the anecdote above amounted to only two typescripts: *A Touch of the Poet* and *More Stately Mansions*. There were no other scripts. The typescript of the latter, as Martha Gilman Bower noted, amounted to 279 pages, at least a couple of pounds of paper that would have been difficult to overlook and then include by accident with other documents in a large shipment. The typescript, too, was a revised draft, not a first handwritten draft that might have blended in with other documents, almost all of which O'Neill had written with pencil. The hefty appearance of the whole package makes it hard to believe that it was not shipped on purpose. The Gelbs passively described how *More Stately Mansions* "found its way into the O'Neill collection at Yale."[10] The manuscript most certainly did not "find its way." Carlotta, much stronger physically than her husband at that time, packed the manuscript in a box and sent it to Yale University in 1951.

O'Neill referred to the Cycle as "on the shelf" after he put it aside in June 1939 to write *The Iceman Cometh* and *Long Day's Journey Into Night*. The Cycle literally was on the shelf at Yale, and it remained dormant there for five years, out of circulation and unavailable to the public. In 1956, after granting production rights for *Long Day's Journey Into Night* and *A Touch of the Poet*, Carlotta wrote Donald Gallup at Yale to inquire about any "completed scripts" other than *Hughie* that might be part of the collection. She, according to Gallup, thought that *More Stately Mansions* had been destroyed with the drafts of "Greed of the Meek" and "And Give Me Death" in 1944. Still, there is a good chance that Carlotta contacted Gallup because she remembered the play and knew it was at Yale. She knew what her husband had written, and she definitely knew what she had typed. What scripts could he have possibly completed about which she knew nothing? What other scripts could have possibly existed other than *More Stately Mansions*? Gallup sent her the original typescript on 16 May 1956.[11] In the fall, as Carlotta garnered publicity for the opening of *Long Day's Journey Into Night* and granted interviews to the press, she spoke dramatically about how she and her husband had destroyed the Cycle plays at the Shelton Hotel. But she already had *More Stately Mansions* in her possession at the time of the interview.

By spring 1957, Carlotta granted permission to the Royal Dramatic Theatre in Stockholm to produce a shortened version of *More Stately Mansions* from the original typescript. O'Neill had greatly admired this theatrical organization in the country of his idol Strindberg, whom he had thanked sincerely in his acceptance speech for the Nobel Prize.[12] Carlotta elected to give Karl Ragnar Gierow, director of the Swedish theater, the rights to premiere all of O'Neill's Tao House plays that had been unproduced in his lifetime. *Long Day's Journey Into Night*, the first of the plays to be produced, opened in February 1956 to tremendous acclaim. Prior to the U.S. premiere in November, Carlotta explained that the Royal Dramatic Theatre had revived interest in her husband's work. "America," she told Seymour Peck of the *New York Times*, "was not a damn bit interested."[13] Two years later, Arthur Gelb reported in the *Times* that *More Stately Mansions* had been scheduled for production in Sweden for the next season. But Carlotta maintained that "it will never be published or released for production anywhere else." She explained the one-time exception later in the same article: "I have given this play to Dr. Gierow for production as a tribute from my husband. [He] always felt that Sweden had done his plays better and with greater interest and enjoyment than any other country. I know he would have wanted me to put the manuscript of *More Stately Mansions* in Dr. Gierow's hands."[14]

The contract stipulated that only O'Neill's words could be used for the abbreviated version of the play, and so the production involved an exercise in cutting. Even so, the final running time of the production, delayed until 9 November 1962, reached four and a half hours, including two ten-minute intermissions, a little bit longer than *Long Day's Journey Into Night*. Nevertheless, the production script represented much less than half of the full typescript. Gierow cut the entire first scene set in the tavern on the day of the wake for Cornelius Melody, the bridge between the action of *A Touch of the Poet* and *More Stately Mansions*. Since his was a stand-alone production, Gierow also cut the epilogue and its prophesies for the future (and for the future of the Cycle plays). That cut, too, allowed him to eliminate the appearance of the four sons in the middle of the play with their grandmother, Deborah Harford. Those textual chunks, though, still only amount to a small portion of the entire typescript. Gierow, after lopping off the beginning and the end, and a little bit from the middle, trimmed the rest from the internal acts and scenes, taking out words, lines, and whole speeches. A statement in the program for the production read: "There is not a scene, not a passage, not a line in the drama which is presented tonight that is not by O'Neill himself."[15] The advertisement for textual purity belied the editorial importance, and even dominance, in this case, of Gierow. The words may have been all O'Neill's, and they may have appeared in the order in which he wrote them, but there were definitely fewer of them, and the ones that he wrote were not necessarily contiguous with each other any longer. The new context of dialogue, scenes, and acts in the edited and shortened version may have been effective, but the truncated version of the play was surely not as O'Neill envisioned.

Despite her earlier claims that *More Stately Mansions* would never be published or produced in the United States, Carlotta next engaged Gallup, with whom she had become friendly, to make a reading version in English from the Swedish production script. Comparing it to the original typescript at Yale, Gallup used a Swedish dictionary to convert the Swedish translation of O'Neill's typescript back to English. Yale University Press published this volume in 1964 as a play by Eugene O'Neill, with a further citation that appears on the title page: "shortened from the author's partly revised script by Karl Ragnar Gierow and edited by Donald Gallup." Gallup's prefatory note to the text outlines the chronology of events that this chapter relies upon with respect to how the typescript changed hands from the O'Neills to Yale, back to Carlotta, and then to Gierow. It ends with a strange claim, one that amounts to a complete fabrication, for Gallup's very shaky and shady enterprise. "Shortened by a friend in whose judgment he had confidence," Gallup concludes with reference to Gierow, "the text is one which O'Neill himself might well have authorized for publication."[16] No evidence suggests that this might be so.

Layers of adaptation piled higher still when Carlotta decided to authorize an American production in 1967, directed by the eminent O'Neill interpreter José Quintero and starring Arthur Hill, Colleen Dewhurst, and Ingrid Bergman. The production first opened the new 2,000-seat Ahmanson Theatre in Los Angeles for a six-week run, and then moved to the Broadhurst Theatre in New York and played from 31 October 1967 to 2 March of the following year, a total of 142 performances. The appearance of a healthy run, however, masked a rather indifferent critical reception of the play. The quality of Dewhurst's acting and the exotic star power of Bergman kept audiences coming for a while, but the production did not leave them wanting more. *More Stately Mansions* has not appeared on Broadway since its initial production. About that production, critic Clive Barnes labeled it "a curious thing indeed [. . .] an abridgement of a play by O'Neill that O'Neill not only failed to finish, but which he specifically wished to die with him."[17] While the question of whether O'Neill finished the play or not remains for further review, the fact of its "abridgement" for the initial productions is incontrovertible.

Though not billed as such, Quintero was really the author of this production. He used the Gierow/Gallup version as the basis for the script, but he restored the first scene of the play in the Melody tavern, and then made many more cuts to reduce the final running time from a three-act play in four and a half hours with two intermissions in the Swedish version, to a two-act play in three hours with one intermission for the U.S. version. The audio recording of the production runs just over two hours. The production script runs only seventy-five typed pages, and a discrepancy exists between the scene breakdown and the actual contents. Act 4, scene 3, the final scene, is listed as "Cabin on the lake, 1842," but this scene does not exist in the body of the production typescript—it is also not included in the recording of the Broadway production.[18] There is no act 4, scene 3 in O'Neill's original typescript. This scene is the epilogue that both Gierow and Quintero excised from their productions. The inclusion of what would have been the epilogue in the scene breakdown for the 1967 production script is quite possibly the vestigial remains of what might have been proposed at one time during the rehearsal period, but was cut from the final production plan.

Gallup recalled that the production could not run past 11:00 P.M. without incurring overtime rates for the stagehands. Quintero had already added the first scene from the typescript. Consequently, he had to cut "ruthlessly" the second half of the play.[19] Unlike the Gierow production, which took pains to announce that it only used O'Neill's own words, Quintero took liberties with stage directions, the final one of which reads: "A soft, strange light comes inside the summerhouse and through the spider web of vines which covers the summerhouse we dimly see Deborah lost in her dream performing a courtly gesture."[20] O'Neill did not write such a thing. Quipped Barnes in his review, "With friends like Mr. Quintero, the shade of O'Neill might think he needs no enemies, and being his own worst enemy was the privilege O'Neill always retained for himself." Quintero cut roughly one and a half hours of playing time from the English version, edited by Gallup, translated from the Swedish production script of 1962, that had used less than half of O'Neill's original typescript. More than twenty years would pass before scholars, theater practitioners, and the general public would realize that what they may have read or seen of *More Stately Mansions* was far less than what O'Neill actually wrote.

The breakthrough in knowledge and perception came quite by accident, but definitely through the dogged persistence of a graduate student in search of a dissertation topic. Martha Gilman Bower's advisor at the University of New Hampshire pointed to the phrase in Virginia Floyd's *Eugene O'Neill at Work* regarding the prohibition to publish anything about the Cycle plays and encouraged her to travel to Yale to see what she could see. By 1983 she gained permission from Yale to read and publish material on the Cycle (the ban was supposed to last only twenty-five years after O'Neill's death). She finished her dissertation and eventually published her book *Eugene O'Neill's Unfinished Threnody and Process of Invention in Four Cycle Plays* (1992). Her thesis that O'Neill created an original character in these plays, the woman hero, influenced the direction of my study.

In the course of her dissertation research, Bower made an even more important discovery. Working through the folders and boxes of material at the Beinecke Library, she encountered both O'Neill's original typescript of *More Stately Mansions* and the much shorter Gierow/Gallup version that had been published in 1964. The tremendous differences between the two scripts astonished her. After all, accounts of the Gierow/Gallup version had always emphasized that only the words of O'Neill had been used. Articles in the *New York Times,* too, had implied, and even stated, that the shortened version followed the explicit editorial direction that the playwright had left behind in writing. Arthur Gelb reported that Gierow "came across some notes by the author on how the play could be cut." Two years later, another article by Gelb quoted a further elaboration from Carlotta O'Neill about the manuscript that she had typed: "It included extensive notes written by my husband as to how he wanted to cut the play."[21] In fact, the many revisions that O'Neill indicated on the typescript suggested a completely different experience, and definitely a much longer one, than the previously published version had provided.

After earning her Ph.D. and accepting a teaching appointment at the University of New Hampshire, Bower returned to Yale and received permission to publish the complete edition of *More Stately Mansions* on 22 May 1986. Naturally, she restored the first act of the play, included in the Broadway production but never published, and the epilogue, as well as the first part of act 3, scene 2, in the garden where the four children appear with their grandmother. But the hard task was to incorporate everything that O'Neill wrote on his typescript into a single master document. Bower's editing task was not to reduce the text, but to include all the handwritten supplements to the typescript—on the lines, between the lines, and in the margins. O'Neill had not left instructions on how to cut his play—he had simply made many changes on the typescript as he edited. To be fair to the previous "edition," Bower did not work under any production constraints in terms of making the play viable for a performance. The Gierow/Gallup/Quintero versions critiqued O'Neill as the Emperor in *Amadeus* advised Mozart: "There are simply too many notes, that is all. Just cut a few and it will be perfect."[22]

Oxford University Press published Bower's "unexpurgated" version in September 1988. In her Introduction, Bower proclaimed: "I see *More Stately Mansions* not as an 'unfinished work' but as a play that O'Neill edited with a sense of artistry and logic. [. . .] [W]ith the exception of one missing page—absent when Carlotta sent the script to Yale—the play is complete and the action whole. And if it is to be published at all, perhaps O'Neill would rather we read the whole script than a fraction of it."[23] Beyond her estimable and informed opinion, ample evidence from the original typescript, O'Neill's *Work Diary,* and Carlotta's daily diary, all housed at the Beinecke Library, supports her claim for *More Stately Mansions* as a finished work.

Confirmation, however, requires answers to a few questions about the typescript. Why, for example, did O'Neill seemingly edit only the first three acts of the four-act drama? Why did his revisions of only two scenes in act 3 constitute the completion of the third draft of the play in January 1939? When did Carlotta type the play and how do the dates listed at the end of certain scenes correspond to the composition of three distinct drafts of the play? In turn, the answers to these and other questions validate the dynamic process through which O'Neill created *More Stately Mansions* over an intense ten-month period from late March 1938 to mid-January 1939.

The title page of the typescript says a lot about possessiveness. At the top, in thick black ink, Carlotta Monterey O'Neill flourished her signature across the entire page to announce ownership of the property, under which she had typed her New York address at the Lowell Hotel, 28 East 63rd Street (between Madison and Park Avenues), where she resided after the death of her husband. She undoubtedly made these additions to the typescript after she reclaimed it from Yale, but before she handed it to Karl Ragnar Gierow on his way back to Sweden to create the shortened version of the play. In the middle of the first page, underneath the title, O'Neill's own shaky hand inscribed in pencil: "a play in four acts and epilogue by Eugene O'Neill." He must have added this later in the 1940s when his tremor had increased. The fragility of his handwriting here contrasts greatly with the strength of his blue pencil on the next page that declaims the typescript as "Unfinished Work."

Why would O'Neill labor to describe his play as "a play in four acts and epilogue by Eugene O'Neill" when he planned to destroy it "in the case of [his] death"? The bottom half of the title page lists the scene breakdown, but once again the text shows evidence of changes over time. Act 4 lists five scenes, but O'Neill crossed three of them out in blue pencil to reflect the final count of two in the play. This indicates, too, that O'Neill cut the scenes after Carlotta had started to type the manuscript. Those extra scenes do not appear in the typescript. O'Neill, it seems, must have elected to delete the scenes sometime after Carlotta began to type the play, but long before she finished.

The manuscript runs 279 pages on college-ruled, three-hole-punched 8.5-by-11-inch notebook paper, not proper typing paper. According to Yale, two pages are missing. Page 16 is gone, acknowledged by Bower, but page 83 appears to be lost as well. However, upon further review, no dialogue is lost: page 82 goes only three-quarters of the way down the page and connects perfectly with the next page (84), a sign not only of O'Neill's editing, but also of Carlotta retyping certain sections as she spliced her husband's edits into the previously typed manuscript. Indeed, heavy edits pervade the first three acts of the typescript, pages 1–206. O'Neill indicated cuts in the text using a blue pencil or crayon. He wrote additions using a blue ink pen in his immaculate, yet tiny combination of print and script. O'Neill reserved for red pencil the task of marking the change in name from "Abigail" to "Deborah" when it appeared in dialogue. He evidently made this decision late, not during the period in which he worked on the play, and these minor changes are likely the only ones that he made to the typescript after 20 January 1939. While deletions and additions fill the first three acts of the play, the final act and the epilogue (pages 207–79) have none. The pages are clean. This is undoubtedly why the published version of 1964 referred to the manuscript as "partly revised."

Page numbers and dates in the typescript suggest the unique manner in which the playwright and his wife composed the play. The first two acts (pages 1–102) display a running count of Arabic numerals at the top left of each page. Beginning with act 3 (page 103), typed Arabic numerals at the top left begin with 1 at the start of each scene, and a running count at the top right, also in Arabic numerals, in pencil begins with 103, 104, 105, and so forth. In addition, pages numbered, for example, "62a," 62b," and "62c" replace or supplement or splice pages to accommodate extensive edits and create a number of quarter-, half-, and three-quarter-filled pages. Such revisions indicate that Carlotta retyped many parts of the original typescript. Finally, a sequence of dates marks the completion of seven scenes, including the epilogue, in the typescript. Bower includes them in her "unexpurgated" version and claims that they refer to when Carlotta finished typing each scene.[24] Dates progress chronologically, from April to December 1938, until the epilogue, obviously the last scene in the play, records an earlier time of 8 September. That date accords with when O'Neill finished the first draft of *More Stately Mansions*. How, then, to account for subsequent dates and drafts, yet no edits on the pages of the fourth act or epilogue?

These questions and mysteries resolve as the process and circumstances of composition of *More Stately Mansions* come to light. Evidence from the *Work Diary* of the playwright and the daily diary of Carlotta, together with the typescript of the play, describes a dynamic process between the writer and his typist. The exchange of papers between them, O'Neill writing in his walled-off study on the second floor, Carlotta typing on the first floor, fashioned an extremely lengthy drama during an intense working period of a little less than one year. At one point, it did not look promising that O'Neill would even start *More Stately Mansions*, let alone finish. In December 1937, after he struggled to complete the first draft of the new version of "Greed of the Meek," formerly called "And Give Me Death," O'Neill wrote in his *Work Diary:* "To hell with the Cycle."[25] Three months later, having moved at last into his new home, Tao House, his mood changed as well. On 26 March he recorded that he had read again the scenario for act 1 of the fourth play in his Cycle, *More Stately Mansions*, and liked it. He had previously started the first act of the play in the week before leaving Georgia, in late September and early October 1936. Now, eighteen months later, he was finally ready to start anew. He continued reading the scenario and decided to go ahead with the play two days later, on 28 March 1938. O'Neill began the first draft of *More Stately Mansions* on 2 April and, working almost every day, finished the first three scenes in rapid succession on 12 April, 9 May, and 20 May, respectively.

Carlotta noted in her diary that she began to type the play on 17 May, conclusive proof of a mistake by Bower—the dates in the typescript correspond to when O'Neill finished scenes as opposed to when Carlotta typed them. Bower lacked access to Carlotta's diaries when she conducted her research. The end of the first scene also includes a second date, 11 May, when O'Neill, according to his *Work Diary,* reviewed the first two scenes and made necessary revisions. With Carlotta beginning to type in mid-May after O'Neill started to write in earnest in April, the two of them followed interactive tracks as they worked on *More Stately Mansions.* O'Neill scrupulously recorded everything he wrote each day in his *Work Diary.* Carlotta's diary naturally recorded many things other than information about her husband's plays. She includes just enough markers about her progress on a play to allow the reader to speculate about the entire process. On Saturday, 28 May 1938, she records that she finished the first scene (pages 1–29 of the typescript). Given that O'Neill had already written and revised that scene, Carlotta typed what amounted to a second draft. O'Neill wrote by hand in pencil, she typed the pages, he edited them further, then she retyped them as necessary, often creating new pages to splice between edits. O'Neill made further edits on the retyped pages. The single typescript that Carlotta produced in nine months included all of O'Neill's revisions. And, taking into account all the changes that O'Neill made, Carlotta typed the extremely long play more than once. "Carlotta typed it twice for her sins," Elizabeth Shepley Sergeant slyly noted in her interview with O'Neill in 1946.[26]

O'Neill wrote relentlessly throughout the spring and summer and made steady progress on the play, winding up act 3 on 10 July 1938. Carlotta worked almost every day on the play as well and often noted the typing in her diary, but she did not regularly indicate what scenes she completed. She did note O'Neill's concerns about act 3, scene 3, in which the three main characters appear together while speaking their inner thoughts (much as in *Strange Interlude*). She also noted that on the following night he shared his worries with her about his health and his ability to continue writing in the future. Carlotta lamented her inability to do anything to help her husband. That she also showed no sign of having read the scene indicates that she had not caught up with his writing and that she was probably bogged down with retyping earlier pages. O'Neill wrote in minuscule script (he had written *The Emperor Jones* in 1920 on three faces of two pages of 8.5-by-11-inch sheets of paper) and bragged that Carlotta was the only person who could decipher his hand, often with a magnifying glass.[27] She was beginning to experience difficulty with her vision and eventually had to correct the problem at Stanford Hospital. O'Neill blamed his handwriting, but the operation proved successful.

Work on the fourth and final act between 11 July and 3 September, almost two months, did not go as smoothly as on the previous three. O'Neill decided to write a new scenario for the entire act and dispensed with the last of five scenes, encapsulating it within the previous one to reduce the total number of scenes to four. He finished the epilogue a few days later and noted the date in his *Work Diary* for completion of the entire first draft as 8 September 1938. That date also appears in Carlotta's diary and on the typescript, as well as in Bower's unexpurgated version of the text. His quip that *More Stately Mansions* was as long as *Strange Interlude* turned out to be badly understated. The Library of America three-volume edition of O'Neill's *Complete Plays* provides a format for ready comparison. While *Strange Interlude* fills 189 pages in Volume 2, *More Stately Mansions* runs to a whopping 276 pages in Volume 3, almost one and a half times the length of his earlier nine-act Pulitzer Prize–winning play.

O'Neill immediately launched into the second draft of his play the next day. This included "going over" the first three scenes from 9 to 22 September (pages 1–72 in the typescript); "going over and rewriting" the second scene of act 2 from 23 September to 6 October; rewriting all of act 3 from 7 October to 26 November; and then "going over and revising" the rest of the play, act 4 and the epilogue, in December 1938. The first scenes required much less attention than the later ones because he had already spent considerable time on the start of the play in what previously amounted to almost two drafts. He had written and revised the first three scenes before his wife started to type them. As they both progressed through the play on their separate tracks, Carlotta, who had initially lagged behind her husband, began to catch up. This closure in the gap of time between O'Neill's drafts by hand and Carlotta's typed copy of those drafts perhaps necessitated a change in the numbering system on the typescript. Carlotta abandoned the running count of numbers after the first two acts and began each subsequent scene with "1" on the top left of the page. On 26 November, she indicated in her diary that she had finished typing act 3, the longest one in the play, pages 103–206, and had pulled even with O'Neill. She typed the date at the end of act 3, scenes 2 and 3, the only instances in the typescript when her progress corresponded with O'Neill's. His *Work Diary* entry for 26 November confirms Carlotta's report. He finished rewriting the third scene of act 3 on that date.

Illness had stopped O'Neill cold the previous month for four days and assisted Carlotta as she tried to pull even with her husband. The slew of health issues that had frequently slowed him down on the Cycle did not bother him as he progressed with *More Stately Mansions*. Miraculously, a few sick days were the only casualties to work that he suffered during the entire ten-month writing stretch of the play. It was an enormously productive period in which O'Neill, faced with the prospects of his imminent physical decline and mortality, wrote three consecutive drafts of a triple-length play.

At the end of November 1938, Carlotta had nothing further to type and had to wait for O'Neill to move forward into the final act with the play. Instead, O'Neill reverted to act 3, scene 2 again, which Carlotta had already typed, and made more changes from 27 November to 2 December. He reverted further to act 1, scene 2 for the next several days and changed, among other things, the opening of the scene at the cabin by the lake (for which Carlotta created page 33a), before moving ahead to act 4 from 7 to 11 December. According to her diary, Carlotta finished typing act 4, scene 1 on Saturday, 17 December, but she added that this scene—in which Simon degrades Sara as a greedy prostitute—is "full of evil—it upsets me." O'Neill created a new second and final scene, act 4, scene 2, throughout the rest of the month, ending on 30 December, by collapsing what had been three scenes into a single one in Deborah's garden. He reviewed the epilogue again and concluded the second draft of *More Stately Mansions* on New Year's Day 1939.

Carlotta began typing the new scene the following day, 2 January, and felt "deeply moved by scene between Sara and Abigail [Deborah]." She finished typing act 4 and the epilogue on 12 January, a timetable that explains why the typescript shows no signs of editing on the pages of the final act and epilogue. Carlotta typed the scenes only after O'Neill had made his final revisions. He had spent almost two months the previous summer constructing an entirely new scenario for the act and trimming the number of required scenes. Then, he spent all of December revising the fourth act again, eliminating two more scenes and arriving at the final arrangement of only two scenes. By waiting for O'Neill's revisions, Carlotta incorporated all of them when she typed the end of the play in the first two weeks of 1939.

Meanwhile, O'Neill began to revise, rewrite, and mark cuts and additions for act 3 on the typescript. Carlotta's previous typing of that act in November had so quickly followed his second draft that he had only revised one scene on the typescript before pushing on with pencil to the fourth act. Now he went back, starting with the first scene of the third act, worked from 1 to 10 January, and then skipped the second scene in favor of the third, which he revised over a week's time, 11–17 January. Since he had already spent several days revising the second scene of act 3 at the end of November and beginning of December, after Carlotta had typed the act, he did not need to attend to it further. Carlotta had typed "Nov. 26" at the end of act 3, scene 2, and O'Neill let that stand (Bower's published version shows this date), but he crossed out that same date in blue crayon on the typescript after act 3, scene 3 to indicate that he did not finish that third scene in November. Before completing work on that last scene of act 3, however, in mid-January 1939, O'Neill observed a rare holiday from work, the only day so marked in his *Work Diary* during the entire period in which he wrote *More Stately Mansions*. Good friends Miguel and Rosa Covarrubias were scheduled to lunch with O'Neill and Carlotta at Tao House, but they could not come at the last minute, and the O'Neills went to visit them in San Francisco. "Day off in SF with the Covarrubiases," O'Neill recorded. The next day, though, O'Neill was back at work and completed his revisions for act 3, scene 3 on 20 January.

Carlotta typed all morning on both 16 and 17 January, but did not list what she did. Based upon the typescript, she likely retyped a few pages of act 3, scene 1: pages 6–8 and 25–27½ are clean and contain no edits, possibly because Carlotta retyped them at this point. Likewise, she may have retyped the initial stage direction of act 3, scene 3 and three more random pages before eight consecutive pages at the end of the scene, all of which are clean in the typescript. Only then did Carlotta likely repaginate the typescript, beginning with act 3, page 103, in pencil using Arabic numerals at the top right of each page. O'Neill, who never exaggerated about the logistics of his work, labeled his work in January the completion of the third draft of the fourth play of the Cycle, *More Stately Mansions*. He had certainly reviewed every aspect of the entire drama a minimum of three times. On 19 January, Carlotta remarked about a conversation with her husband: "Gene talks to me of doing 'Dive' play—excellent idea." *The Iceman Cometh* was already in his mind and he would turn to that in less than six months and leave the Cycle behind.

Bower's unexpurgated version of O'Neill's massive Cycle play skillfully and carefully collates O'Neill's handwritten edits with Carlotta's much-revised typescript to create a master text (Fig. 6). She created the text that Carlotta would have done if she had typed the entire manuscript yet again. Hailing the edition as one of the major publishing achievements during O'Neill's centenary year, Marc Maufort described *More Stately Mansions* as "far from unfinished" and argued that it showed "O'Neill at his most innovative—as far as dramatic structure is concerned—and at his most poetic—as far as his often denigrated literary style is concerned."[28]

A series of unfortunate events, however, eclipsed the release of Bower's complete edition of the play and robbed her of due acclaim. At almost the same time as her new edition of the play, the Library of America came out with *Complete Plays* in three handsome volumes edited by Travis Bogard, and the *New York Times* mistakenly announced that these O'Neill volumes included "the first unabridged text of his late play *More Stately Mansions*."[29] Parenthetically, the article noted that Oxford University Press was simultaneously publishing the play in a single volume. Oxford had actually published the play the previous month. The Library of America edition used Bower's version of the play, but the *Times* article did not mention her name. After all the hard work she put in to secure a publishing contract, Bower upstaged herself at a rival press. Somehow, Library of America got permission from Oxford University Press to publish Bower's work in Bogard's edited editions. According to Bower, Bogard maintained that he had not been aware that she was ever working on the text of *More Stately Mansions*. Oxford University Press published his revised edition of *Contour in Time* in 1988, only a few months before Bower came out with her full version of *More Stately Mansions* from the same press, with only a single footnote to acknowledge the existence of the original typescript.[30] The left hand apparently did not know what the right hand was doing. Despite the fact that

even that I had started studying, ~~history~~. But perhaps you did not
take it seriously. I was always studying something, wasn't I? The
time I have wasted ~~instructing~~ my mind!

Simon: (rebukingly) ~~Mother! That! too bitter.~~
Don't tell me you regret -- (abruptly) You didn't write to me, that
kind of history.

Abigail: (Smiles at him teasingly) No doubt I was
ashamed to confess. ~~Oh, I have been studying Roman history, too,
especially the lives of the Roman Empresses.~~ But I find the French
Eighteenth Century the most instructive and congenial. ~~It is still so
near - at least, to me. I can conjure it back to life~~, at home in it.

Simon: (Abruptly changing the subject) ~~But~~ What of
your old passion for Hindoo Philosophy? Don't tell me you have given
that up!

Abigail: ~~(with defensive curtness)~~ Yes. Long ago.
Or, to be exact, a year ago.

Simon: (looking at her - puzzledly) Why? You seemed
to believe in the doctrine of Brahma so enthusiastically. The Sacred
Books of India were like a Bible to you.

Abigail: (with a bitter smile) ~~I have always has an
infinite capacity for deluding myself -- until Life rudely awakens me.
When I awoke one day to Life sneaking out my door deserting me,
and the Sacred Books became merely a rubbish of words. Just another hiding-place, in which I had implacably discovered myself. Brahma
had failed me. Or I had failed Brahma. There was no faith left in my
soul, but only the ghost of an intellectual conception in my brain of the
vague All which is the Nothing-At-All. I could not loose myself in
Brahma. Brahma was lost in me. In the end there was only I as an absurd celebrant offering the sacrifice of self in worship before the al-
tar of myself. (She laughs wryly) A sufficiently ridiculous tableau,
if you like - and not without humor, if one can have the hardihood to
laugh. And there was an end to Brahma, and the cowardly swindle of self-
renunciation.~~

Simon: (worried and puzzled - matter of factly) Yes.
~~I don't think Eastern philosophy is suited to our Western~~
are too young, too in love with the world of appearances and possessions.
(He adds slowly) Too wise, perhaps.

Abigail: ~~(impatiently)~~ East, West. I see no differ-
ence, except a superficial one. Hindu or Yankee, there is in the end only
oneself, a man or, woman, a lonely animal who dreams. As for my excursion
into Oriental ~~thought, it was like~~ the flight of one who, bored at home,
blames the surroundings, and sails for ~~the~~ far ~~thrown~~ lands, only to find
a welcoming figure waiting there to greet one - ~~and the figure~~ oneself! (She smiles bitterly) And straightaway the exotic palm ~~trees~~

FIGURE 6. Page 42 of the typescript of *More Stately Mansions*, act 1,
scene 2. O'Neill made extensive cuts and revisions on this page. See
O'Neill, *"A Touch of the Poet"* and *"More Stately Mansions,"* 219–20, for
Martha Gilman Bower's inclusion of O'Neill's edits (also *More Stately
Mansions*, CP3, 324–25). The 1964 Gierow/Gallup version of the play
excised this entire section. (Courtesy of Eugene O'Neill Papers, Yale
Collection of American Literature, Beinecke Rare Book and Manuscript
Library. Copyright © Yale University. All rights reserved.)

Bower's work represents 25 percent of the third volume of *Complete Plays* (*More Stately Mansions* runs more than 250 pages), her name only appears in the notes section in the back of the book.

Things did not improve much for Bower in terms of name recognition in the ensuing years. A decade later, the Gelbs wrote an article that appeared in the *Eugene O'Neill Review* that referred to the publication of the "original unfinished, uncut script," but did not list Bower as the editor. In a later article also in the *Review,* they talked about the Cycle plays and *More Stately Mansions* without mentioning the unexpurgated version at all. Worst of all, Donald Gallup adopted the passive voice to skirt the subject of Bower altogether in *Eugene O'Neill and His Eleven-Play Cycle:* "O'Neill's original draft was published in its entirety in 1988." Only in the bibliography, once again in the back of the book, does Bower's name appear. Even that reference to her work, though, does her no credit. She did not publish O'Neill's "original draft"—she collated all his revisions of what amounted to three drafts into a single master document that revealed many more aspects of *More Stately Mansions* than had ever been imagined.[31]

Thirty years after the Broadway production, Ivo van Hove directed *More Stately Mansions* at the New York Theatre Workshop (NYTW) in 1997. Robert Brustein, who had dismissed the play in a concluding footnote in *The Theatre of Revolt,* raved about the production and cited the event as an example of how performance could save a deficient text.[32] Despite the avant-garde production elements (minimal set, emphasis on lighting, geometric design, balletic movement, full-frontal nudity), the production still used the Gierow/Gallup text and inspired a comical controversy in which the Gelbs and Bower appeared by accident to be on the same side of the argument.

Steven Drukman's coverage in the *New York Times* drew the battle lines between the O'Neill producers on one side and the O'Neill biographers/ scholars on the other. Artistic director James Nicola of NYTW billed the production as "a play by Eugene O'Neill, as adapted by Karl Ragnar Gierow." Before the production opened, Nicola added a phrase to allay complaints raised by the Gelbs: "by Eugene O'Neill, as adapted by Karl Ragnar Gierow from O'Neill's unfinished manuscript." Nicola, welcoming dissent, invited the Gelbs to write an addendum to the program and they complied with a 2,000-word essay that restated the same arguments that they had advanced since their 1962 biography. For emphasis, the *Times* article repeated the Gelbs' claim: "Whatever the merits or faults of *More Stately Mansions*, it obviously cannot be evaluated as a play by Eugene O'Neill, nor can any stage production on which it is based."[33] Incredibly, Drukman's article juxtaposed this strong statement by the Gelbs with one from Bower in which she appeared to agree with her longtime antagonists. "I'm not happy about this being performed at all," Drukman quotes her as saying, "It gives a false impression of what O'Neill meant that play to be. People who watch this will think, 'This is *More Stately Mansions* by Eugene O'Neill,' which is wrong."

While the Gelbs disavowed any production of *More Stately Mansions*, Bower discredited this one because of the use of the Gierow/Gallup short-ened version of the play. Bower, unlike the Gelbs, would undoubtedly have welcomed her "unexpurgated" version of the play, the complete and whole version of what O'Neill wrote, which she had labored to recreate in her published version almost a decade earlier. The misunderstanding came in consequence of the publication of a vastly shortened abridgement of the text before the original was ever noticed and known in its complete state. In the inverted chronology of *More Stately Mansions*, the complete version of the text did not surface until 1988, almost twenty-five years after the Gierow/Gallup adaptation appeared in print, and thus the original type-script became known as just another version of the text. The Drukman piece gave the final word to the artistic director, James Nicola: "The difference in scholarly opinion about authorship is not news. The story here really is Ivo van Hove's bold, unexpected approach to O'Neill."[34]

Sales of Bower's edition predictably floundered in competition with the impressive, three-volume set of *Complete Plays* from Library of America, and the book soon went out of print. But Yale University Press took over the copyright and published Bower's version of *More Stately Mansions*, pre-ceded by *A Touch of the Poet*, in a single-volume softcover edition in 2004 that remains available at this time. The blurb on the back of the book claims that with this volume the only two "surviving" plays of the Cycle are printed together for the first time. That is good public relations, but it is also true that only here, in the thick pages of a single volume, with Bower's Introduction and her edition of the long play, does the reader get a sense of the substantial remains of the Cycle. While O'Neill at one time envisioned each of the eleven plays to be presented separately and to stand on its own, these two plays achieve new meanings and are far more effective when considered together as a single action. The Cycle reveals its form in the completed and conjoined plays of *A Touch of the Poet* and *More Stately Mansions*. Together as one, these two plays, the center of the Cycle, represent O'Neill's final and finest statement on the corruption of the human soul.

CHAPTER FOUR

SARA MELODY AND THE AMERICAN DREAM

O'Neill remarked in the 1940s that critics had never paid any heed to his Irish heritage.[1] The three major monographs on his works at that time, Barrett H. Clark's *The Man and His Plays* (1929), Sophus Winther's *A Critical Study* (1934), and Richard Dana Skinner's *A Poet's Quest* (1935), made nothing of it. They could be forgiven for this lapse, though, because an actual Irish voice had only been heard faintly in O'Neill's plays, and not for a very long time. Only a few memorable Irish characters emerged from the disparate dialects and ethnicities in the boiler rooms and barrooms from O'Neill's early works: Driscoll in *Bound East for Cardiff*, Mat Burke in *"Anna Christie,"* and Paddy in *The Hairy Ape*. Few remembered the autobiographical Ned Malloy in *Exorcism*. The Provincetown Players produced it in 1920, but the text disappeared, much to O'Neill's liking, and did not resurface until a lone copy was discovered in 2011. The Murrays of *Abortion* had never been seen onstage, while the one in *The Straw*, Stephen Murray, along with the Carmody clan, premiered at the Greenwich Village Theatre. O'Neill's big works of the 1920s that culminated with *Mourning Becomes Electra* in 1931 did not mention the Irish at all as they chipped away at New England Puritanism and WASPy sexuality.

Clark made it clear in a revised version of his book in 1947 that he limited his study to the published works of O'Neill. In a section called "Temporary Retirement," he wrote: "I do not intend to follow in detail the playwright's travels, nor his plans, nor his many bouts of illness, nor his writing labors between the year 1934, when *Days Without End* was first seen in the theatre, and 1946, when *The Iceman Cometh* opened in New York. It was a period of almost incredible activity."[2] Unbeknownst to Barrett Clark and the rest of the theater world, O'Neill's "incredible activity" consisted of writing almost exclusively about the Irish and Irish characters since 1935 in the most remarkable series of plays, in terms of ambition and quality, of his entire career. This list includes the Tyrones and Hogans of *Long Day's Journey Into Night* and *A Moon for the Misbegotten,* but also three generations of the Melodys from the Cycle plays of American history: Cornelius and Nora, their daughter, Sara, and her four children, Ethan, Wolfe, Jonathan, and Honey.

Sara Melody, the Galway girl, stands out as the protagonist of the extant Cycle plays, *A Touch of the Poet* and *More Stately Mansions,* when they align in sequence. Major Melody may be the star of the former play, but his wake begins the latter. Simon Harford, Sara's husband, appears to be the central character in *More Stately Mansions,* but he is only an offstage character in *A Touch of the Poet.* Only Sara appears as a principal in both plays, and she embodies O'Neill's theme that greed and materialism destroyed the promise of America. Her story, not Con's, and certainly not Simon's, who, among other things is decidedly not Irish, personifies the title of the proposed Cycle: "A Tale of Possessors Self-Dispossessed." An Irish immigrant and member of an oppressed class and ethnic group, Sara determines to rise and make it socially and economically in America. She plots to seduce a rich Yankee gentleman, Simon Harford, and stake her claim for economic and social growth through marriage. But it is not as simple as that. She also wants to wipe the sneer against her poor father from Deborah Harford's face.

Sara doggedly pursues a divide-and-conquer strategy to separate mother from son and take Simon for herself. Simon is both the object of Sara's desire and the obstacle blocking her desire for revenge. In spite of her calculations, or in addition to them, Sara genuinely loves Simon, and the fierceness of her love softens and compromises her ruthlessness to reach all of her goals. Her greed conflicts with her love and the struggle between irreconcilable desires forms the crucial contest. Edward Shaughnessy, who sees Sara as the most important character in the Cycle, defines O'Neill's version of sin in terms of a Catholic sensibility: "one person's violation of another which, because he recognizes the evil of his deed, causes the perpetrator to feel guilt."[3] The tripartite structure of sin, guilt, and redemption gives impetus and shape to the whole Cycle. In terms of sin, Sara knows she does wrong against her husband in pursuit of material things, but she cannot check her greedy impulses.

O'Neill's rhetorical injunction from the Bible critiques the danger and ultimate futility of Sara's actions: "But what shall it profit a man, if he shall gain the whole world, and lose his own soul?" Sara knows right from wrong, and her guilty conscience creates a back-and-forth volley of actions and reactions, assertions and recantations, attacks and apologies.[4] Ultimately, Sara redeems herself and renounces her craven materialism in an attempt to save her husband. The final tableau offers a moment of rest, a break in the oscillation between opposing impulses, reminiscent of the so-called happy ending in *"Anna Christie."* O'Neill then adds a few more lines to show that such peace is but a brief pause, a comma, before the cycle of greed begins to churn again.

Though Sara triangulated from the beginning of *A Touch of the Poet,* Simon articulates the tactic in *More Stately Mansions:* "I have learned only too well in my life here the strategy of dividing in order to conquer—of creating strife and rivalry, and waiting until the two opponents are exhausted destroying each other—then I step in and take advantage of their weakness to possess them both."[5] Simon speaks here both of his business practice and of his personal method for dealing with his wife and mother as well. He attempts to assert his mastery of his house by causing a rift in the bond between Sara and Deborah and then relegating the former to his office as his mistress and business partner, and the latter to her garden as his nurturing confidante. Deborah also participates in the game and shifts her allegiances in the course of the action. First, she tries to reclaim her hold upon her son and wages war against Sara. Unsuccessful in that attempt, she befriends Sara and her children in order to spite Simon. Thwarted by him, she turns on Sara again to win Simon for herself. Edward Shaughnessy coined a splendid phrase to describe perfectly the relentless action:

"Each victory is the result of an attempt by one to move the other off the board like a spent checker. The reader himself becomes exhausted by their ceaseless maneuvering and release of psychic energy."[6] The push and pull among all three characters plays out in all possible permutations, always two against one, and threatens to destroy them all.

Beginning with his first big success in the theater, *Beyond the Horizon,* the Pulitzer Prize winner of 1920, O'Neill exploited the theatrical possibilities of triangular relationships. Two men, brothers in this case, love the same woman, a formula O'Neill repeated later without the sibling tie in *The Great God Brown.* In *"Anna Christie"* and *Desire Under the Elms,* O'Neill replaced one of the male lovers with a father and increased sexual tension in both plays. *Strange Interlude* and *Mourning Becomes Electra* featured a series of shifting triadic formations. Much as a stage director shifts focus and changes the angles of interest and tension within a scene, the drama of Nina Leeds plays out between her and her many men: her dead lover, her father, her avuncular friend, her lover, her husband, and her son. Similarly, the interlocking triangular entanglements in *Mourning Becomes Electra* transfer from mother/her lover/daughter to mother/father/daughter to mother/son/daughter to mother/her lover/son to brother/sister/her lover, in a dizzying array of incestuous possibilities. O'Neill exploits all possible permutations with only three characters in *More Stately Mansions:* Simon Harford (son and husband), Deborah Harford (mother), and Sara Harford, née Melody (wife). In the family hothouse, relationships do not grow—they feed on each other. Each character attempts to supplant another in order to form a provisional bond with a third member of the triangle.

Outlined in this way, Simon appears to reign at the apex. He is the titular character of *A Touch of the Poet,* and in *More Stately Mansions* he endeavors to distinguish his spiritual relationship with his mother from his physical relationship with his wife. Seen from this angle, the play exhibits, according to Laurin Porter, an exclusively male perspective in which Simon seeks peace and tries to put his two women in place. Simon, in Porter's well-drawn scheme, tries to integrate Sara's materialism and Deborah's spirituality into a complete sense of self: "Their [Sara and Deborah's] signifying function is to represent the divisions in Simon's psyche."[7] It's only a small leap from here, then, to cast Simon Harford as another self-portrait of the artist. O'Neill often teased Carlotta that she should return to the stage in the role of Deborah, but the wife in this formulation appears even worse. Among his last notes for revisions of the Cycle in October 1941, the playwright concluded: "In the end Sara wins through the greater strength of her primitive unscrupulousness and ruthlessness."[8] Sara defeats Deborah, certainly, but she also triumphs over Simon in the final image.

This self-pitying portrait of an artist (Simon dreams of being a writer) tortured by two women inspires a maelstrom of misogynistic readings, the most damning of which comes from Travis Bogard, who concludes in *Contour in Time:* "the cycle was to show woman as the destroyer of ideals, dreams, and even life." Bogard does not stop there, but elaborates: "Woman's dream is of corruptive and spectacular power; man's dream is of perfect, idealistic freedom. The cynical monarchial motivations of women conflict mortally with the democratic concepts that move men. Woman's power is achieved through control of man, and she sets herself to destroy his dreams that she may in owning him live free of his desire." Such attacks do not come only from male scholars. Virginia Floyd labeled Sara as "the most avaricious woman in the canon" and sees her not only as the destroyer of Simon in *More Stately Mansions,* but as one "riding roughshod over her father" in *A Touch of the Poet.* Even Porter puts Sara in the same camp with, say, Maud from *Bread and Butter,* as she "takes her place with O'Neill's other dream-destroyers." Not surprisingly, given these unchanging dynamics between men and the women who constrain them, Bogard concludes that the worldview of the Cycle depicts a "desperate fall to a frightening end in a world that offered only vicious struggle as a way of life."[9]

In the schemas above, women take the active and aggressive role in the battle of the sexes while men only passively respond. If men are the victims of women in these familiar readings, then women, it stands to reason, should enjoy at least the privilege of power. The Broadway program cover for the 1967 production of *More Stately Mansions* splendidly captured these roles (Fig. 7). A lobotomized-looking Arthur Hill, as Simon, stares blankly into empty space; Ingrid Bergman looks down in profile past her son to her female adversary; Colleen Dewhurst as Sara grabs primary focus. The slight tilt of her body and face allows the camera to capture the intensity of her eyes. Sara's left hand cradles Simon's head, but it also reaches up to wrest him from Deborah. Simon may be in the center of the group, but

FIGURE 7. Ingrid Bergman as Deborah, Arthur Hill as Simon Harford, and Colleen Dewhurst as Sara in *More Stately Mansions,* 1967, directed by José Quintero. This image adorned the *Playbill* cover for the Broadway production after its run at the Ahmanson Theatre in Los Angeles. Dewhurst (1924–1991) received a Tony Award nomination for her performance. She played leading parts in many O'Neill plays, including Abbie Putnam in *Desire Under the Elms* (1963), Christine Mannon in *Mourning Becomes Electra* (1972), Josie Hogan in *A Moon for the Misbegotten* (1973; Tony Award winner), Essie Miller in *Ah, Wilderness!* (1988), and Mary Tyrone in *Long Day's Journey Into Night* (1988). (Photo by Maurice Manson. Courtesy of the Museum of the City of New York.)

Sara seems to be the most actively engaged character in the scene. Sara knows what she wants and boldly stakes her claim.

In addition to his passivity, Simon Harford's lack of Irishness relegates him to a supporting role. The fact that he comes from a rich family also makes him an object of scorn for O'Neill. The Harfords in the Cycle plays are not all that different from the Chatfields in *Long Day's Journey Into Night,* to whom Tyrone theatrically bows as if he were making a curtain call. "He's right not to give a damn what anyone thinks," Edmund comments approvingly.[10] O'Neill sticks it to the Irish oppressors in all of his plays, but never more famously than in his late autobiographical masterpieces. "Proudly Irish," biographer Louis Sheaffer contends, "the playwright son never forgave the first families of New London who had looked down on James O'Neill and his family."[11] The Standard Oil millionaires Harker in *Long Day's Journey Into Night* and T. Stedman Harder in *A Moon for the Misbegotten* prove no match for the crafty Irish wits of Shaughnessy and Phil Hogan in those respective plays. In each case, the underdog Irish win a "glorious victory" over the wealthy Yankees. Harker and Harder, too, sound very close to Harford.

Harford is also just a voiced consonant away from sounding like Harvard, the elite institution from which Simon graduated. While O'Neill derides the value of a college education in the aforementioned plays, he also makes a guilty villain of the privileged Jack Townsend, a college athlete responsible for the death of his Irish "townie" sometime girlfriend in *Abortion*. Townsend, at least, commits suicide when he fully recognizes what he has done, but Simon Harford implores his mother to murder his wife after he first convinces his wife to kill his mother! Harvard is not just any college, but the direct object of the playwright's scorn. O'Neill decided in the 1940s to distribute most of his early manuscripts to the Museum of the City of New York; manuscripts from his middle period, from *The Straw* to *Desire Under the Elms*, went to Princeton; Yale received all of his late work. He added this coda to a letter to his son, Eugene, Jr., in 1942: "Perhaps, as a just man, I should have asked Harvard if it wanted any, but I'm not a just man where Harvard is concerned (early Princeton influence, perhaps). I just don't like the damned place."[12] O'Neill's antipathy to the rich, powerful, and elite, epitomized by access to Harvard, works against a portrayal of Simon Harford as the central character.

A shift in perspective and rotation of the triangle place Sara Melody at the apex. The production of *More Stately Mansions* at the New York Theatre Workshop in 1997, directed by Ivo van Hove, staged a triangular tableau among the three principals at the beginning of each of three acts. Deborah stood upstage between Sara and Simon in act 1 (the first two acts of O'Neill's full text); Simon, instigator of the divide-and-conquer campaign, was the central figure in act 2 (act 3 in O'Neill's script); but Sara received primary focus in the third and final tableau (act 4 of O'Neill's script). Each character gets its due, but Sara performs her most important functions leading up to and during the climax of the play. Martha Gilman Bower argues that O'Neill creates with her character a new kind of woman hero who possesses the Nietzschean will to power typically reserved for male literary characters. Despite her appalling ambition and ruthlessness, which O'Neill does not shy away from depicting, Sara generates the life force in the drama. Bower notes that the playwright changed his estimation of her over time, and he grew to admire her strength and courage.[13]

Born on an estate near Galway, Sara immigrated with her parents to America as a very young girl after her father resigned in disgrace from the British army for trying to seduce a Spanish nobleman's wife. Despite having left Ireland when she was just a little girl, and despite her present poverty, Sara thinks of herself as an aristocrat quite apart from the other Irish immigrants in her Massachusetts community. She emphasizes the family difference in terms of educational and social status, if not economic status, to her mother with reference to Father Flynn, the local priest, early in act 1: "You ought to tell the good Father we aren't the ignorant shanty scum he's used to dealing with" (23). The family settled in a town outside Boston where her father, Cornelius Melody, bought an inn with the understanding that a new coach line would stop there and provide steady business and income for years to come. Unfortunately, the Yankees swindled him in the transaction—no coach line opened near the inn and the property returned little on the investment. Humiliated, Melody salved his wounded pride by playing the part of an English, not Irish, gentleman, and refused to do any work. He hired a bartender and required his devoted wife, Nora, and his only child to work as cook and waitress at the inn. He, though, bought a thoroughbred mare to ride around the countryside and rule the land as if he were a lord.

Sara, twenty years old at the start of *A Touch of the Poet*, resents her father on three related counts. First, she accuses him of living in a world of dreams and fantasies and avoiding the facts of life as they present themselves. Second, she hates the way her father pretends to be above having to perform any labor and leaves all the hard work of running the inn to her and to her mother. She cannot understand how her mother still loves such a man and sees the physical toll that Nora has paid for her devotion to Con. Only forty years old, Nora's body breaks in service of the man she loves. Sara recognizes that her mother was very pretty as a young woman, and Sara fears the same future hardship for herself. Third, Sara holds her father responsible for the family poverty. She remembers a life of privilege, but the present is a daily struggle that shows no sign of ending anytime soon. She understands that predators fooled her father as a novice businessman adrift in a new land, but she does not understand or forgive him for not getting back on his feet after an initial setback and attempting another plan in search of success. Sara, unlike her father, sees America as a land of opportunity: "He had education above most Yanks, and he had money enough to start him, and this is a country where you can rise as high as you like, and no one but fools who envy you care what you rose from, once you've the money and the power goes with it" (22).

Unlike her father, Sara is proud of her Irish origins, but she also looks to the future with confident optimism. Her father cannot recover from the slights of the past. He regrets the lack of funds that prevents him from investing in railroads (an industry in which his future son-in-law and one of his grandchildren will later thrive), but otherwise sees no action for him to take in the United States. Con cannot or refuses to bend with new times and the ways of a new country, but Sara has youth on her side, and she eagerly embraces what the future might hold for her. As John Patrick Diggins says about her, "Sara Harford agrees completely with Tocqueville that democracy is the victory of will over birth and that America is an open field of opportunity for the ambitious."[14] Historically, only men enjoyed the freedom to pursue their ambitions, and Sara complains about her father's wasted opportunity and her lack thereof: "Oh, if I was a man with the chance he had, there wouldn't be a dream I'd not make come true" (22).

Present circumstances at the Melody Inn, however, present Sara with one of the few opportunities available to a woman of that time, and she intends to capitalize on it. Simon Harford, son of a rich and established Yankee family, had rented Melody's nearby rustic cabin by the lake to write poetry, theorize about radical social and economic justice, and escape from the daily slog of his father's lucrative shipping business. Recently, though, he became ill and the Melodys, fearful that he might die, brought him to the inn, where Sara and her mother nursed the young man back to health. Simon's extended bedrest gave Sara all the time she needed to fall in love. Significantly, although she knows that he comes from a wealthy family, Sara loves Simon because he's "different" from other men and "didn't like being in trade." In Sara's words, Simon wants to "think great thoughts about what life means, and write a book about how the world can be changed so people won't be greedy to own money and land and get the best of each other but will be content with little and live in peace and freedom together, and it will be like heaven on earth" (24). Sara allows that Simon has not actually written any part of this book yet, just taken a lot of notes, but the idea of it is enough to set him apart in her eyes and distinguish him as the one for her.

Nora voices concern that the young man, well above Sara in social and economic class, might desire her only for sexual fulfillment. Sara assures her, though, that she will seduce him long before he resolves to advance upon her. And Sara is not about to lose her head in a silly romance that leaves her victimized and broken-hearted. Sara loves Simon, "[b]ut not too much. I'll not let love make me any man's slave. I want to love him just enough so I can marry him without cheating him, or myself. (*Determinedly.*) For I'm going to marry him, Mother. It's my chance to rise in the world and nothing will keep me from it" (25–26). Sara resents the ways in which her father exploits her mother and has worn her down through the years. Her father always holds himself as superior; when he got married he was, technically, an aristocrat and Nora was a peasant. But when Nora got pregnant with the child who became Sara, Melody did the honorable thing and married her, though he never forgave himself for stooping below his station and made it clear that such an unfavorable match led to his ruin. Sara cannot understand how Nora continues to love unconditionally such a man and vows not to make the same mistakes as her mother. Later, though, after Simon finally kisses her and Sara knows that a marriage proposal is imminent, she seems transformed with happiness. Still, she angrily protests: "I'm too much in love and I don't want to be! I won't let my heart rule my head and make a slave of me!" (54).

Despite Simon's advantages of birth and family wealth, Sara considers him her equal, and she sees from the outset that she will be able to help him succeed. Although possible interference from Simon's mother concerns her, the question of whether Henry Harford will disinherit his son does not bother Sara at all. She recognizes that Simon has a force of will and an independent streak that matches her own. She likes the poet in him and his ideas for a just society, but she also sees his raw ambition and desire to achieve great things in business, and she instinctively knows that she can assist and motivate any of his lucrative pursuits. Sara sees and appreciates Simon's steely and stubborn resolve behind his mask of meekness: "When it comes to not letting others rule him, he's got a will of his own behind his gentleness. Just as behind his poetry and dreams I feel he has it in him to do anything he wants. So even if his father cuts him off, with me to help him we'll get on in the world" (27). From the very beginning, then, Sara recognizes the complexity and contradictions in Simon. She loves him because she sees the full panoply of his attributes. She tries to ration her portions of love in an attempt to hold on to her independence and sense of self.

Cornelius Melody fears his daughter's clear-eyed resolution and willingness to pursue what she wants. He tries to dismiss her relationship with Simon as purely ambitious and manipulative. When he catches her walking up to his room wearing her Sunday best, he interjects: "Faith, the poor young devil hasn't a chance to escape with you two scheming peasants laying snares to catch him" (49). He includes Nora in Sara's plot and sympathizes with Simon's plight as if it were his own from years ago. He adds, with reference to his own tragic fate, "And if all other tricks fail, there's always one last trick to get him through his honor" (50). Nora cuts through his bitterness by voicing what she calls her sin as a young woman with Con. Chastened, Con admits that he seduced Nora and asserts that there was no shame in their union: "It was love and joy and glory in you and you were proud" (51). With Sara now upstairs, Melody tells Nora that he will consent to Sara's prospective marriage provided that he and the senior Harford can agree upon a proper settlement. Happily, Nora imagines that this marriage will give their daughter her opportunity to rise in the world. Nora speaks almost rhapsodically about the future: "We'll see the day when she'll live in a grand mansion, dressed in silks and satins, and riding in a carriage with coachman and footman" (52).

The prospects of a happy and uncomplicated future with a united family splay in the third act. Sara agrees to work one last time as a waitress for her father's celebratory feast on the anniversary of his greatest military victory at Talavera in 1809. However, she cannot hide her contempt for what she considers her father's life of many illusions. Fed up, she announces that she has had enough: "I'm going. I don't want to listen to the whiskey in you boasting of what never happened—as usual!" (89). Perhaps realizing that in another year she will be married to Simon and never appear again at this dinner, the most meaningful night for him each year and almost the only thing to which he looks forward, Melody stops his daughter with a barrage of insulting comparisons of her "thick wrists" and "ugly, peasant paws" to the dainty limbs of his thoroughbred mare. Melody then plays out an elaborate and well-crafted joke regarding his private conversation with Simon (offstage) about the prospective marriage arrangements and the financial settlement between the two fathers. Of course, Sara knows that her father has no money to provide a dowry. But she does not care: it is an outmoded custom and she feels she needs no assistance from her father to get a start in the world. Still, Melody's rhetorical skills compel her to listen and react emotionally to his words. Finally, her father delivers the punch line: "Well, to be brutally frank, my dear, all I can see in you is a common, greedy, scheming, cunning peasant girl, whose only thought is money and who has shamelessly thrown herself at a young man's head because his family happens to possess a little wealth and position" (94). Melody goes on to suggest that his barkeep, Mickey Maloy, would make a much more suitable match: "He can give you a raft of peasant brats to squeal and fight with the pigs on the mud floor of your hovel" (95). Stung, Sara retorts that her father must be thinking of where his own father was born and raised. With his back to her, Melody finally relents, offers a heartfelt apology for his brutal assault, and waits for a word of forgiveness. Hearing no response, he turns to discover that Sara has left quietly without him noticing. The last chance for reconciliation slips away.

The end of the act unfolds as farce with the entrance of Nicholas Gadsby. After identifying the visitor as a lawyer in Henry Harford's employ, Melody incorrectly assumes that Gadsby has come to negotiate the dowry

settlement for the prospective marriage. In fact, Gadsby is prepared to offer a monetary incentive to Melody if he will forgo any hope of such an alliance between the two families, sell their inn in Massachusetts, and move
west as far as Ohio. The comic misunderstanding results from Melody's
pride—he does not recognize the difference in class between the Yankees
and himself and regards the lawyer as little more than a toady. The scene
also suggests that Melody fabricated the exchange with young Harford in
which he counseled the young man against marriage to Sara. Melody's
willingness to discuss terms with Gadsby casts doubt that he ever had the
frank conversation with Simon that he reported to his daughter. Once
he fully feels the thrust of Gadsby's counterproposal, Melody explodes
with anger, literally kicks Gadsby out of the inn, and prepares to challenge
Henry Harford to a duel.

In consequence to this affront to his honor, Melody forbids Sara to
marry Simon for certain and claims that it is a question of honor. In a
classic division of male and female perspectives, Sara counters that it is a
matter of her happiness. She defies him or anyone to come between her
and Simon. Her father said previously that if she were to trick Simon into
bed, he would give his consent to the marriage. Now, she threatens to do
that very thing in order to secure her future happiness. After Con and his
cohorts depart for the Harford mansion in search of a fight, Sara insists
to her mother that she can win her own battles: "I won't let him destroy
my life with his madness, after all the plans I've made and the dreams
I've dreamed. I'll show him I can play at the game of gentleman's honor
too!" (109).

Act 4, the final act, begins at midnight. Sara joins her mother to wait
for the return of the men. Stage directions indicate a noticeable change in
Sara's general attitude: "All the bitterness and defiance have disappeared
from her face" (114). Her mother gives voice to her longstanding fears that
God will punish her for the mortal sin she committed with Con before
they married. "You're living in Ireland long ago, like Father," says Sara,
who has just made love to Simon in the upstairs room (117). She feels the
same honor and love for Simon as Nora does for Con, but none of the
shame and sin. In defense of her actions, she asks: "Would you have me
do nothing to save my happiness and my chance in life, when I thought
there was danger they'd be ruined forever?" (119). Sara did not perform

as brazenly as she bragged. She and Simon both turned shy in the face of love and ended up in bed together through a kind of mutual, sweet gravitation. Although she had tried to seduce him, all she could do in the end "was stand and gape at him and blush!" (120). Simon, it seems, had been making plans all along for their future. He proposed to buy a small cotton mill and earn just enough to survive: "just enough to be comfortable, and he'd have time over to write his book, and keep his wisdom, and never let himself become a slave to the greed for more than enough that is the curse of mankind. Then he said he was afraid maybe I'd think it was weakness in him, not wisdom, and could I be happy with enough and no more" (122).

At this point, Sara regards all her former dreams of riches as the foolish boasting of a girl, not the woman in love that she is now. Her mother, whom she had considered weak, would do anything for Con, but Sara realizes that she would do the same for Simon. She feels that she has learned a valuable lesson from her mother and now regards Nora as a wise woman. Of her own experience in bed, Sara confides: "I'd got to the place where all you know or care is that you belong to love, and you can't call your soul your own any more, let alone your body, and you're proud you've given them to love." Moments later, she adds: "It's love's slaves we are, Mother, not men's—and wouldn't it shame their boasting and vanity if we ever let them know our secret?" (125). Earlier, Sara feared that she might give too much of herself away in love to Simon. Now, she reasons that she has given herself to love and not to Simon, that she serves not him, but love. Filled with the same kind of pride for love as her mother, Sara understands and admires her mother's relationship with her father for the very first time in her life.

The noisy return of the men, beaten and bruised from a humiliating brawl with the police outside the Harford mansion, interrupts the reverent atmosphere created by the two women. Jamie Cregan, Con's distant cousin and corporal from long ago, describes what transpired and insists that they fought to defend Sara's honor. As if challenged to a duel of her own, Sara responds forcefully: "I can revenge my own insults, and I have! I've beaten the Harfords—and he's [Con] only made a fool of himself for her [Deborah] to sneer at. But I've beaten her [Deborah] and I'll sneer last" (134). Alone with her mother in the previous scene, Sara had lapsed into reciting dreamy idylls on love. Faced with her father and his friends, though, she regains an aggressive composure that frames her lovemaking as a victorious battle. While Con tilted at windmills under the window of Deborah Harford, Sara slept with Deborah's son and secured his marriage proposal without any help from her father. She claims that she tricked Simon into bed per his suggestion, faces him directly as he recoils from the news, but then flinches when he draws his dueling pistol and aims it at her. "I know you've great ambition," he tells her in the thick Irish brogue that he now assumes, "so remember it's to hell wid honor if ye want to rise in this world" (142). He does not shoot, but a few moments later he offers a final prophesy regarding his only child: "I'd lay a pound, if I had one, to a shilling she'll see the day when she'll wear fine silks and drive in a carriage [. . .] behind spankin' thoroughbreds, her nose in the air; and she'll live in a Yankee mansion, as big as a castle, on a grand estate av stately woodland and soft green meadows and a lake" (145).

Melody no longer resembles the proud major, one time of His Majesty's Seventh Dragoons, but is just another Irish lout, indistinguishable, really, from O'Dowd, Riley, or Roche, the idle spongers whose tongues hang to lap up Con's booze. After having wished wholeheartedly to bring her father down from his high horse, and after repeatedly stating that he needed to face reality and abandon his dreams, Sara now fervently tries to restore the father whom she once knew and prevent him from retreating to the bar with the drunken crowd. She goes so far as to say that she won't marry Simon because she is "too proud to marry a Yankee coward's son!" (149). She insists that she is proud to be Con's daughter, but he begs her to stop and release him. He goes, and Sara adds a simple requiem: "May the hero of Talavera rest in peace!" (152).

More Stately Mansions, the sequel to *A Touch of the Poet*, begins at the same tavern four years later for the wake of Cornelius Melody. Con never recovered his former spirit after the beating he received from the Harfords. Cregan complains that "his own daughter turnin' traitor and marryin' Harford's son" did not help (162). Maloy speculates that Sara, who has never returned to her former home, will not attend the wake, either, because she is "too high and mighty" to interact with "poor Irish relations" (163). Nora, forty-five, "a typical Irish peasant woman with a shapeless, heavy figure" (164), defends her daughter as similar in nature to her dead husband: "Sara had great pride in her, her father's own pride, and great ambition to raise herself in the world, and maybe she's grown shamed of me" (166). Sara allays her mother's fears, though, when she arrives with her husband. Stage directions characterize the young couple in "as loving and contented a marriage as one could find" (169).

Pregnant with her fourth child, Sara explains that Simon insisted that they give Irish names to two boys (Wolfe Tone and Owen Roe), while Sara chose Yankee names for the other two (Evan and Jonathan). She remains bitter regarding her father and refuses to acknowledge any resemblance of her children to their late grandfather. Sara blanches, too, at the prospect of paying off her mother's debts that her father accrued. She does not want to tap resources that she and Simon "slaved to save." Nevertheless, she realizes that her mother has "been a slave to this drunkard's roost too long" (180). Sara and Simon conclude that it is their duty and desire to help Nora. Pride, though, stops Nora from accepting her daughter's charity, and she reverts to her refrain on Sara and Simon's success from the previous play: "I want you to rise in the world, an' own the things your father once owned an' you was born to—wealth an' a grand estate an' you ridin' in your carriage like a Duchess wid coachmen an' footman, an' a raft av servants bowin' an' scrapin'" (185). Nora plans to relinquish all of her worldly possessions and enter a convent, but she does not want the same for her daughter. Sara knows that she must help her mother financially, but she resents that her father continues to draw her into conflict even from the grave. Business at the mill with Simon has been good, and he has plans to buy out his partner and make even more money, but new priorities to redirect funds and pay off Con's debts promise to delay the expansion.

While Sara continues to say that she loves the poet in Simon, she encourages him to excel in business and recognizes that she has an aptitude for the work as well. Proudly, she asserts: "I've got brains for more than just sleepin' with the man I love an' havin' his children an' keepin' his house" (187). She reverts to Irish brogue as she speaks, a sign, according to O'Neill's earlier stage directions, of Sara at "moments of extreme emotion" (169). She, clearly, is not just the force behind Simon in business, but a partner with him. She supports most of his decisions, though she criticizes his purchase of the cabin by the lake where they first fell in love as sentimental. Still, she figures that the land might be an ideal site on which to build a gentleman's estate in the future. Prospects seem wide open for Sara at this point, and she is confident that she and her husband and her sons will continue to be very successful financially. She believes strongly that her country, the United States, affords a wealth of opportunities to those who are smart enough to recognize them and work hard enough to seize them. As Sara embraces the possibilities in a new land, she also distances herself from her father who lived too much in the past: "this is America not poverty-stricken Ireland where you're a slave! Here you're free to take what you want, if you've the power in yourself." She further goes on to voice the capitalist credo (and the myth of America and the American Dream): "for where is the glory of life if it's not a battle where you prove your strength to rise to the top and let nothing stop you!" (188; 189).

At the same time, Sara senses that something is wrong with her rationale for rapaciousness. She records the ambivalence that Simon registers about the rigors of daily trade, but she tries to justify her encouragement of him by suggesting that she knows what he really wants, and that his fanciful dreams of writing books for a just society are little more than indulgent detours from his primary directive to make lots of money. "Sure, when he's himself," Sara reasons, "there's no one takes more joy in getting ahead." Still, apart from what Simon does, Sara can say about him with passionate conviction: "I love him more than ever any woman loved a man" (189). She may spot the reservations that Simon has about thriving in trade, but Sara has enough self-awareness to see the contradictions in her own character as well, and she takes herself to task for her greedy inclinations: "I'm a fool always dreaming of wealth and power and pride, even while I know in my heart that doesn't matter at all, that your [Simon's] love is my only wealth—to have you and the children. But I can't help dreaming, Darling. I've known what you haven't—poverty—and the lies and dirt and hurt of it that spits on your pride while you try to sneer and hold your head high!" (194).

Sara's love for her husband and desire to get ahead in the world are not always in opposition—she does know what is most important in human relationships—but the above passage hints at a conflict that simmers at this point in the action and threatens to boil as the action unfolds. Just before she discounted her dreams as foolish, she lamented to Simon that coming home again had reminded her of her father. "Ah, why can't he be dead," she asks, "and not have his ghost walk in my heart with the sneer on his lips!" (191). Pride defined and destroyed her father, but Sara claims the same pride and wears the same sneer on her lips as she tries to escape the poverty of her past and the Yankee oppressors who would keep her down.

Sara holds the Harfords, especially Deborah, responsible for her father's demise and does not want to offer forgiveness until she beats her. Simon Harford, then, is more than the man she loves; he is the scion of the family that represents all the hateful snobbery in the world, that conspired first to swindle and then to kill her father, and that now threatens to snub her as well. In the struggle for Simon's love against his mother, Sara certainly plays to win; but the love she feels for Simon also competes with the violent hatred that fuels her revenge against Deborah in her father's name. Although Sara constantly feels the burden of making her mark in the world, she cannot entirely forget her father. She wants to keep his old battle alive and this time win it for him. In her own way, Sara wants to challenge the Harfords to a duel. Sara knows that such practice is antiquated and illegal in modern times—thus, she settles to gain satisfaction economically in the battle of trade.

She may hate the Harfords, but Sara remains wildly possessive of Simon. She identifies his mother, Deborah, as her prime adversary, and when a message arrives from her to request a private meeting with her son outside the old cabin, Sara determines to go, though not with Simon, and spy upon them. She betrays the trust of her husband, but, to her, the end of protecting what is hers justifies any means: "Ah, the divil take honor! It's something men made up for themselves! As if she'd [Deborah] ever let honor stand in her way!" (203). But when Sara overhears Simon laugh at his mother's dreams and humiliate her pride, Sara emerges after he departs to express empathy for her opponent. First, though, Sara flaunts her physical superiority. Next, she abruptly takes Deborah's side against her husband: "How can a man know about the truth of the lies in a woman's dreams?" (235). Deborah had dismissed Sara as a craven Irish biddy, but Sara assures her that she sees only the part that she wants to see. Sara would give up everything in the world for Simon, she insists, were it not for the children, whom she wants to raise as gentlemen. Still, she adds, she will stop the pursuit of riches when they have accumulated enough money not to want or need any more. How much is enough, though, Sara cannot say. Sara boasts that she was born in Ireland in a castle, but then denies any pride in her father and decries his penchant for lying and pretentiousness. Finally, she confides to Deborah that she seduced her son out of love for him, but she admits that she would have slept with him to force a marriage if that action would have been necessary to procure the desired result. She makes it emphatically clear to Deborah that "Simon is mine now," and then walks away with a renewed sense of ownership (238).

Four years later, in June 1936 (act 2), Sara still "exudes an atmosphere of self-confident loving happiness and contentment" (267). Simon, on the other hand, looks strained from too much hard work. He had been trying to balance his daytime job with attempts to write his book at night, with discouraging results. He now realizes that he will probably never write his book in the vein of Rousseau about a utopian society in which men and women are naturally good. Simon blames Sara for making him face the facts of his limitations, and for doubting his abilities and even inclinations to complete such a formidable treatise. On this particular night he decided to face up to reality and discard his old idealistic dreams. "I threw all I've done in the fireplace and burned it," he claims. "Not that there was much beyond notes. I've destroyed so many beginnings at different times" (273). Shedding the pipe dream of writing such an idealistic and philosophical book, Simon prepares to face the world and accept himself as the greedy trader that his mother, his wife, and now even he believe him to be. Ironically, his new outlook on his role in life inspires an idea for a new book, "a frank study of the true nature of man as he really is and not as he pretends to be" (274). In this revaluation of virtues that anticipates Stirner and Nietzsche (O'Neill avidly read both), human nature is good as far as it is true to itself. Simon believes that Sara has goaded him to take this stance, but, truly, his new philosophy allows him to pursue unscrupulous business practices without worry of conscience to slow his velocity.

Simon plots for the future and further expansion of his mill at a time of tremendous economic uncertainty in the United States. He sees opportunities, also, to scoop up other business bargains as they fail around him. His goal, he tells his wife, is to make his company completely self-sufficient. With that in mind, he eyes his father's shipping business as a mode of transport for his cotton. He contemplates buying railroads to haul his cotton across the land and considers buying banks as a ready means of finance for his business. The prospects for making even greater sums of money are dizzying—even when he and Sara seem to have enough already. At that moment, a knock at the door produces Deborah and her other son, Joel, to make an offer to Sara and Simon that they cannot refuse: the helm of the late Henry Harford's shipping company.

Deborah sequesters Sara for private conversation; Joel talks to Simon in his study. By separating Simon from Sara, Deborah anticipates the divide-and-conquer strategy that her son will articulate in the next two acts. Joel tempts Simon to take their father's mantle, which Simon accepts as long as he can absorb that company into his own and erase his father's name. Deborah, meanwhile, says that she will deed her famous Harford mansion to Sara and her family as part of the new deal. Stage directions describe Sara with "eyes gleaming again," and she readily accepts the offer (291). The prospect of owning the very house in which her father suffered his most humiliating defeat represents a crowning victory for Sara in her personal war against the Harfords. Both Simon and Sara accept offers without consulting each other, a first-time offense that hurts Sara, who takes great pride in her business acumen. Simon resents the way Deborah flaunts her new friendship with Sara and feels that the women gang up on him. In an understated tone, he prophesies a future filled with conflict: "it will be a difficult matter when two such opposites as you are have to live together in the same home day after day, with continual friction and conflict of character developing" (310).

Another four years pass before the start of act 3 in 1840 and the scene shifts to the office of Simon Harford, Inc., a business that has expanded from a single mill to five. The thirty-five-year-old leader, Simon, has absorbed his father's old business and turned it into his own marine division. On this very day he prepares to add a railroad to the portfolio. Simon's brother, Joel, warns against his unscrupulous practices and the "ruthlessness with which you take advantage of others' misfortunes." Though his methods might destroy the company in the present times of economic uncertainty, Simon remains resolute: "The only moral law here is that to win is good and to lose is evil. The strong are rewarded, the weak are punished" (316). Simon's business aggressions have nevertheless taken a physical toll upon him, and he looks older than his years. What's more, Simon had anticipated that his mother and wife would not be able to get along with each other, but he now suffers from loneliness and feels that his wife and his mother have formed an alliance that excludes him. Merely the breadwinner, Simon endures "this daily grind of slavery to an unscrupulous greed for power—the ambition to be a Napoleon among traders" (321). He recalls abandonment by his mother as a child as the first cause of his unhappiness, but he also blames Sara for encouraging him as a "cotton good's Napoleon" (324). He invites her to his office with a plan to make her shoulder some of the burden of his soul-crushing business.

The influence of Deborah has given Sara a "more passive, satisfied contentedness," but Sara comes quickly when Simon beckons (324). Although she enjoys her friendship with Deborah (it represents a victory over desire to vanquish her rival), Sara recognizes the divide that now exists between her and her husband. She has been increasingly worried about their relationship and his health as he seemed to pull away emotionally and physically from her. She fears that he has found another woman, vows to fight any rival, and refuses to step aside. "You're mine till death, and beyond death," she claims, "and I'll never let you go, do you hear!" (334). Sara makes it clear to Simon that he comes first for her, before either Deborah or the children. Relieved, Simon plots with her to deprive his mother of influence and stop her from coming between them. In truth, he wants to separate Sara and Deborah from each other and then develop his own relationship with his wife in the office and his mother at home in her private garden.

Simon promises Sara that she can be his wife, partner, and mistress if she agrees to work in his company (342). But, he warns, she will have to work hard for this opportunity. He agrees to sell the company to her, piece by piece, but she will have to earn each acquisition by having sex with him in the office. Earlier in the scene with his brother, Simon recalled Sara's courtship as "unscrupulous and ruthless as a whore selling herself!" (323). Under the present business stress, Simon recollects that Sara forced him to marry her as if she were swindling him in the same manner that Simon now manipulates and takes advantage of his business adversaries. He simply cannot imagine pure love as a motivational force for any meaningful action. For her part, Sara recalls her mother's pledge to Con at the end of *A Touch of the Poet* to "play any game he likes and give him love in it" (152). Beyond games of love and the thrill of sex to rejuvenate the marriage, the prospect of owning the company excites Sara very much. She has always wanted to work for the business and admits that life in the domestic sphere as a mother has proved quite boring. She feels fit to use her brain and business skills to excel at the office. Going forward, Simon plans to train Sara as if she were "an understudy learning to play my part" (354). She will take his place in the company if the need arises, though it may be a matter of when, because thoughts of his escape through the summerhouse door in his mother's garden already fill his head. To further motivate Sara to perform well, he instructs her to draw up plans to build the grand estate about which she has always dreamed. Sara responds enthusiastically and happily informs her husband that she can always dream bigger dreams than she ever previously imagined.

The final act, act 4, returns to Simon's office in midsummer the next year, 1841, and opens with Sara dressed "provocatively female" and "as nakedly as the fashion will permit" (446; 447). Two new additions to the office entwine prostitution, trade, and capitalism. First, a garish sofa possesses "the quality of a painted loud-mouthed bawd who has forced her way in and defied anyone to put her out" (446). Its placement in the room suggests what Joel says later in the scene: that Simon and Sara have transformed the workplace into a brothel. Also, tacked on the wall above her desk, Sara displays the architectural drawings for her prized prospective mansion of the future: "a pretentious, nouveau-riche country estate on the shore of a small private lake with a beach in the foreground on a wharf with small pleasure craft moored to it" (446). This plan represents the lavish upgrade from the simple cabin where love began between Sara and Simon. Sara has taken practically everything from Simon's business by this point, and she brags to Joel that, despite the highly leveraged situation in which the business exists, she can take care of it as well as her husband. Regarding plans for the new mansion, she tells Joel: "That's one debt I'll make him pay—the debt the Harfords owe my father's daughter" (451). Earlier, of course, Sara sought to right the wrong against her father. Now, though, she casts herself as the aggrieved party in the third person and seeks direct compensation.

The transformative effects of greed and materialism play out in terms of Sara's sexual frankness, aggression, and even promiscuity. She nearly seduces Joel, who seemingly cannot resist Sara despite his protests and moral disgust. Amazed herself, Sara slips into brogue as she appraises her newfound sexual power: "Who'd have dreamed it Sara Melody—you in your beauty to have such power over bright and mighty men! By the eternal, as my father used to swear, I think you could take what you wanted from any one of them!" (453–54). Bravado masks fear, however, that she will never be able to quell or even quiet her own greed. Simon enters in a dream-like state, having ceded the operation of his company to Sara, and encourages his wife to expand further her plans for a grand estate. Triumphantly seduced, Sara coos that the banks her husband bought will be "crammed with my gold," and that Simon only has "great need to love me!" (463). In tune only with her own glory, Sara does not listen to Simon's recitation of Oliver Wendell Holmes's "The Chambered Nautilus" and misses the irony of building ever greater shells that block the sight of heaven, the ultimate mansion.

As a final audition for her role as future head of the company, Simon steers her to one of his rival bankers, Tenard, and directs her to finish him off. Having played the first half of the scene almost as a prostitute, Sara adopts the role of a ruthless businesswoman to destroy one of Simon's competitors. At the summit of conquest, trade does not equal prostitution, for that would suggest some kind of transaction. In dealing with Simon's rival one on one, trade is survival of the fittest in which only one can win: trade equals destruction. The beating she gives Tenard is not physical, but it is no less humiliating than the blows that her father took years ago on the Harfords' front steps. Sara has become monstrously robotic in pursuit of profit. She informs Tenard matter-of-factly of what she has done and will do: "I am not interested in moral attitudes. You owned something I desired. You were too weak to hold it. I was strong enough to take it. I am good because I am strong. You are evil because you are weak. Those are the facts" (493). There is no sign of human compassion left in Sara. She has far outperformed her husband and taken over his company. Sara is the company at this point.

Sara pauses for a moment with second thoughts about what she has done and how she has acted, but Simon taunts her with the fear of return to a life of poverty and potatoes. Unable or unwilling to face such ignominy, she continues on the "cursed treadmill of greed!" (477). The final goal of the company, Simon advises, is for it to achieve complete self-sufficiency. In order to do that, Simon and Sara must close the cycle of trade and exert control over every aspect of the production of raw materials, transportation, manufacturing, distribution, and sales. Despite all that they have achieved, Simon points out that there is still much unfinished business: "You still have to have stores to retail our cotton goods. Your own plantations worked by your own nigger slaves. Your own slave ships and your own slave dealers in Africa. That will complete the chain on the end" (479). Moments later, Simon spots yet another idea to consider in order to monopolize profits: "Of course, it would be the crowning achievement if I could conceive a scheme by which the public could be compelled to buy your cotton goods and only yours—so you would own your own consumer slaves, too. That would complete the circle with a vengeance!" (479). Newly convinced, Sara agrees to play any game that Simon desires. "If it's a whore you love me to be, then I am it, body and soul, as long as you're mine!" (481). She would do anything to keep him and not allow his mother to come between them. He suggests, without specifically saying so, that she could murder Deborah as a final solution. Sara listens with "horrified eagerness" as the scene ends (483).

In the next and final scene, Sara experiences an epiphany that draws her back from all that she has become. She enters Deborah's garden that night looking like "a prostitute the morning after a debauch" and intends to taunt her rival into madness (490). Once she sees Deborah, however, she cannot execute her plan. In fact, she intercedes to prevent Deborah from walking through the summerhouse door to crazy dreams that lie within its confines. Deborah views Sara's compassion as weakness, but, as Sara later says, "If I'm humbled, it's by myself and my love, not by you" (540). They reconcile, but before they can leave the garden together, Simon intercedes and dispatches Sara to the house to tend to the needs of the children, a scheme devised to buy time alone with his mother.

He no longer asks his mother to kill his wife, but he does beg Deborah to escape with him to whatever lies behind the summerhouse door, what he hopes will be the "lost life of peace and truthful faith and happiness" of his childhood (525). Deborah accepts his plea and leads him up to the very door. Sara, though, returns from the house just in time before they enter and likely disappear forever, and, out of love for Simon, agrees to give him up to his mother if she will only shut the door and lead him to safety. At this moment, Ed Shaughnessy contends, "Sara's willingness to give him up springs from a motive of self-abnegation and generosity."[15] After all the damage that she has done, this moment shows that she, too, is worthy of redemption. Deborah rightly does not trust her, but Sara simply says, "I've told you I'm beyond scheming. I'm too—dead" (541). Sara's plea to save Simon and give up her hold on him, to break the triangle, is an opportunity for her to rejoin the living and recant her former ways. Deborah, still in competition with Sara, releases Simon and enters her summerhouse of insanity alone. If Sara had not intervened, Simon would surely have been lost. Even so, he remains damaged, ill, and part of Sara's penitence demands that she nurse him back to health.

O'Neill discarded the epilogue he wrote for *A Touch of the Poet,* but he kept the one he wrote for *More Stately Mansions.* The scene takes place a year after the fateful events in the previous scene and returns to the Thoreauvian cabin-by-the-lake where love began between Sara and Simon. In only a year's time, Sara drove the company into bankruptcy and allowed creditors to take everything. Happily, Sara reports that Simon and she are "as poor as Job's turkey." They are free to begin again with a fresh start: "We're back where we started with only our love for riches! (*Hastily.*) And it's more than enough! It's the greatest treasure in the world!" (561). In the last image of the play, Sara cradles and caresses Simon as he falls asleep on her breast. Soothingly, she murmurs: "Ah, sleep, my Darlin'. Sleep on my breast. It's yours like the heart beating inside it! Rest in peace. You're home at last where you've always wanted to be. I'm your mother now, too" (567). Love wins. Simon is Sara's. She possesses him in a pose that foreshadows that of Josie and Jim in *A Moon for the Misbegotten.* In the later play, though, Josie's gesture appears as a sacrifice when she agrees to play the part of Tyrone's mother. In *More Stately Mansions,* Sara cannot help but gloat about her near-complete possession of Simon. Deborah has left for good and Simon will depend on his wife for the rest of his life. Sara takes stock of her victory as if to suggest that her deep strain of possessiveness and acquisitiveness has not died entirely.

O'Neill's scenario for the next play to follow, *The Calms of Capricorn,* which he wrote in 1935 prior to *A Touch of the Poet* or *More Stately Mansions,* verifies that the schism in Sara's soul between her abundant love for Simon and her love of abundance never completely mends. Still at the cabin, now a potato farm in 1857, Simon never fully regained his former strength and vitality, and finally succumbed to pneumonia and died. Sara mourns his loss with a speech that reveals the full depth of her love for her husband:

> Wasn't it a beautiful life I've lived, even the sorrow in it? How many women have known what I have known, the feel inside that your heart has borne the man you love into life, and in your heart he's grown and become a man and your lover and husband and yet always remained a child, and at the last his death is only a return behind the gates of birth to sleep at peace again forever in the love of your heart. [. . .] Yes, I thank Almighty God for you, Simon, and for the beauty of the poet's love, and the passion of a man's love, and the tender dependence of a child's love you brought me. And it's the sweet life I've lived with you and I wouldn't change it if I had a choice of all the lives other women have ever lived in the world![16]

Moments later, Sara follows this beautiful tribute to love with a bitter attack on her way out the door: "Free of me—free of me—and you've set me free—I've a new life starting and I'll do as I please now and as I've always wanted and I've four strong sons to work with me and to help me to the wealth and power of this world and all I've dreamed."[17] The close juxtaposition of such radically opposite expressions of love and resentment does not champion one over the other or negate either one, but suggests that the two sentiments, however irreconcilable, are also inseparable. The composite picture of Sara presents a woman very much in love with her husband, but also one who asserts an independent existence outside the bonds of love and possession. The war she wages against the Harfords, and with herself, continues unabated despite her valiant attempts to check her worst impulses.

For all intents and purposes, O'Neill was done with the Cycle when he tore up the prologue for *The Calms of Capricorn* in 1939. In January 1942, however, prior to the fourth and final draft of *A Touch of the Poet*, he penciled a few notes in consideration of the whole Cycle: "Add, general theme throughout—tragic battle of the opposites—aspect expressed in Latin quote I remember—translated for this purpose—'I know the good way (Tao) and I believe it is Truth, but I follow the bad way.'"[18] What Sara's lines disclose above and what O'Neill's notes suggest is that the splits within characters are not exactly even, and the fight within them is not exactly fair. Sara knows what to do, she feels better when she does the right thing, but nevertheless she is not always able or willing to do it. Self-interest, be it pride or ambition, even when it rules against what is best for the self, trumps love without vigilance and constant reassessment. O'Neill goes on to say that something within men and women such as Simon and Sara and even Deborah keeps them distant from each other and prevents them from getting the very things that they say they want and need. O'Neill adds, specifically, that they know what they are doing as they transgress against themselves and those whom they love: "The Harfords always know in their hearts what is Truth & Salvation, but a demonic fate in them makes them deny this in their living, and do the opposite—a defiance, a pride—a 'better to rule in hell, than serve in heaven' complex—and instinct toward self-destruction—revenge—."[19]

The "demonic fate" in the Melody Harfords is always the notion that they need to assert their will upon others in order to get ahead in life. They may want to love and live simply, both Simon and Sara, but they fear that such love might diminish them in the eyes of the other. The revenge they seek against others is never much more than a vicious attack against themselves for their own guilty thoughts and deeds. The epilogue that closes *More Stately Mansions* seems to end the story of possessors. The four Harford boys gather around their mother, who, in the last lines of the play, breaks the peaceful tranquility with a startling reversal. While she and Simon have rediscovered the love that brought them together in the first place and celebrate the fact that they have finally broken free of the American Dream and capitalist desire to rise in the world through an accumulation of riches, Sara now condemns her sons to the same capitalist fate of conquest that nearly killed Simon and turned her into a monster: Ethan will own a fleet of ships; Wolfe will have his banks; Jonathan will run railroads; and Honey will be in the White House. All that Sara seemingly learned vanishes in an instant as she forces her sons to imbibe the hair of the dog that choked the whole family line. Enlightenment, the way of love, proves nearly impossible to follow for more than a few fleeting moments.

CHAPTER FIVE

CLIMBING THE HARFORD FAMILY TREE

Together, *A Touch of the Poet* and *More Stately Mansions* encapsulate the whole story of the Cycle. Deborah, Simon's mother, appears only once, in act 2 of the former play, but she delivers a monologue in her scene that condenses the entire history of the Harfords into one long speech. In that speech, she details the quest for freedom among the Harfords that goes back to the Revolutionary War, and emphasizes that the male prerogative to pursue such complete freedom enslaved the women who loved these men. The same dynamics that draw blood between Simon and Sara, Deborah implies, were at work through at least three prior generations of Harfords. As for the future, the epilogue in *More Stately Mansions* and a couple of earlier scenes in act 3 project the rest of the unwritten Cycle, a ninety-year span from the conclusion of the play in 1842 to the end of "The Hair of the Dog" in 1932. The original four brothers appear as young boys. Each has his own dream, each his own sense of destiny and happiness, but each wants to make his parents happy and proud as well. The forecast is poignant by virtue of the fact that the children are both naïve and innocent. Ethan, Jonathan, Wolfe, and Honey have no sense of the autonomy that they voluntarily relinquish to serve blindly their parents' business.

On a page of general Cycle notes, O'Neill listed "Bondage/Freedom" as one of six pairs of opposites.[1] This one, in particular, comprises not a diametrical opposition but an inversion. Sara longs to be free, but her pursuit of freedom leads to future and further enslavement, capped off by her syntactically convoluted final line in *More Stately Mansions:* "[O]ne slave is enough for any woman to be owned by!" (568). Marriage, in her construction, is slavery; Simon owns Sara—that makes her a slave—but she casts him as a slave as well. Who owns them? Capitalist ideology enslaves them both in the name of freedom.[2] The action couches Sara's rise in the world from rags to riches as inevitable from the moment her mother mentions her progress in *A Touch of the Poet.* Sara decides that there is nothing worse than poverty and targets Simon as a means of escape from it. She gets what she wants, marriage to Simon, and they start life together with a new family and hope for the future. By the end, though, Sara loses almost everything on her journey.

Sara shares a dream with her husband to make just enough money to live well and enable Simon to retire early to pursue his literary interests. The questions arise at several points in *More Stately Mansions:* How much is enough? When is it enough? Is enough ever enough? Moving into the Harford mansion did not slake Sara's thirst for revenge against the family that destroyed her father. Neither did it satisfy her ambition to gain a seat at society's table. She cannot quell a compulsion to build an even more impressive estate and for Simon's company to reap even greater profits through constant and ruthless expansion and acquisition. The independence that Sara seeks through the accumulation of wealth turns into a horrid fantasy that transforms her into a lascivious bawd. She pursues freedom through ownership, but the company enslaves her as a willing accomplice to her own servitude. The articulate, scheming, and confident Sara Melody of *A Touch of the Poet* disappears, and a desperate and debauched Sara Harford takes her place prior to the last scene of *More Stately Mansions.* She recognizes, at last, the trap of the value system into which she has fallen, but she cannot pull free of it.

The battle of inverted opposites plays out interpersonally in the love story of Sara and Simon, but also ripples to the first four plays of the Cycle that O'Neill never wrote, as well as to the last five plays that he never completed. O'Neill conceived the history of the Harfords as going back before the American Revolution, but he carefully showed in *A Touch of the Poet* how the pursuit of pure freedom in those prior generations ultimately ended in enthrallment at Napoleon's coronation in 1804. *More Stately Mansions,* set during Jacksonian democracy, travestied liberty with tales of government corruption and unregulated greed. As he wrote these plays, the modern world turned dark with the rise of fascism. On 1 September 1939, only three months after O'Neill stopped work on the Cycle, Hitler attacked Poland and soon the world was at war. The playwright did not need to add anything more to his work. In a letter to Kenneth Macgowan on 10 September, he wrote: "Jesus, the incredible, suicidal capacity of men for stupid greed!"[3]

Just over two years earlier, after O'Neill finally recovered from the infection that nearly killed him, he attacked the Cycle project with renewed vigor. He noted in his *Work Diary* in June 1937 that it was "grand to feel creative mind alive again." On 20 June, O'Neill began to review his notes for the second, third, and fourth plays of the Cycle: "Greed of the Meek," "The Hair of the Dog" (soon to be renamed *A Touch of the Poet*), and the first act of *More Stately Mansions* (the last thing he wrote before leaving Georgia). On 11 and 12 July, O'Neill spent considerable time and effort drafting an elaborate Harford family tree (Fig. 8). This schematic revealed what he had dramatized thus far, as well as the future direction of the Cycle as it spanned seven generations and almost 180 years of American history.

The diagram is drafted on stationery bearing the heading "Le Plessis" (home of the O'Neills in France where he had written *Mourning Becomes Electra* in 1931), crossed out and amended as Woods House, the home O'Neill rented in Lafayette, California, during the construction of Tao House in Danville. O'Neill rotated the sheet to what we now call "landscape" configuration and numbered a column on the far left side of the page from 1 to 7 to designate the generations of the family. He displayed all his character names between horizontal and vertical straight lines in his characteristically precise and elegant script that is barely readable to the naked eye. The overall composition reveals O'Neill's playwriting tendencies as well: solid construction, patterns that repeat again and again, names that recur as well through the generations, and generations that tend to mirror one another. Thus, the four children of Simon and Sara in the fifth generation mirror their four grandchildren in the seventh generation. Similarly, the third and fourth generations of the Melody family on the right side of the diagram in the center, headed by Cornelius Melody, and

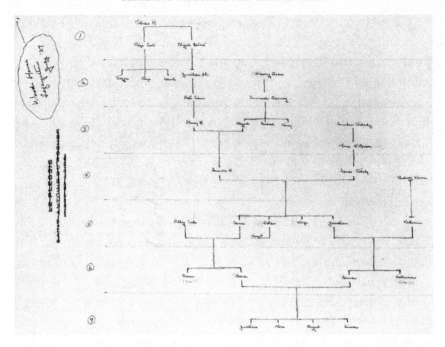

FIGURE 8. The seven generations of the Harford family tree drafted by O'Neill
in July 1937. Simon Harford and Sara Melody meet on line 4. The Cycle
originated with four plays about their sons (line 5). (Courtesy of Eugene
O'Neill Papers, Yale Collection of American Literature, Beinecke Rare Book
and Manuscript Library. Copyright © Yale University. All rights reserved.)

his wife, Nora, and followed by his daughter, Sara, correspond to the third
and fourth generations of Harfords that show the marriage between Henry
and Abigail (later renamed Deborah) and their son, Simon. The marriage
between the Yankee Harfords and the Irish Melodys produced four sons,
two with Yankee names (Ethan and Jonathan) and two with Irish (Wolfe
and Owen).

O'Neill had committed to a nine-play Cycle, but he had only written
the second and third plays at this point. "Greed of the Meek" explored
Deborah's life around the time of her marriage to Henry Harford and introduced her father and siblings as well as Harford's aunts, Maggie, Eliza
(originally Maya), and Hannah (Fig. 8, line 2, left). These elderly women
fascinated O'Neill, and the new first play that he was planning to write
would include much younger versions of the three. He decided to give
this new first play the same title as the old one, "Greed of the Meek," and

the play that he had completed with that name he changed to "And Give Me Death." Although O'Neill struggled to complete drafts of these plays, both of which he later destroyed, the family tree shows the importance he placed upon the three sisters in the overall structure of the Cycle. The Harford branch on the left side of the diagram shoots straight up from Henry Harford to Jonathan Harford and then crowns Ethan Harford as patriarch at the top. Ethan had two wives, though, and his first wife delivered three daughters, who in the plays became known as the Three Sisters, or even the Blessed Sisters. Hanging down from the top of the diagram, these three figures hover over the entire family saga, reminiscent of the trees through which O'Neill framed the action in *Desire Under the Elms*:

> They bend their trailing branches down over the roof. They appear to protect and at the same time subdue. There is a sinister maternity in their aspect, a crushing, jealous absorption. They have developed from their intimate contact with the life of man in the house an appalling humaneness. They brood oppressively over the house. They are like exhausted women resting their sagging breasts and hands and hair on its roof, and when it rains their tears trickle down monotonously and rot on the shingles.[4]

The importance of the Three Sisters stuck in O'Neill's imagination regarding the conflict between freedom and enslavement even after he had mostly put the Cycle aside. Notes dated 3 February 1940 read: "There is a struggle throughout the Cycle of free will versus destiny (the past which is oneself) and therefore to conquer oneself in order to be free, to conquer outside one the symbols of the past that are in one (or evade, escape them)."[5] O'Neill toyed with the idea of adding the Three Sisters to both *A Touch of the Poet* and *More Stately Mansions* but gave up on 1 October 1941 without ever making the revision.

After finishing his Harford family tree on 11 July 1937, O'Neill wrote notes on the fifth through eighth plays on 25 July, the original quartet about the four brothers. The following day he turned to the "Bessie Bowen" material, the ninth and final play of the Cycle. Striving for a sense of closure, O'Neill decided that Honey (Owen), the youngest child of Simon and Sara, should appear in the ninth play and live until its end. Sara is pregnant with Honey in her first appearance in *More Stately Mansions*, set in 1832. The final play goes to 1932, a span that makes Honey 100 years old. This idea required an extra generation that does not show up on the diagram but intervenes between the sixth and seventh generations—Sara II, daughter of Owen (Honey) and Abby Cade (Fig. 8, line 6), has a single female child named Lou (the "Bessie" character from old material) who marries a mechanic-inventor and births the four children identified at the bottom of the diagram (line 7). Honey, then, is their great-grandfather. This change allowed O'Neill to keep the same time frame he had developed over the years with the "Bessie Bowen" material (1900–1932) and to provide continuity throughout the Cycle with inclusion of a familiar character.

The diagram of the family tree tilts left toward the Harford branch, which possibly represents a weakness in the overall plan. In the end, O'Neill chose to dramatize the independence and isolation of the Melody line—graphically located on the right side of the diagram, but still in the center of it all—to tell his story. Along the horizontal axis in the middle of the diagram (Fig. 8, line 4), the marriage between Sara and Simon joins the two families, Irish and Yankee, and balances the past and the future in the ongoing struggle between freedom and enslavement.

A Touch of the Poet is a generational battle between Cornelius (Con) and Sara. The father was born in Ireland, but the action is set entirely in New England. O'Neill did not bother to create any lineage for Con back on the Old Sod. There are stories in the play, to be sure, about his parents, particularly his father, and about Nora as a young girl, but O'Neill saw no point in committing any of that to his family tree. Family history nearly suffocates the Harfords, much as it did the Mannons in *Mourning Becomes Electra,* but the lack of genealogy gives Cornelius Melody an opportunity for free expression. Swings between the King's English and Irish brogue, heightened and affected manners, outrageous flirtatiousness, Byronic posing, and military bearing contribute to the sense that Melody approaches daily living as if it were a kind of theatrical performance. His daughter Sara, also born in Ireland, makes it clear that America is a place where you can be anything that you want to be. Sara's chief complaints against her father are that he cannot be the person he pretends to be for any appreciable length of time and that he does not know who he is.

In *More Stately Mansions,* Deborah recites the same verses from Byron's *Childe Harold's Pilgrimage* to Ethan, Wolfe, Jonathan, and Honey in act 3, scene 2 that Cornelius Melody mouthed for himself in the mirror in *A Touch of the Poet.* She brokers a truce with Sara in order to get to know her grandchildren, and holds court with them regularly in her garden. That she and Con both gravitate to Byronic poetry suggests similarities with respect to their rebellion against commercial trade and the unrelenting pursuit of the almighty dollar. Both of them achieve comfort by clinging to the past—Melody through recollections of his time as major in His Majesty's Seventh Dragoons, Deborah in her playacting of scenes from eighteenth-century French memoirs—rather than face the tumult of current events and modern living. The garden wall shields Deborah from the outside world, and she relishes the possibility of never venturing beyond its confines. Within her sanctuary, however, Deborah welcomes the opportunity to interact with the four boys and to teach them things that go beyond what they need to succeed in the world of business. She tries to inculcate a different kind of moral sensibility in her grandchildren than they have learned from their parents. She emphasizes individualism and freedom, in keeping with Byron, and encourages the children to "rely on themselves, to own their own lives and be what they want to be" (386).

Simon and Sara, in strident opposition, determine that their sons must meet the growing needs of the company if it is ever to reach self-sufficiency. Simon outlines his plans to Sara in act 3, scene 1: Ethan must manage the marine division, Wolfe needs to handle the banking branch, Jonathan will become a railroad executive, and Honey will enter national politics in pursuit of the highest office (341). Simon reminds Sara that the lofty ambitions they have for their sons argue for limiting Deborah's influence and contact with them. Even after Simon collapses at the end of the play and Sara notes the dissolution of the company in the epilogue, she still pushes her sons toward the same arenas. With the hazardous toll of these capitalistic endeavors plainly evident in the physical demise of Simon and the moral lapse experienced by Sara earlier, the four boys will likely not face a kinder fate and future than their parents.

The dreams of the father degrade over time, and the scenario and outlines for the plays about the four brothers, though never turned into actual plays, suggest a desolate resolution to the family quest. With no marine division to run, Ethan settles as a first mate on a clipper ship in *The Calms of Capricorn*. He does not seek spiritual and sexual escape in the South Sea Islands as, say, Brant does in *Mourning Becomes Electra*, but races for a new speed record around Cape Horn to San Francisco. About the voyage,

Ethan claims at the outset: "I want this chance to accept the sea's challenge, that's all. If I win, I possess her and she cringes and I kick her away
from me and turn my back forever. If I lose, I give myself to her as her
conquest and she swallows and spews me out in death."[6] After failing to
break the record and feeling guilty for having murdered the ship's captain,
Ethan dives overboard and drowns in the sea.

The rest of the brothers meet similarly sad fates in the subsequent outlines.
Wolfe devolves from the prospective bank executive in his father's plan to
a daring gambler in San Francisco. He, too, commits suicide at the end of
"The Earth Is the Limit" after losing the woman he loves in a bet with his
younger brother. The politician, Honey, ultimately must resign from the
Senate in "Nothing Is Lost but Honor" amid evidence of a railroad scam
that he orchestrated on behalf of his brother Jonathan. Honey leaves public
office in disgrace but makes ten million dollars in the shady deal. The tenth
play of the Cycle, "The Man on Iron Horseback," focuses on Jonathan's
struggles at the Stock Exchange in New York to finance the transcontinental railroad. Although he wants "to be responsible to no one but himself,"
he leaves everything behind and returns to San Francisco when he learns of
his mother's imminent death.[7] He dies, too, once Sara passes. On his death-
bed, he realizes that the money he had amassed illicitly no longer means
anything to him. Honey, his younger sibling, swears an oath at the end: "I'll
never draw another sober breath till the day I die, so help me God. I'll puke
in the face of life!"[8] The tyranny of capitalism and the will of the father,
Simon, overpower Deborah's small voice for individualism and the pursuit
of happiness. Each of the brothers experiences early success in business and
politics as a new kind of enslavement. Simon condemns his sons to the same
"slave pen" of trade that left him "crucified on this insane wheel" (357).

Deborah's chronicle of the past in *A Touch of the Poet* predicts the same
battle between inverted opposites among her four grandsons at the end
of *More Stately Mansions*. The history of the Harfords, as Deborah tells it,
proved to be particularly hard for the female family members who bore
the brunt of decisions made by men in the name of freedom. Deborah
outlines how the movement for independence transformed over time from
the search for complete liberty in the American Revolution to submission to supreme authority with the rise of Napoleon barely one generation
later. While American independence and the coronation of Napoleon as

emperor in the early nineteenth century seem to represent opposing political structures of belief and ideology, Deborah's long monologues in act 2 show how one quickly leads to the other. Having previously visited with her son upstairs and realizing that she cannot dissuade him from marrying Sara, Deborah warns her prospective daughter-in-law about the Harford family. She cannot bully Sara. Moreover, she has compassion for Sara in light of the fate that awaits her as a woman among the Harfords. Her speech prophesies the future even as it fills in the blanks of three prior generations.

Deborah first mentions Simon's great-grandfather Jonathan (named Ethan on line 1 of Fig. 8), who died at Bunker Hill in the early days of the Revolution, which for him "was a personal war, I am sure—for pure freedom" (69). His son, Evan (named Jonathan on the diagram [line 2]), Simon's grandfather, grew even more fanatical in his cause for "pure freedom" and joined the Jacobins of the French Revolution. He later built the little Temple of Liberty that stands in Deborah's garden as her summerhouse and died wearing his old uniform of the French Republican National Guard. "But the point is," Deborah informs Sara, "you can have no idea what revengeful hate the Harford pursuit of freedom imposed upon the women who shared their lives" (69). Both Jonathan and Evan abandoned their wives. Deborah reports that Evan's half-sisters, Jonathan's stepdaughters, ultimately had to "embrace the profits of the slave trade" and "escape the enslavement of freedom by enslaving it."[9] The freedom of one, O'Neill suggests, almost requires the enslavement of another, if only to ensure the former of the illusion of freedom. Deborah implies, then, that Simon's dream of a world of pure freedom inspired by nature might come about only if Sara were to sacrifice her dreams for the future for those of her husband (69).

Deborah makes it clear that the Three Sisters would have embraced Sara as one of their own: "They would see that you are strong and ambitious and determined to take what you want. They would have smiled like senile, hungry serpents and welcomed you into their coils." Deborah allows that she hated the Sisters—"Evil old witches! Detestable . . ."—but she admired their strength in the same way as she admires and appreciates the differences between her and Sara (69). Deborah retreats from the world, and fantasizes that she "is entirely ruthless and lets nothing stand in the way of the final goal of power she has set for herself, to become the favorite of the King and make him, through his passion for her, her slave!" (226).

But while Deborah's life is largely one of imagination, centered on the Temple of Liberty in her secluded garden, Sara lives a life of ambitious means and acquisition rooted in everyday life, far removed from Deborah's imaginative space. In an unpublished interview with Elizabeth Shepley Sergeant in 1946, O'Neill said that Sara ran through much of the Cycle because she was "such a grand character." Talking about other characters from the "Bessie Bowen" material, O'Neill described them in ways that fit Sara perfectly as a type of physical and driving force. "The family are people with guts," O'Neill allowed. "When they feel negative they burn the building." He added: "They are the kind of people who go after success, and succeed, and then fall but never stay fallen."[10] Sara is fleshy and grounded in the soil. Deborah, on the other hand, is often described as pale and looking like a ghost. She eluded the grasp of the Three Sisters through her lack of physical stature. "I managed to escape," she says, "because there was so little of me in the flesh that aged, greedy fingers could clutch" (69).

Deborah's alignment of Sara with the Sisters is inaccurate in one important sense. While Deborah both admires and recoils from Sara's eagerness to take what she wants, the Sisters' main attribute reads as hypocritical meekness. Early in *A Touch of the Poet,* Cornelius Melody bursts out suddenly: "I hate the damned meek of this earth," a sentiment that Sara certainly shares with her father (30). Hannah Harford presented "meekness as fatalism—it is nature's law that [she] should possess—appears to notice nothing, to be stolidly indifferent, but nothing escapes her beady black eyes." Eliza Harford, with "a plump greedy health about her," represents the "social-conformity meek." The eldest sister, Maggie Harford, maintains "a fierce will to possess beneath an outward seeming of meekness bowing before the will of God." She wears "the grim mask which uses religious conformity to get what its greed desires—to make someone else get it for them so it comes to them."[11] The violence and greed that belie their meek appearance set them apart from Sara. While Simon and Deborah frequently describe Sara as greedy, and Sara laments her acquisitiveness, she never lies or fails to acknowledge her avaricious and rapacious impulses. She is not a hypocrite. She catches herself giving voice to base desires, and then she reckons with these expressions.[12] She always knows when she acts wrongly and confesses her weaknesses, a marked difference from the corrupted souls of the Sisters, whose meek visages hide black hearts and greedy desires. Their kind of meek does not wait to inherit the earth. They will take and take and take.

They all share admiration for Napoleon, as Deborah allows near the end of her speech in *A Touch of the Poet*. The Sisters idolized him and agreed (without a trace of humor or irony) that he was the only man they would ever have agreed to marry. Deborah, for her part, admits that even she had dreamed of Empress Josephine. Her marriage to Henry Harford represents a social upgrade and a stake of ownership in the Harford mansion, but it does not lead to happiness. She remembers that all of them, including the Three Sisters, traveled to Paris on her honeymoon in order to attend the emperor's coronation. The road to freedom and independence ends up at the foot of a new despot.

Deborah takes no interest in her husband's business and shows contempt for his "conservative, material dream" (68). The couple, as Deborah relates, rarely talks about anything. Deborah is surprised to learn in *More Stately Mansions* that her husband possessed a gambling streak that led him to speculate wildly on western lands during the early 1830s. Unfortunately, he gambled and lost, and when he died in 1836 (prior to act 2) he left his company exposed to takeover and complete collapse. Henry's death and the crippled state of the company force Deborah to revisit Simon and Sara after four years and tempt them with offers that they cannot refuse. Deborah's disingenuous desire to see her son "become a Napoleon of finance" signals the end of freedom for all three of them (300).

Before Deborah exits *A Touch of the Poet*, she imparts a farewell anecdote that frames enslavement in historical and racist terms. Her story concerns her black coachman, Cato, a former slave, who Deborah notes has always acted as a self-possessed free man. Simon, who "emancipated" himself from the Harford family business, embarrasses Cato by frequently shaking his hand whenever they meet (72). Cato does not appear in *A Touch of the Poet*, but he does bring a message from Deborah to Simon at the end of the first act of *More Stately Mansions*. In their brief exchange, Simon welcomes Cato vigorously and sticks out his hand to greet him, which the Black man takes "*embarrassedly.*" Simon is not just proving his own likability but straining to adhere to his own moral code in which all people are equal. "Cato and I are old friends, aren't we, Cato?" (197–98). Such a friendship is surely not based on a principle of equality. The older man is an employee of the Harfords, dressed in uniform to wait upon them. It gives Simon pleasure to think of Cato as his friend, but the Black man knows the limits of the relationship and acts accordingly. He smiles and defers and grins, as if he were delivering a performance of servitude. What he really thinks of the Harfords, including Simon, remains a mystery behind his congenial demeanor.

The institution of slavery undergirds the company that Simon buys and builds in *More Stately Mansions*. Simon and Sara are not slave owners per se; they live in Massachusetts, but their cotton mill refines the raw product harvested by Black slave labor in the South. They trade with Southern planters and depend upon them to maintain and grow their business in the North. Business as a cotton mill owner forces Simon to compromise his values in order to prosper. Sara, ever the pragmatist, insists that she wants to free the slaves within reason, "if they can find a way to do it that won't ruin the country" (268). She means, of course, that she would welcome emancipation if it did not compromise profits at her cotton mill. Simon, more confusedly, is an abolitionist (on the sly), but at the same time supports John Calhoun's doctrine of nullification. Simon explains to Sara: "I see State rights as a symbol of the individual's right to freedom" (269). Simon does not see the contradiction in the two positions. Perhaps they are both examples of the "pure freedom" that his ancestors sought going back to the American and French Revolutions. These pursuits, though, as Deborah traced them above, inevitably lead to new forms of enslavement and servitude. Simon abandons his dream of equality and a new society in favor of the world of business in which only the strong and the smart survive and flourish. He and Sara, "accumulation addicts" in Joel Pfister's splendid phrase, can never escape the fact that their material success is due to the labor of Black slaves.[13] Unfortunately, they discover that in the process of pursuing success, building their company, and expanding its resources, they become enslaved to a soul-crushing ideology that nearly destroys their marriage.

Meanings of *slave* and *slavery* proliferate as the Cycle unfolds. In act 4 of *A Touch of the Poet*, Sara shares a scene with her mother, Nora, while they wait late at night for the return of Cornelius Melody and his cohorts, who galloped away earlier to attack the Harford estate. Sara has just come from Simon's bedroom (where they made love for the first time) and now appears more humble than in the past. She has always looked down on her mother, despite loving her, for obeying Con's every wish and command. Sara proudly boasted from the outset, despite her genuine feelings for Simon, that she would not make herself a slave for any man. Nora had insisted in the opening act: "There's no slavery in it when you love!" (26). Now, at the end of the same day, Sara appraises her mother differently:

> Sure, I've always known you're the sweetest woman in the world, Mother, but I never suspected you were a wise woman too, until I knew tonight the truth of what you said this morning, that a woman can forgive whatever the man she loves could do and still love him, because it was through him she found the love in herself; that, in one way, he doesn't count at all, because it's love, your own love, you love in him, and to keep that your pride will do anything. (125)

Sara refuses to consider herself a slave to another man, but she does picture herself in service of another power: "It's love's slaves we are, Mother, not men's," she concludes (125). Simon reiterates this sentiment early in *More Stately Mansions* during the meeting with his mother at the cabin by the lake. Deborah, who has not seen her son since visiting him on his sick bed at the Melody tavern four years earlier, interrogates him about his marriage and accuses him of being Sara's slave. "Oh, to love I am a willing slave," Simon responds. After four years of marriage and with four young sons, the couple live in a home of "comfort and moderate prosperity," which allows Simon to devote his days to work and nights to his private literary matters (211, 266).

The life they lead seems much like what Sara described in *A Touch of the Poet* as Simon's ideal when they lay in bed together for the first time in 1828:

> [H]e could easily make a living for us from this mill—just enough to be comfortable, and he'd have time over to write his book, and keep his wisdom, and never let himself become a slave to the greed for more than enough that is the curse of mankind. Then he said he was afraid maybe I'd think it was weakness in him, not wisdom, and could I be happy with enough and no more. So I kissed him and said all I wanted in life was his love, and whatever meant happiness to him would be my only ambition. (122)

Deborah's entrance to Simon and Sara's home in act 2, scene 2 of *More Stately Mansions* incites the action with invitations/temptations for Simon to take over his father's failing business and for Sara to inherit the Harford mansion as its mistress. Enough will never be enough once they accept those bargains. However, the cracks in their relationship begin to show prior to Deborah's arrival. Simon informs Sara that he has abandoned his plans to write his book and has burned all the notes. He needs to free his mind, he says, for difficult business decisions regarding the mill. Financial opportunities may arise from the bankruptcy of other mill properties during this time of rapid market fluctuations and frequent crashes. Simon plots to capitalize upon the weakness of his competitors. Nevertheless, he blames Sara for never really believing in his utopian fantasy about a perfect society and claims that she encouraged him to write the book only to prove that he could not. Sara does not bother to disagree with him, so delighted is she that the literary prospect has disappeared. She declares that they have saved fifty thousand dollars, but Simon announces that they will soon have the hundred thousand they had set as their goal. "But wouldn't two hundred thousand, say, be better than one?" Simon asks temptingly, rhetorically (277).

Simon begins to imagine the company expanding beyond a single mill, to include shipping, railroads, and even banking. The possibilities are wide open, he believes, and these acquisitions will preserve and protect the assets of the company as it moves toward self-sufficiency. Excitedly, Simon envisions vast business prospects now that he has laid the book aside, but while the book was about the possibilities for a free society, he realizes that his new path promises to enslave him as a ruthless and greedy trader. He chides himself for once believing in the essential goodness of humanity, but his decision to put aside what he considered his important life's work in favor of business betrays his former self-concept no matter how hard he tries to believe otherwise:

> What a damned fool a man can make of himself by clinging to the irresponsible, sentimental dreams of his youth long after he has outgrown them and experience has proven how stupidly impractical they are! Keep on deliberately denying what he knows himself to be in fact, and encourage a continual conflict in his mind, so that he lives split into opposites and divided against himself! All in the name of freedom! As if Freedom could ever exist

in Reality! As if at the end of every dream of liberty one did not find the slave, oneself, to whom oneself, the Master, is enslaved! (280)

As Con Melody killed the major in himself, so does Simon rip asunder his poetic side. He blames Sara for this act of self-destruction but does not consult with his wife about his plans, instead assuming that she will be pleased to have at long last eradicated this aspect of his personality. In fact, Sara loves the poetic nature of Simon and fell in love with him because of it. Nevertheless, she would prefer that Simon keep his literary ambitions in check as he labors to earn for the family. Sara believes that Simon will thrive in the workplace with his mind focused solely upon his job. And he does. He becomes a moneymaking machine as he plots a new course for the company. While Cornelius Melody assumed the role of a drunken lout in *A Touch of the Poet,* Simon, with his "touch of the poet," plays the part of a ruthless and wildly ambitious businessman. In a time of economic turmoil, he assumes ever greater risks in the marketplace and tries more daring financial exploits than any of his competitors. He recognizes the endless loop he follows and the unforgiving treadmill upon which he runs. Melody begged Sara to let him get off and cavort with the other patrons at the bar; but, here, Simon hates Sara for exposing the lie he had told himself about the goodly nature of himself and humanity. He bears a grudge, and the first argument between the couple threatens to tear the marriage apart.

Under the weight of the business, Simon's behavior becomes more monstrous in act 3, four years later in 1840. He looks older than his thirty-five years, while Sara has seemed to prosper at home with the children in the company of Deborah. Simon and Sara formerly made decisions jointly and lived in a true partnership. Now, Simon manages the office domain at the company, while Sara rules the mansion. At home, Simon has moved into a separate bedroom and no longer sleeps with his wife. At work, he is bound to "this daily grind of slavery to an unscrupulous greed for power." Despite his labor and force of concentration that nearly kill him, Simon still believes that the "possession of power is the only freedom" (321). He knows this is false—the thesis of his book would have argued the exact opposite—but he seems incapable of changing directions and blames his wife's greed for encouraging him in the wrong direction. "[I]t was Sara's lust," he claims, "dreaming of Irish castles in Spain and a landed lady's estate, that has made me a cotton good's Napoleon!" (324). Simon now hatches a plan to shift the blame and responsibility for what he has done back to Sara. Prior to the first scene of act 3, set at Simon's office, he solicited Sara to stop by for the first time in years. She meets him there because she has had almost no time of late to see him privately, but also because she has genuine concerns for his health. Sara admits that she has been preoccupied with the children and that she has enjoyed the love and companionship of Deborah at home, but she makes it clear to Simon that he remains her first priority and that she will do anything for him.

Relieved, Simon offers Sara a new way for them to be together more and an opportunity for Sara to share the business as well. Sara will serve as Simon's new secretary, but she will function more as his mistress at work. Fearful that Simon has decided to throw her over for another woman, Sara jumps at the chance to play any game Simon chooses so long as she has him exclusively. He pitches the sex games with her as an opportunity to spark renewed intimacy between them, and Sara eagerly accepts his terms. She even thinks that it will be fun "playing I'm a wicked, lustful, wanton creature and making you a slave to my pleasure and beauty" (351). The game that Simon proposes, however, is not innocent but a scheme to burden Sara with the company that he no longer wants to own. He will sell it incrementally to her, he says, for every sexual act that she performs. Sara recognizes that this bargain amounts to prostitution, but the temptation to own the company proves too much. She never suspects that Simon's plan is to slip away from her forever. Instead, she continues plans to build an even bigger and more impressive mansion than the Harford home. Simon encourages her dreams and ambitions but insists that she can build nothing now, "before the company can be free and independent and self-sufficient" (355). Simon reassures her that her dream house will someday become a reality when they have enough money. The original goal had been $100,000. At this point they have amassed much more than that modest sum, but enough, it seems, is never quite enough.

Sara had accepted becoming a prostitute in the previous scene. A year later, 1841, in act 4, scene 1, she dresses the part as well. But after nearly seducing Simon's brother and then humiliating one of Simon's business rivals, Sara begins to take stock of her husband's manipulations and how they have exposed her as a "cruel greedy whore" (474). She recognizes that he swindled her into control of a company that is now encumbered with debts and highly leveraged. She threatens to bring the whole house of cards down and move with her children back to the old farm, where she'll be free to "live like a decent, honest woman working in the earth!" (474). Simon does not take her threat seriously and counters: "You would have to work like a slave for a bare living" (475). Now is not the time to stop, he argues, and encourages her to enjoy the thrill of risking everything to defeat her enemies. "You must go on to more and more!" he tells Sara, overriding her pleas to leave the business with more than enough to survive (478). Undeterred, Simon props up the ever-elusive and receding goal of self-sufficiency for the business: "Keep your whole mind and will concentrated on what must still be accomplished before your Company can be out of danger, safe and absolutely self-contained, not dependent on anything outside itself for anything, needing nothing but itself. Until that is done, how can you enjoy any true security or freedom within yourself—or any peace or happiness. Surely you must see that clearly, Sara?" (478–79).

Simon next outlines the work that remains to be done to close the business loop: first, Sara will need to own retail stores to sell her finished cotton goods. At the other end of production, however, it would be beneficial if she owned the plantations and slaves to pick the cotton. And, if she really wanted to control her business, it would be helpful, Simon points out, if she owned the slave ships for transport from Africa and could negotiate privately with her own slave dealer on that continent. Maybe, too, Simon further reasons, it is not enough to own the stores where Sara sells her products. It would be even better, he thinks, if she could compel consumers to buy only her products—in that way she could then enslave her consumers. She would then own the slaves who made her goods, as well as the slaves who bought them.

Simon's vision of the perfect business plan escalates to an absurd level, but it also reveals the depth of depravity of the amoral business model. Enslavement dehumanizes victims, but the owner loses all vestiges of humanity as well. Despite the fact that Simon has maneuvered her into heading a company on the cusp of bankruptcy, Sara remains as faithful to him as her mother did to Con Melody, and just as willing to do anything for him that he says he wants: "If it's a whore you love me to be, then I am it, body and soul, as long as you're mine!" (481).

In the final scene, later that same night, Sara reverses course in time to save Simon and herself. She discovers that enough *is* enough and decides to return to a simple life on the family farm and forget her dreams of a bigger mansion and more money. When she sees Simon almost led away by Deborah into her summerhouse of mad dreams and fantasies, it is as if she realizes what she has done to Simon by pushing him into business and encouraging his basest motives for profit and return investment. In this moment, she finally sees what the incessant drive to earn more money has created and vows to turn back before losing her husband, and maybe herself, forever. She discovers the wisdom of relinquishing control over another human being. She does not try to subjugate Simon to her will as she admits she once did. She simply explains to Deborah: "I see now the part my greed and my father's crazy dreams in me had in leading Simon away from himself until he lost his way and began destroying all that was best in him!" Now, with time not on her side, she pledges a new strategy for Simon's full recovery: "But I'll give my life now to setting you free to be again the man you were when I first met you—the man I loved best!—the dreamer with a touch of the poet in his soul, and the heart of a boy!" (544).

Sara dissolves the business "to prove my love for you and set you free from the greed of it" (544). On the farm where they first met, she vows to do the manual labor with her sons and give Simon time to write his philosophical books on freedom, equality, and a new society. In the epilogue, Sara assures Simon, who has recovered from his bout of brain fever, "You're free as you always wanted to be in your heart." She promises him that she will do anything in her power to preserve his health and happiness, then adds: "You can be in your dream of a world free of greed where men are good" (561, 563). Sara does not necessarily believe that such a world can exist, but she is willing to pretend for Simon's sake. In the end, Sara creates a refuge from which Simon does not change the world, but that saves him from self-destruction. She proves her love for him through action.

In her explanation to Simon about her earlier motives, though, Sara admits: "Nothing would do me but you must become a Napoleon of business" (559). Sara's incentive to make just enough money in order to be comfortable vanished with the image of the French conqueror. Much as Deborah described the Harford pursuit of freedom winding up in praise of Napoleon in *A Touch of the Poet*, Sara worships the same conqueror as an analogous all-powerful leader of business who might consume all of his rivals in *More Stately Mansions*. And, sadly, it is a Napoleonic ideal to which she holds her sons, despite her own repentance for her craven attitudes and desires. There are only three references to Napoleon in *A Touch of the Poet,* all of which occur in act 2, beginning with Deborah's entrance and ending immediately after her departure, the scene in which she recalls the past and outlines the Harford history. In *More Stately Mansions,* references to Napoleon spike to thirty-four. Simon is called a "Napoleon of finance" (300) or a "Napoleon among traders" (321), the "Company's victorious little Napoleon" (386), a "Napoleon of facts" (401), the "conquering Napoleon" (405), and the "reincarnation of Napoleon" (502). In world politics or local business, the drive for absolute freedom can transform over time into a need for complete submission to authority. Simon espouses the philosophy of Jean-Jacques Rousseau at the beginning of *More Stately Mansions* but has become the "cotton mill Napoleon" by the end (516). How torturously, then, the fight for freedom and independence devolves into new expressions of tyranny, power, and domination.

O'Neill was still a young man and a fledgling playwright when the Great War broke over Europe. James O'Neill paid to print his son's first batch of plays in 1914, the same year that Eugene enrolled in George Pierce Baker's English 47 playwriting workshop at Harvard. One of the plays he wrote for school, an antiwar one-act called *The Sniper,* while not very good, sincerely conveys the senselessness of war. Having lived through one world conflict, even from the safety of the United States, O'Neill anticipated a second bitter drink from the same cup in the late 1930s. He withheld production of *The Iceman Cometh* because he did not think an audience would accept the bleak message until the war ended (and maybe not even then). He had already determined that an audience would never accept the Cycle as he had conceived it.

Around the time he diagramed the Harford family tree in the summer of 1937, prior to moving into his last grand residence, Tao House, O'Neill decided to give Honey, the youngest son of Simon and Sara, the last word in the final play, "The Hair of the Dog." Aged 100 years, Honey had seen it all and recognized that humanity had learned little from its experiences and mistakes. Although he refers to his own family, his last speech addresses a worldwide audience on the brink of mass destruction:

That's right! A hair of the dog that bit you! That's the ticket! We Harfords have been bitten by 111 dogs—and they're all the same dog, and his name is the Greed of the Living and when he bites you there's a fever comes and a great thirst and a great drinking to kill it, and a grand drunk, and a terrible hangover and headache and remorse of conscience—and a sick empty stomach without greed or appetite. But take a hair of the dog and the sun will rise again for you—and the appetite and thirst will come back, and you can forget—and begin all over![14]

Honey's speech would have wrapped up the Cycle nicely by saying that it would never end. O'Neill had already said as much, though, with the two completed middle plays. Upon Cornelius Melody's first entrance in *A Touch of the Poet*, Nora responds to his difficult disposition and encourages him to imbibe a "hair of the dog" to steady his nerves. He refuses at first but quickly acquiesces and, despite his condition, manages to pour a drink, raise the glass to his lips, and drain the contents. His mood changes for the better as the alcohol begins to take effect in his ravaged system. That which makes him ill and will destroy him over time also allows him to continue to function and tolerate the dawn of another day. Similarly, the greedy and materialist impulses that threaten to destroy the Melodys and Harfords in the subsequent generations of *More Stately Mansions* are the same dominant traits and characteristics that started innocently enough as vain hopes of someday hoarding just enough to stop playing the vicious game of capital conquest. Sadly, Sara and company can never save enough, or say "enough," and the pursuit of freedom collapses into its ugly opposite—new bonds of enslavement. Long before World War II ended, indeed before it even started, O'Neill predicted that Americans would never be truly free.

CHAPTER SIX

STRIPPED STARK NAKED

About his latest script, O'Neill confided by letter to Lawrence Langner in August 1940: "there are moments in it that suddenly strip the secret soul of a man stark naked, not in cruelty or moral superiority, but with an understanding compassion which sees him as a victim of the ironies of life and of himself. Those moments are for me the depth of tragedy, with nothing more that can possibly be said."[1] O'Neill referred to *The Iceman Cometh*, which Langner had just read and liked, but in his previous play, *More Stately Mansions*, several characters used the same phrase, "stripped naked," in ways that seemed to foreshadow the grand effect in the later drama. Simon instructs Sara midway through the play: "You will have to strip life naked, and face it. And accept it as truth. And strip yourself naked and accept yourself as you are in the greedy mind and flesh" (353). Later, regarding Sara, Deborah asks, rhetorically: "is there any one of us whose soul, stripped naked, is not ugly with meanness?" (413). *The Iceman Cometh* seemed to provide the last word and definitive answer to this question by dramatizing the need for illusions to shield against the harsh realities of everyday existence. People cannot honestly face themselves as they are, and their pipe dreams provide an indispensable crutch for living. Both *A*

Touch of the Poet and *More Stately Mansions* seem to lead in the same direction as O'Neill's investigation of pipe dreams in *The Iceman Cometh*.

But the two Cycle plays ultimately function quite differently than O'Neill's "dive" play. The Cycle dramatizes compulsive behavior and the inability to stop; *The Iceman Cometh* showcases the art of denial and the refusal to move forward. While the principal female characters in the latter play remain unseen and offstage, created solely through the dialogue and stories of male characters, Sara Melody stands out as a strong female protagonist in the Cycle. Moreover, while her husband strips her naked, literally and figuratively, Sara rejects the humiliation that Simon inflicts upon her. In fact, Sara transforms the violence of stripping herself naked into a rite of purification in keeping with her Catholic sensibility. Over the course of the plays, Sara sins against herself and her husband because of her passionate and greedy nature, but, unlike the characters in *The Iceman Cometh*, she acknowledges what she has done and atones through guilt and suffering. Ultimately, too, she redeems herself and her husband through action and self-sacrifice. Sara gains wisdom through suffering over the course of the action, recognizes where she has strayed, and tries to repair the damage she has done.[2] She sinks almost as far as the derelicts do in *The Iceman Cometh*, but she does not stay sunk. Instead, Sara rejects the singular polarities that Simon and Deborah apply to her as either a "whore" or an "Irish biddy" (323, 409). Sara can see such designations as a part of her character, but not exclusive descriptions. She is also strong and smart and honest. Sara knows that a single modifier fits her best for only a moment and that she is capable of change over time.

The Cycle does not represent a rough draft, then, of *The Iceman Cometh*. Unfortunately, a hardy critical tradition represents O'Neill's late plays, beginning with *The Iceman Cometh*, as the ultimate goals of the playwright's career. The fact that these plays were published and performed before much was known about the Cycle created a hole in O'Neill's resume that critics filled as best they could or sometimes entirely ignored (for instance, Barrett Clark's monograph cited at the start of Chapter 4). Instead of appreciating the Cycle seriously, then, with its own goals and obstacles, over time critics came to view the period from 1934 to 1946—from *Days Without End* to the Broadway production of *The Iceman Cometh*—as an interlude that bridged stages of O'Neill's artistic development and ultimately prepared the way for his artistic genius to manifest fully with the final Tao House plays. For example, Virginia Floyd, among the first scholars to publish material from the O'Neill archive at Yale, argued that O'Neill's work on the Cycle deviated from his principal work but added that "after veering off course slightly, he continued in his work his life's journey." Even Martha Gilman Bower, who wrote her dissertation on the Cycle and then published the unexpurgated edition of *More Stately Mansions*, mapped the Cycle period as a "rehearsal stage for all the great plays he was to write."[3]

In 2004, Bower reiterated this judgment in the Introduction to her edition of *A Touch of the Poet* and *More Stately Mansions*. The Cycle plays, in her estimation, represented stages in development, not important and independent works, as O'Neill gathered momentum to write the now-famous late plays.[4] In this vein, Normand Berlin and Travis Bogard considered *Long Day's Journey Into Night* the ultimate literary goal or even confession to which O'Neill aspired. Berlin categorized *A Touch of the Poet* and *More Stately Mansions* as preludes in which O'Neill first had to take an oblique approach to his family situation before he could dramatize it directly in *Long Day's Journey Into Night*. "In *Poet*," according to Berlin, "the autobiographical pressure comes from the father; in *Mansions* it comes from the mother, Deborah Harford, an earlier portrait of Mary Tyrone. It seems that O'Neill had to suffer through the history Cycle in order to confront more directly his personal life."[5] Berlin cites the similarity of the physical descriptions of Deborah and Mary (and Mary Ellen "Ella" O'Neill, the playwright's mother) as proof that they are the same character, and equates the former's aloofness/insanity with the latter's drug addiction. Deborah's retreat to her summerhouse equals Mary's withdrawal to the upstairs spare bedroom. Only in the final plays did O'Neill gain the courage to tell the truth and present the O'Neills as themselves without unnecessary and distracting adornment.

After having valorized the Cycle in *Contour in Time* as one of the greatest works of literature that was never written, Travis Bogard changed his mind by 1993 in his last book, *"From the Silence of Tao House,"* and sided with the critical mainstream. He went further, actually, and claimed that O'Neill's "writing of the Cycle suggests a kind of madness in its author." While Berlin described O'Neill's oblique approach to his personal narrative, Bogard outlined O'Neill's desperate attempt to avoid writing the inevitable tale about his family. O'Neill, in this view, tried without success to stave off the Oedipal fate that he would master artistically only in his final great plays, especially

Long Day's Journey Into Night. Rejecting the rehearsal metaphor of Bower and Berlin, Bogard sides with Floyd and discredits the Cycle as an elaborate diversion from his main autobiographical task. "The Cycle can be looked on," according to Bogard, "as can many of his earlier plays, as a way of not writing the central truths of his life."[6] O'Neill, according to Bogard, did not prepare to write *Long Day's Journey Into Night* by writing the Cycle; rather, he wrote the Cycle in order not to have to write *Long Day's Journey* at all.

Disguised portraits of his parents in O'Neill's early plays possibly say as much about the psychological relationship between James and Ella O'Neill, perhaps more, than the representation in *Long Day's Journey Into Night*. In the one-act *Ile* (1917), Captain Keeney takes his wife on a long voyage to hunt whales, and she goes mad amid the loneliness of the interminable trip and the static relentlessness of the icy seascape. Is this not reminiscent of Mary Tyrone's descriptions of waiting alone "in that ugly hotel room hour after hour" for her husband to return from the theater?[7] O'Neill did not even bother to disguise his parents' names, Jim and Ella, in *All God's Chillun Got Wings* (1923). Here, the racial antagonism between a Black man and the White woman who both loves and hates him is a visual expression of his parents' marriage as a union between opposites.

O'Neill's bold portrayals of his parents early in his career cast doubt on arguments for a sudden shyness about that subject in later years. Bogard recasts his "Cycle as madness" thesis in vain when he suggests that O'Neill's reluctance to write *Long Day's Journey Into Night* is analogous to Deborah Harford's flirtations with insanity in *More Stately Mansions:* "O'Neill's characters surely chart his own way of being, and it is perhaps not too much to suggest that the Cycle was itself an elaborate daydream, and that O'Neill shut himself in his study much as Abigail [Deborah] shut herself in her summer house losing herself by telling romantic stories about the French Court."[8] Bogard essentially asks the same rhetorical question as Floyd, Bower, and Berlin: "Was the Cycle a way of disguising a truth which [O'Neill] ultimately gained the courage to present?"[9]

On this basis, Bogard represents the final portraits of the Tyrones (O'Neills) in *Contour in Time* as a more sophisticated rendering of the Harford and Melody alliance in the two extant Cycle plays. Con Melody is Tyrone (James O'Neill); Nora/Deborah is Mary (Ella O'Neill); Simon Harford is Edmund (Eugene O'Neill). Thus far, Bogard's straightforward equations are easy to follow, but he still has to account for Sara, and he stretches credulity when he surmises that "perhaps" she is Jamie. Other than quarreling with her father as Jamie spats with the senior Tyrone, Sara has little in common with Jamie. While she is the vital life force in *A Touch of the Poet* and *More Stately Mansions*, Jamie is more than "a little in love with death," and Josie Hogan describes him prior to his first entrance in *A Moon for the Misbegotten* as a "dead man walking." By the end of the play, Josie realizes that Jamie has "died already."[10] The fact that Sara does not fit neatly in Bogard's formulations suggests a difference in O'Neill's conceptualizing of the Cycle and the late plays; the fact that Sara in essence defines the unique arc of the Cycle plays would seem to settle the matter. Sara has no analogue in *Long Day's Journey Into Night*.

Nor has she one in *A Moon for the Misbegotten*, contrary to Bogard's assertion that "Sara and Josie are the same woman."[11] They do similar things, certainly, and they strike similar poses at the end of their respective plays, evocative of a Pietà, when they cradle their lovers and vow to be their mothers. But Sara can hardly be both Jamie and Josie. While it is easy to see aspects of Josie and maybe even Jamie in Sara, the leading character in the Cycle faces an array of choices that the other characters do not have an opportunity to explore. The expansive range of Sara Melody surpasses that of any single character in another O'Neill drama.

Nonetheless, in his Introduction to his book on the Cycle plays, Donald Gallup went so far as to suggest that O'Neill's decision to stop work on the Cycle in June 1939 precipitated a critical breakthrough that allowed him to write his final masterpieces: "The change had a remarkable effect. His creative mind came alive again as new ideas flooded his brain. [. . .] After his tortured attempts to get at the complicated motives of his Cycle family, the Harfords, these two autobiographical plays [*The Iceman Cometh* and *Long Day's Journey Into Night*] almost wrote themselves."[12] On the one hand, Gallup's interpretation ignores the relative ease and speed with which O'Neill drafted *A Touch of the Poet* and *More Stately Mansions*. On the other hand, though, by claiming that *The Iceman Cometh* and *Long Day's Journey Into Night* "almost wrote themselves," Gallup robs them of their artful construction and hints that O'Neill was free at last to write the truth of his life.

Scholar Doris Alexander convincingly challenges the notion of autobiographical truth in the late plays. She astutely points out numerous examples of O'Neill manipulating and altering facts to make good drama, down to details regarding the real wedding dress of Ella O'Neill as opposed to the stage property brought from the attic by Mary Tyrone and held by her husband, James, at the end of *Long Day's Journey Into Night*.[13] The true story of the O'Neills has none of the poetic images supplied by the playwright for the fictional Tyrones. The real story does not exploit repetition, does not employ symbolism of light and dark, and does not structure time brilliantly to move forward and backward simultaneously. O'Neill fosters an elegant illusion that a definitive and forthcoming answer will solve the mystery of what happened to the Tyrones and name those to blame for its miseries, but the curtain falls with an unresolved account.

Long Day's Journey Into Night is not a great play because it is more truthful to O'Neill's real-life experiences in 1912. It is great, in part, because an audience confronts its own experiences as it witnesses the event. *The Iceman Cometh*, also set in 1912, refers to people whom O'Neill knew at that time, but it is not really an autobiographical play. While it is convenient to figure Edmund Tyrone as Eugene O'Neill, the voice of the playwright is not heard exclusively from any one character in the earlier play. The mother-son relationship between Rosa and Don Parritt resembles the bond between Mary and Edmund in *Long Day's Journey Into Night,* but *The Iceman Cometh* is a great play to the extent that it addresses the hopes and fears and dreams of an audience, not the degree to which it accurately reflects the playwright's recollection of slumming in New York. In O'Neill's last play, *A Moon for the Misbegotten,* Josie Hogan overpowers Jim Tyrone, a stand-in for Jamie O'Neill, as the most interesting and important character. The one-act *Hughie* (1942), in which a small-time gambler laments the loss of his only friend, has no autobiographical link at all. O'Neill left behind notes for three plays in 1940 that had nothing to do with his personal history. "Malatesta Seeks Surcease" was a comic foil to *The Iceman Cometh* in praise of anarchism. The rise of Hitler and threat of war inspired "The Last Conquest" and another Hitler-like gangster in "Blind Alley Guy." If writing his family truth were his ultimate goal, why did O'Neill continue to write about subjects other than the Tyrones/O'Neills after starting *Long Day's Journey Into Night?*

Bogard hypothesizes that O'Neill wrote all the Tao House plays, including the two plays from the Cycle, with a repertory of actors in mind. O'Neill had envisioned a company of actors performing the Cycle plays at the Theatre Guild, but not individual stars. Stars, he intuited, would never commit to playing in a series of plays over four years or more.[14] O'Neill was excited, even adamant, about putting together a repertory company without having to engage star performers. Bogard's theory that O'Neill conceived the plays for a company of actors to perform them offers a new way of looking at how one play relates to another. Instead of seeing Cornelius Melody or Deborah Harford as the prototypes for James and Mary Tyrone, the theatrical model sees the parts as suited to the range of what certain actors could play. While the notion that Sara Melody *is* Josie Hogan, for example, robs both characters of their individuality, the same actress might perfectly *play* both roles in separate productions.

Similarly, it would be logical to cast the same actor in the roles of Con Melody and James Tyrone, another as Mary Tyrone and Deborah Harford, and a third as either Edmund or Jamie, Simon Harford, or Jim Tyrone. O'Neill carefully distinguished between actor and role when he discussed ideal casting for Con Melody in *A Touch of the Poet:* "What one needs is an actor like Maurice Barrymore or James O'Neill, my old man. One of those big-chested, chiseled-mug, romantic old boys who could walk onto a stage with all the aplomb and regal splendor with which they walked into the old Hoffman House bar, drunk or sober."[15] This same speech has often been invoked to prove that Con Melody was an early portrait of his father or James Tyrone, but read carefully, what he actually says is that the role requires an actor like his father—one with the qualities that his father possessed as an actor. O'Neill did not necessarily have his father, the man, in mind for Melody.

As actor is to role, so playwright is to play. Actors bring a number of personal qualities to a particular role such as the ones O'Neill associates with Barrymore or O'Neill, Sr. Such qualities make an actor fit or unfit to play certain characters onstage, though producers and directors do sometimes cast actors against their traditional types to marvelous effect. Still, range determines limits, and the boundaries define the kinds of roles any individual actor might assume. It is much the same for playwrights. O'Neill possessed certain qualities, inclinations, and literary proclivities that circulated throughout his body of work. An interest in the idea of modern tragedy, the desire to strive for big themes and universal statements, a tendency to make bold theatrical statements, an urge to exhaust language in pursuit of the last word, poetic titles, the need for at least a "hopeless hope" in order to survive, alternating or simultaneous rhythms of love and hate in intimate relationships, the search for God, and the search for a sense of belonging in the modern world—these aspects and features help to identify O'Neill's familiar stamp.

Unlike most dramatists, O'Neill wrote his "plays of a lifetime" at the end of his career. Just as the Tao House plays—*A Touch of the Poet, More Stately Mansions, The Iceman Cometh, Long Day's Journey Into Night, Hughie,* and *A Moon for the Misbegotten*—present roles that could be performed by a company of actors, the plays share many of O'Neill's frequent thematic and stylistic concerns. Neither *A Touch of the Poet* nor *More Stately Mansions* leads to *The Iceman Cometh,* however, despite important similarities. In fact, the ways in which these plays share certain aspects demonstrate the break between the plays. They share a trajectory up to a certain point, but then turn in radically different directions. In the end, *A Touch of the Poet* and *More Stately Mansions* explore identity rather than crave illusion, rebel against prevailing norms rather than passively capitulate to them, and populate the dramatic world with powerful women rather than limit it to a society of men.

The respective settings nevertheless connect the two plays from the outset: Melody Tavern in *A Touch of the Poet* and the first act of *More Stately Mansions* located outside Boston in 1828; and Harry Hope's saloon in *The Iceman Cometh* on the Lower West Side of Manhattan almost 100 years later. Drinking figures extensively in both plays: Con Melody, Sara's father, is an alcoholic in the former play; nearly all the characters save Hickey, only of late on the wagon, are drunks in the latter drama. In both plays, alcohol provides an escape from realities that the characters seek to evade and serves as a tonic for the celebration of happy illusions. Both establishments have rooms for guests upstairs in unseen quarters. Simon Harford convalesces for the entire duration of *A Touch of the Poet;* Sara regularly reports on his recovery. Her seduction of him in that offstage bedroom in the interval between acts 3 and 4 leads directly to their marriage, which becomes the subject of the sequel. Similarly, many of the habitués of Hope's saloon also rent rooms on one of his upper floors. They describe how Hickey proselytizes from room to room and chases each man to create a forced community in the bar.

The layout of the visible playing spaces in these two settings is strikingly similar as well. O'Neill specifies in the opening stage directions of *A Touch of the Poet* that the inn was formerly prosperous and that at one time the barroom and the dining room were one large room. Now, however, the barroom is just offstage, and a wall, of flimsy construction and a poor imitation of the adjoining beams and panels from sturdier times, divides the two spaces. Just so, a dirty black curtain divides the back room of Hope's saloon from the actual bar in the front. Subsequent acts divide the room differently: in the third act, for example, the scene takes place in the front room and focuses on the windows and front door to make the outside world proximate. The artificial partitions in both plays enclose the interior spaces, but they also emphasize the permeable border that surrounds the inhabitants and applies pressure at the same time for those on the inside to escape. The bar in *A Touch of the Poet* and the outside street in *The Iceman Cometh* are destinations where dreams die, and Con and Hope's crew would do almost anything to avoid these life-changing thresholds. They eventually do cross these boundaries, and their confrontations with themselves shatter the illusions that they held. Con does not recover; most of the men in *The Iceman Cometh* do manage to take up their old pipe dreams, but the end of the play does not promise future happiness.

Despite the whiskey that flows like water, the action in both plays stanches the spread of illusions and forces Con's and Hope's gangs to accept themselves as they are. Theodore Hickman ("Hickey"), a traveling salesman with the gift of gab, offers the final word on this subject as he tries to convince his old friends in *The Iceman Cometh* that they don't need to get drunk anymore in order to prop up their tired illusions and pipe dreams about themselves. Hickey preaches salvation, not temperance, but it turns out that he needs illusions as much as if not more than any in his audience. He has just murdered his wife in her sleep because he could no longer endure the guilt-inducing forgiveness with which she responded to his debauched life on the road. He convinced himself, though, that he killed her as an act of mercy and love to put her out of the misery of loving him. Free at last, he heads to Harry Hope's to convince its denizens that they should give up their pipe dreams, as he has done, in order to discover true peace and happiness.

Arriving for Harry's birthday party in act 1, Hickey tells the assembled group: "Well, I finally had the guts to face myself and throw overboard the damned lying pipe dream that'd been making me miserable, and do what I had to do for the happiness of all concerned—and then all at once I found I was at peace with myself and I didn't need booze any more." The partiers at Harry's just want to get drunk and pass out—Hickey's sobriety baffles them and they wonder whether his new act is some kind of comic gag. Hickey presses on, however, in the second act and assures them that the peace he promises is real and that he has experienced it firsthand. He wants each one of the tribe to feel the same way as him: "The kind of pity I feel now is after final results that will really save the poor guy, and make him contented with what he is, and quit battling himself, and find peace for the rest of his life."[16]

To his chagrin, Hickey learns that his old friends suffer miserably without their "pipe dreams." He, too, in the course of explaining and justifying his actions, realizes that he killed his wife not as a gesture of sacrificial love but in an act of violent rage and hatred. After detectives arrest him in the final act, unable to face the true motive for what he has done, Hickey invents a new story and claims that he must have been insane when he murdered his wife. Backed up by Hope and the rest of the gang, who are eager to avoid the truth about Hickey as well as about themselves, Hickey clings desperately to a new narrative of what happened regarding his wife's death in order to avoid the knowledge of the fact that he is ultimately guilty. None of the patrons at Hope's bar, including Hickey, can face life without illusions.

The end of *A Touch of the Poet* leads to the same conclusion. Beaten and bedraggled, Con theatrically gives up his pose as Major Melody and enters the barroom to join a throng of besotted Irishmen. In the end, he trades his Byronic stature for a place in the crowd. Sara, alone among the witnesses, recognizes her father's dramatic drop of pretense: to be stripped naked is something worse than death.

Sara did not always feel that way. As Hickey implored his old pals at Harry's to put down their "pipe dreams," Sara repeatedly begged her father to live in truth in *A Touch of the Poet*. The conflict between father and daughter stems from Sara's realization and lament that her father is not the person whom he pretends to be. Sara hates the manner in which her father treats her mother and the ways that he enslaves her because of a felt class difference only tenuously justified by his family's history. Con uses money the family does not have to feed his thoroughbred mare, upon which he rides about the county as if he were a nobleman and not an American citizen who must work for a living. Nora and Sara labor to preserve Con's pretense of status and to prevent an honest reckoning: the Yankees swindled a naïve Irish immigrant into buying a useless piece of property, the tavern, that will never turn a profit.

Sara resents her father's pose, and she does not hesitate to confront him and express her wish for him to drop the illusions that enslave the family: "If you ever dared face the truth, you'd hate and despise yourself! All I pray to God is that someday when you're admiring yourself in the mirror something will make you see at last what you really are!" (87). Regarding her prospective marriage to Simon, a rich Yankee, Con supposes that the Harfords should be grateful that he would allow his daughter to enter an alliance with a family of greedy traders. Incredulous, Sara refuses to listen further to her father's delusions: "Is it stark mad you've gone, so you can't tell any more what's dead and a lie, and what's the living truth?" (42). Before leaving at the end of act 3 to challenge Harford to a duel, Con forbids his daughter to marry Simon and threatens to kill her if she does not obey. Sara refuses to submit, however, and seduces Simon and secures a marriage proposal in her father's absence. Waiting with her mother for Con's return, she repeats the same wish that she has voiced about her father throughout the play: "All I hope now is that whatever happened wakes him from his lies and mad dreams so he'll have to face the truth of himself in that mirror" (126). When Con finally does hunt down the truth outside the Harford mansion, he discovers, like the homecoming crew in Hope's saloon, that the booze no longer has any kick.

The conflict between father and daughter in *A Touch of the Poet* expands to a triangular tension in *More Stately Mansions* among Sara, Simon, and Simon's mother, Deborah; but the urge for characters to face the truth about themselves and abandon the illusions that they have created remains consistent with the action in *The Iceman Cometh*. Deborah claims in act 1, scene 2 that her son has lost his poet's dream of ever writing a book about utopian society and the goodness of humankind. Now, she says, Simon is a successful merchant, like his father, a devoted husband to Sara, and the father of four young sons. In order to sustain such responsibilities, she implies, Simon will have to give up his former dreams of writing his books in contemplative solitude. He is not the same person, she chides, as he was in earlier years when the bond between mother and son held them close. In order for him to thrive in his new environment, Deborah advises, "you must forget what you once wanted to be and face yourself as you are, and not be ashamed" (229). Four years later, Simon acknowledges the futility of trying to balance two sides of his nature, the poetic dreamer and the ruthless man of business: "There I was at night in my study trying to convince myself of the possibility of a greedless Utopia, while all day in my office I was really getting the greatest satisfaction and sense of self-fulfillment and pride out of beating my competitors in the race for power and possessions!" (272). He destroys the notes for his book but then articulates an idea for a new book to replace the old one. This one, however, will not idealize the philosophy of Jean-Jacques Rousseau; on the contrary, it will strive to present the world as it exists without any flattering embellishment. As his mother suggested, Simon proposes a book that would be "a frank study of the true nature of man as he really is and not as he pretends to himself to be" (274). Simon does not return to the poetic side of his nature again until after he recovers from his collapse during the epilogue, staged once again at the cabin where he first felt inspired to write about nature in the manner of Thoreau.

After the confrontation with his mother, Simon turns around and saddles Sara with several naked truths about herself as well. He devises a game in which she will have to embrace greed and lust as her core impulses. If she ever hopes to gain ownership of his company, Simon panders, she will have to act like the whore she has always been (Fig. 9). In the name of honesty, he describes a new and transparent morality: "Yes, you will have to learn to be shameless here. That is to say, to free yourself from false shame and be what you are" (353). Initially enthralled with the chance to reclaim her husband sexually and excited to take a part of his business, Sara grows sated scarcely a year later and begs Simon to stop. Maniacally, he counsels in act 4: "You must not be weak. You must be courageously and ruthlessly what you are! You must go on to more and more!" (477–78). Simon reduces Sara to a man-eating machine and refuses to let her stop working until she consumes him and the entire company.

The connections between the Cycle plays and *The Iceman Cometh* culminate in the final scene (4.2) of *More Stately Mansions*, in which Simon takes the philosophy of facing the truth and seeing life as it really is as far

FIGURE 9. Jenny Bacon (Sara) and Tim Hopper (Simon) in Ivo van Hove's production of *More Stately Mansions* at the New York Theatre Workshop in 1997. (Image courtesy of Ryder Thornton. Photo © by Joan Marcus.)

as possible. Having torn apart his own dreams (he literally destroyed the notes for his book on a utopian society), Simon now longs to escape to a dream-like past with his mother through the summerhouse door in her garden. All his former business dealings and conquests and gambles have ravaged his soul and left him unrecognizable from the optimistic, thoughtful, and helpful young man who escorted his wife to Cornelius Melody's wake almost ten years earlier. Now, Simon anticipates the arrival of the Iceman in the next play: "But the obvious fact is that [our] lives are without any meaning whatever—that human life is a silly disappointment, a liar's promise, a perpetual in bankruptcy for debts we never contracted, a daily appointment with peace and happiness in which we wait day after day, hoping against hope, listening to each footstep, and when finally the bride or bridegroom cometh, we discover we are kissing Death" (520–21). Hickey is the bridegroom in *The Iceman Cometh* who, as Larry Slade says in act 2 of that play, "brought the touch of death on him!"[17] To give up one's dreams—to face oneself in the mirror without the armature of illusions— leads to death. Hickey represents the last stop on the route that Sara, Con, Deborah, and Simon have traveled.

Simon, though, suggests Larry Slade more than Hickey. Both Simon and Larry express a view of humanity that swaps meliorism for pessimism. Larry had been an active member of the Movement, an anarchist political group dedicated to freedom, equality, and political change. Early in the play, though, he explains his reasons for his permanent withdrawal from the group: "I saw men didn't want to be saved from themselves, for that would mean they'd have to give up greed, and they'll never pay that price for liberty."[18] Similarly, Simon voices a radical spirit in act 1, scene 2 of *More Stately Mansions:* "In a free society there must be no private property to tempt men's greed into enslaving one another. We must protect man from his stupid possessive instincts until he can be educated to outgrow them spiritually" (214). In the course of the play, however, Simon abandons his theories and assumes a much more pessimistic stance about the nature of humanity. Four years later, in act 2, scene 2, he calculates that an individual is only one-tenth spirit, but nine-tenths hog (273). He repeats his equation of man as hog in acts 3 and 4 (321, 504). Slade comes to the same conclusion in act 1 of *The Iceman Cometh:* "The material the ideal free society must be constructed from is men themselves and you can't build a marble temple out of a mixture of mud and manure. When man's soul isn't a sow's ear, it will be time enough to dream of silk purses."[19]

The philosophical poses that Simon and Slade share, however, originate in perceived betrayals by women rather than in reasoned judgment or thoughtful convictions. In Simon's case, his mother, who had been everything to him as a child, abandoned him at a certain point. She confided to him that childrearing had been a kind of slavery for her and that she even wished that she had never birthed him. Rejection by his mother prompts Simon to adopt a withering worldview of humanity. Similarly, Larry loved Rosa Parritt, the leader of the Movement on the West Coast, but she refused to remain faithful because of her political beliefs about women and marriage and a truly "free" society. Slade, like Simon, cannot fully articulate his loss, and concocts a cerebral but conveniently universalist explanation that allows him to dodge the true source of pain in his life.

Simon and Slade have "swallowed the anchor" in their respective plays. That term crops up first in *Chris Christophersen* (1919), the forerunner of *"Anna Christie"* the following year. To swallow the anchor is, according to Second Mate Paul Andersen, "to shrink from any more effort and be content to anchor fast in the thing you are!" Andersen, who morphed into Mat Burke in the successful revision, explains the virtues of this way of life: "I'm free from the sin of ambition, you see. I'm quite content to remain where I am and let others do the aspiring."[20] It's not clear, though, whether Andersen actually believes what he says or merely adopts a convenient pose. He certainly does not believe in it by the time he proposes marriage to Anna and vows to captain his own ship. Unlike Andersen, Simon rejects his wife and asks his mother to lead him through her summerhouse door as an escape from the workaday world to childhood bliss. In *The Iceman Cometh*, Slade already inhabits "the Bottom of the Sea Rathskeller" at Harry Hope's when that play begins: "No one here has to worry about where they're going next, because there is no farther they can go."[21] Simon and Slade sink, and they do not plan to resurface in the world anytime soon.

By contrast, Sara Melody perseveres in the Cycle plays as an ambitious force of a distinctively American capitalism. Unlike her husband or any of the characters in *The Iceman Cometh*, she does not "swallow the anchor" but stands tall with her feet on the ground from beginning to end. If a barroom setting is the most noticeable similarity between the Cycle plays and *The Iceman Cometh*, Sara's strong presence as a female protagonist separates the former from the latter. All women but the three "tarts" remain offstage and never get the chance to speak in *The Iceman Cometh*. Instead, the male characters speak for them. In O'Neill's later one-act *Hughie*, the titular character never appears but comes to life through the monologues of his only friend. The technique allowed O'Neill to reveal as much about the speaking character as it did about the subject. And so it is with Marjorie Cameron, Bessie Hope, Rosa Parritt, and Evelyn Hickman in *The Iceman Cometh*. The stories about them as told by the men who knew them says something about the women, but it shows even more about the men who blame the departed and unseen women for tormenting them.

James Cameron (Jimmy Tomorrow) blames his wife Marjorie's extra-marital affair for driving him to drink. He admits later, though, that he preferred to drink rather than spend time with her and that she left him only as a last resort. Bessie Hope, Harry's wife, constantly harangued her husband to keep the place respectable. Given the fact that Harry surrounds himself with spongers in his bar—including Bessie's brother, Ed Mosher, who appears to be the most shiftless character in the play—her demands do not seem so extreme. Rosa Parritt, whom her son labels a "bitch" and her former lover calls a "whore," may not have been a doting mother and a faithful partner, but she is a strong leader of firm convictions, and her position prevents her from accepting conventional relationships. Nevertheless, the fact that her son seeks to atone for what he has done to her and that Larry Slade still loves her suggests that she has more dimensions as a character than the slurs against her would indicate. Hickey describes Evelyn Hickman, the most prominent of the unseen characters, as a saint. Not until the very end do his own words take him by surprise as he calls her a "damned bitch."[22] Such polarities suggest that she is neither one type nor the other, but rather occupies a medial position as an independent character with virtues and vices, thoughts and feelings. Hickey blots out any variety in the creation of his wife. He needs her to be a saint or a bitch in order to justify his homicidal rage.

Simon treats Sara much the same way as the men do their women in *The Iceman Cometh*: he makes her responsible for what he has done. For example, he blames her for pushing him into business rather than encouraging him in a literary career. While Sara shares some culpability for that decision (she acknowledges her part), Simon becomes a "Napoleon of finance" for his own reasons that have nothing to do with Sara—to rebel against his mother's neglect and to side with his dead father against her as an act of revenge. In the epilogue of *More Stately Mansions*, Sara ministers to Simon, just recovered from a bout of brain fever, and attempts to inform him of all that has happened since he hit his head in the last act of the play. Sara accepts the blame and says that Simon did what he did out of love for her. Simon responds, *"eagerly"*: "Yes, now that you've said it yourself, that is the real truth of it, Sara" (563). So much for chivalry . . . and so much for Simon reading the scene with any nuance at all. Indeed, Simon refuses to view the world with any awareness of its complexity. In order for him to maintain stability, he demands that Sara represent sexuality and that his mother stand for spirituality. He cannot integrate evidently contrary forces within a single female character. Ultimately, he determines that he must choose between Sara and Deborah.

Not surprisingly, he picks his mother, the past instead of his future. Deborah, too, is a fixed character who hides behind the high walls of her garden and seldom ventures outside to encounter life as it is lived. Simon remembers his idyllic youth with her and longs to return to his former position outside her summerhouse door, waiting for as long as it might take, until Deborah "opened the door and welcomed him home and they were both happy ever after" (401). But life with Sara offered no such fairy-tale ending. Simon has diminished her to a whore and transformed his office into a brothel for their elaborate daytime trysts and assignations. Although Sara has been willing to play his game, just as her mother had humored Con, she realizes that Simon has pitted her against his mother in a loser's death match.

Sara resists the downward pull to face herself as she is, to rid herself of illusions, to deal with facts, and to sink to the bottom. She both expresses her desire to be more than she is and takes action to prove that she is capable of change and growth and worthy of redemption. Sara does not agree with her husband that people are "hog[s]" and that life is hardly worth living. She stands in opposition to Simon's negativity and refutes the theme of *The Iceman Cometh* regarding the need for pipe dreams and illusions and the impossibility of seeing life clearly. Sara welcomes the possibility and has the courage to want to become a better person. This requires honesty to accept responsibility for her many failings and shortcomings, but also a desire to seek redemption and forgiveness. Notably, in *A Touch of the Poet*, despite her many disagreements with her father, she sees that her father's pose is not mere pretense but an aspect of who he is. She recognizes his heroic stature and charisma when he dons his red military uniform, and she laments the fact that he cannot live up to the standards that the image projects. Amazed, though, she asks: "Oh, Father, why can't you ever be the thing you can seem to be?" (74). Melody has not given up at that point. He aspires to greatness that he cannot achieve or maintain, but Sara admires the effort. Sara alone mourns his demise at the end of that play, for she hears his brogue and sees his drunkenness as signs of his willful resignation: "swallowing the anchor" and sinking to the bottom where nothing can bother him ever again. Sara vows that the same thing will not happen to her.

Deborah and Simon dismiss her as greedy, but Sara acknowledges the unwelcome presence of that trait, which she cannot always hold at bay. She is much more than a singularity, and she knows it. At the end of act 1, scene 2 of *More Stately Mansions*, Sara emerges from behind the door of the cabin by the lake to confront her mother-in-law and display a full range of characteristics. First, she asserts her dominance and physical power over Deborah and declares that Deborah will never take Simon from her. "Life is too strong for you!" Sara brags. "But it's not too strong for me! I'll take what I want from it and make it mine!" (234). Next, though, Sara softens and extends her compassion. Earlier in the scene, Sara eavesdropped on Deborah and her husband and overheard Simon humiliate and laugh at Deborah and then walk away as if he had done nothing. Now she kindly apologizes on his behalf in a heartfelt and gentle manner that astonishes Deborah. Poverty made her greedy, Sara admits, but she insists that Deborah simply does not know everything about her. She continues: "But the thing you don't know is that there's great love in me too, great enough to destroy all the greed in the world" (236). A series of statements and immediate counterstatements further complicates the composite image of Sara: she would gladly give up all material things to live in a hut with Simon, but she wants their children to grow up as gentlemen; she boasts that her father lived in a castle in Ireland but decries his lying pretenses; she confesses that she seduced Simon for love but that she would have done it to get financial freedom as well. A successful performer in this part might be one who does not try to reconcile the contradictions of the role but exposes and exploits them instead.

The proof of Sara's ultimate goodness and the triumph of her character, with its many flaws, emerges in the last act. Sara appears twice in the final scene as an intruder into Deborah's garden, an outsider at a strategic disadvantage, but she discovers a redemption that sets the Cycle apart from *The Iceman Cometh*. At the end of the latter play, two detectives lead Hickey away to the jailhouse, and probably the asylum or the electric chair; and Larry Slade sends young Parritt upstairs and off the fire escape to his death. In *More Stately Mansions*, Sara enters Deborah's garden with a plan to push her mother-in-law into her summerhouse and a world of madness. She discovers that she cannot do it. Greed and possessiveness motivated many of her actions up to this point, but Sara relinquishes her psychological hold on Simon and her physical advantage over Deborah at the play's climax. She offers to give Simon up permanently to save him from madness or death. That Deborah subsequently makes her own sacrificial gesture does not diminish the magnitude of what Sara did. If she had not interceded in time, Simon would have been lost.

Sara reports to her husband in the epilogue: "creditors stripped us clean" (561). They have nothing now and face the prospect of starting over. At the beginning of the previous scene, Joel Harford had warned Sara that Simon had rashly overleveraged the company. Competitors, he said, lurked everywhere to "strip you of everything you possess" (450). In response, Sara reasoned that she "could strip him [Joel] bare" with her beauty and seductive power; earlier in the scene, she had referred to the banker Tenard as "stripped bare" (453, 448). Anticipating what O'Neill later said about *The Iceman Cometh* to his friend Langner, the phrase drives home the theme of reduction and diminishment that runs the course of *More Stately Mansions* and *The Iceman Cometh*.

Yet the image of "stripped bare" or "stripped naked" takes on quite different meanings at the end of both plays. In *Iceman*, the illusions with which Slade wrapped his life are torn away, and he must face the fact that he sentenced Don Parritt to death for crimes against his mother. He must admit to himself that he sent the young man away because of his own love for Rosa and the devotion and guilt that it has inspired in him. Despite all his protests, life has drawn him back into its fray and exposed the fraudulence of his beloved philosophy. He can honestly claim for the first time that he is ready for death. While Slade remains vulnerable without the "pipe dreams" that shielded him from the truth, events in *More Stately Mansions* purify Sara Melody. Her nakedness manifests as newborn innocence. She and her husband have returned to the cabin by the lake where they first met and where Simon once envisioned that he would write his books about a free society in quiet contemplation. With nothing but themselves, their boys, and a farm to work, they escape momentarily from the cycles of greed that imprisoned them and poisoned their relationship with each other. Sara remains undaunted by the realization, brief though it may turn out to be, that they actually have enough in order to survive and that, in fact, the genuine love that she can now see in Simon will enable her to face a future shorn of illusion.

CHAPTER SEVEN

BEYOND THE THRESHOLD

The collapse of Cornelius Melody at the conclusion of *A Touch of the Poet* mirrors that of Simon Harford in the final act of *More Stately Mansions*. The reflection, however, casts each in the opposite direction: Con through the barroom door to the drunks who gladly offer a hand down from his high horse of gentlemanly pretense; Simon away from the tensions of workaday life to the make-believe fantasies in his mother's summerhouse. Sara Melody, witness to both events, manages, with an assist from Deborah, to pull her husband back from the edge and save him. In the former play, however, her father begs Sara to let him go, and she can do nothing but watch as he disappears into the drunken throng. While Nora prays that Con might finally find the peace that has always eluded him, Sara recognizes this discovery as the peace of death. Having prayed all her life for Con to face the truth, Sara now sees what appears to be his admission of that truth as another lie and would prefer her father as he formerly pretended to be instead of the seemingly honest lout who just departed. "Why do I mourn for him?" she asks in her last line (153). Sara says nothing more, but her subsequent actions in the sequel play suggest that she learned to admire her father's ambition for, if not realization of, nobility of spirit and greatness. Sara determines to carry that legacy forward as she advances in the new world of *More Stately Mansions*.

In that second play, Simon cannot sustain his competing roles as a poet and businessman, son and husband, spiritual idealist and material realist, just as Con cannot ultimately reconcile his dueling parts as both Major Melody of His Majesty's Seventh Dragoons and son of a "thievin' she-been [illicit bar] keeper" (9). The touch-of-the-poet mixture in Simon and Con fosters an elaborate masquerade that shields their true identities from themselves as well as others. As things play out, though, the action in both plays questions the authenticity and primacy of such opposing personas and even hints that one front may be no more genuine than another.

In June 1939, O'Neill updated Richard Dana Skinner on the Cycle's progress and indicated that he longed for a vacation after laboring on it for well over four years. He noted how difficult it had been to coordinate all the disparate parts of each individual play in preparation for when "the curve completes its circle." He reported that he had finished four plays, with five yet to go. Three plays were "double length or over," but he was trying to bring the fourth play [*More Stately Mansions*] down to normal size.[1] Such length, O'Neill explained, stemmed from his "attempt to get a deeper, more revealing, more complicated motivation into character—to get all the aspects of the inner strength of opposites in the individual which is fate—keeps me constantly overreaching the medium."[2]

O'Neill's conception of character highlights contradictions in order to produce a sense of depth. Con is both gentleman and drunk, Simon is part Thoreau and part Napoleon, and the characters, and by extension the playwright, struggle to keep all aspects of identity in play. O'Neill becomes novelistic as he describes the evolution of characters over time and through the years in *A Touch of the Poet* and *More Stately Mansions*, and he experiments with ways to convey inner processes that go beyond the dialogic form. His methods threaten to crush the drama under voluminous pages.

O'Neill represents Sara Melody as no less split than her father or her future husband with her initial entrance in *A Touch of the Poet*. His lengthy stage directions describe her physical appearance as a blend of aristocratic and peasant characteristics. She has a well-shaped head with a "fine forehead," a nose that is "thin and straight," small ears and a slender neck, but her mouth has "a touch of coarseness and sensuality and her jaw is too heavy." Her figure is "strong and graceful," but she has "large feet and broad, ugly hands with stubby fingers." Her voice and speech sound educated, but she lapses into brogue in times of emotional distress. Sara wears a dress of cheap material, but "she wears it in a way that gives a pleasing effect of beauty unadorned" (12). Stage directions about Sara in *More Stately Mansions* list some of the same attributes: "There is a curious blending in her appearance of what are commonly considered to be aristocratic and peasant characteristics." The time is four years after *A Touch of the Poet*, Sara is visibly pregnant with her fourth child, yet the same catalogue of descriptions still applies, and concludes with a list of the same common defects: "thick ankles, large feet, and big hands, broad and strong with thick, stubby fingers" (169).

The assumption easily follows that Sara inherits the aristocratic features of her appearance from her father and the peasant ones from her mother. Con was a gentleman in Ireland, and he married a poor girl, Nora, who worked on his father's estate. Ned Melody attained rank and privilege through crooked means, and he passed his son off as gentry by an exchange of money. Con, as his nickname suggests, acts the part of a gentleman at times, but such status is a matter of pure invention. He despises his Irish heritage and considers himself British, scoffs at the American Yankees and their desire to make money, yet his own penchant to proclaim what he pretends to be his true identity labels him as a self-made man and a true American citizen. O'Neill describes Nora, only forty years old at the start of *A Touch of the Poet*, as disheveled and riddled with rheumatism. But Con remembers her as a beautiful young woman when they married. Sara looks now as her mother did only twenty years prior. "Aristocrat" and "peasant" do not speak to the facts of Sara's birth and her genetic inheritance. They are simple codes for a descriptive shorthand meant to suggest Sara's full range of physical characteristics that are impossible to reconcile. They simply exist.

The contradictory aspects of Sara's appearance via O'Neill's stage directions suggest the range and depth of character differently than how O'Neill expressed depth for either Con or Simon. For the male characters, the mask concept assumed that something of substance or depth lay underneath. The outer mask projected one aspect of character to others and protected the inner face of private experience from scrutiny and examination. The mask, whether material or metaphorical, became a theatrical means for O'Neill to create the illusion of depth and complexity of characterization that could rival a novelist's ability to describe interior processes. The mask relied nevertheless upon narrative sequence in order to convey the sense of depth: a character dons one mask, then exchanges it for another, and the perception of that change or the moment, however brief, between the appearance of the first mask and the adjustment for the second, produces an illusion of character.

The physical descriptions of Sara, however, provide a new means of theatrical representation that produces the illusion of depth without use of the theatrical mask. Sara's "aristocratic" and "peasant" features—a straight nose and fine forehead, but a coarse mouth, stubby fingers, and thick ankles—are plainly evident at all times. Beyond physical descriptions, though, she possesses a varied mix of attributes—psychological, spiritual, moral—that are simultaneously present and in potential conflict from one moment to the next. That the audience cannot take in all aspects of her character at once is a matter of perspective. Sara reveals herself more fully in and through time. It is impossible to see the complete dimensionality of Sara at any one time, but her body in motion reveals all sides, and new facets become visible with even a slight turn of her head, twist at the waist, or pivot of the foot. O'Neill conceives of character as a body on a stage, and the tension between the actor in space and character in an environment resonates with theatrical meanings for an audience as it follows Sara through a performance.

The comparison in the preceding chapter between the two Cycle plays and *The Iceman Cometh* demonstrates how Sara deviates from the pattern of diminishment in both plays in which other characters reveal themselves as less than what they are in the process of facing the truth about themselves and their world. O'Neill stripped the characters naked and unmasked them. Sara, though, does not wear a mask of any kind. Just as her physical characteristics are present at all times, Sara keeps no secrets, lacks guile of any kind, and freely admits her faults as well as claims her virtues. She confesses her greedy nature to Deborah in act 1, scene 2, for example, but also claims that she loves Simon greatly and would do anything for him, a foreshadowing of what she does in the final act. The late revelation of character does not hide throughout the earlier parts of the play. Sara advertised early that she possessed the quality that the dire situation at the end later requires.

Prior to the Cycle plays, O'Neill exploited the mask as a means to reveal character through the illusion of surface and depth. He used actual masks in several of his plays in the 1920s, beginning with *All God's Chillun Got Wings,* an expressionistic play about the ill-fated marriage between a Black man and a White woman in which the wife stabbed a Congolese mask to express her rage and penchant for racial violence against her husband. The pageantry of *Lazarus Laughed* required many masks, but O'Neill fashioned the device most pervasively and confusingly in *The Great God Brown.* In that play, the three principal characters wore masks, put them down, exchanged them, and put them back on enough times to destroy consistency of meaning. O'Neill suggested, clearly, that all people wear masks and that no one dares to allow another to see what lies underneath. The two male protagonists, Dion Anthony and William Brown, represent the artist and the businessman as opposite types. Businessman Brown steals Dion's identity (and dons his mask) but dies from the burden of carrying two divergent identities (and from a policeman's bullet). Before the end, though, Brown offers a little moral to his story in the form of an aphorism that became a favorite of O'Neill's: "Man is born broken. He lives by mending. The grace of God is glue!"[3] The mask theatricalizes a psychological problem of the modern condition: the inability to integrate outward appearance with interior experience.

Mourning Becomes Electra (1931) did not use masks even though the original actors in Greek tragedies, the source plays for O'Neill's adaptation, all wore them. Instead, O'Neill's stage directions refer to all the Mannons as having a mask-like appearance and skin that looks less like actual flesh than a death-like mask. The Mannon death mask is intractable, and O'Neill describes even the painted portraits of the Mannons that adorn the walls as having that same look. Within the action of the play, Christine, a Mannon by marriage, and Lavinia, her daughter, try to pry the death-like visage from their faces, but discover that their destiny precludes such freedom. Christine almost succeeds and escapes with her lover aboard his clipper ship, but her son murders Adam and drives Christine to despair and eventual suicide. Lavinia does sail to the South Sea Islands and enjoys a temporary respite from New England Puritanism as she explores sexual freedom far from home, but the Mannon dead eventually call her back. Lavinia's resolution to oversee the end of the Mannon line until her last breath concludes the play. She dons the Mannon mask and no longer fights to remove it. The double meaning of the play's title appealed to the playwright as one of his favorites. The black dress of mourning befits Lavinia—it is her best color, it becomes her. But mourning the Mannon dead is also her fate. She inters herself with all the family ghosts and guilt.

The following year, 1932, O'Neill wrote a three-part series of articles, "Memoranda on Masks," published in George Jean Nathan's *American Spectator Magazine,* in which he asked, rhetorically, "For what at bottom is the new psychological insight into human cause and effect but a study in masks, an exercise in unmasking?"[4] This series proved to be O'Neill's only foray into dramatic theory, but he focused on his chief device that he had used and continued to advocate to reveal character and sustain the illusion of surface and depth that would allow for dramatic revelation. He used literal masks in only one more production, *Days Without End,* in 1934. He split his protagonist named John Loving into two characters, "John," the sincere yet guilty half, and his shadow, "Loving," his cynical twin who tried to convince his better half that he could never atone for the betrayal of his wife and should not try. "Loving," a Mephisto type, wore a mask to further distinguish him from John, but in the end lay defeated at the foot of the cross in a Catholic Church. John's victory over his twin rival, a victory over himself, vindicated the claim in *The Great God Brown* that God could glue humanity together.

The best examples of unmasking come not from the plays that actually used masks but from ones that featured a metaphorical mask. Two early expressionistic plays, *The Hairy Ape* (1921) and *The Emperor Jones* (1920), feature a dramatic action that strips the protagonist in each play to his bare-naked essence. In *The Hairy Ape,* Yank, along with his mates covered in coal dust, appears to be more of an ape in a cage than a man in the stokehole of an ocean liner. In the final scene, Yank squares off against a live gorilla at the zoo and suddenly realizes for the first time what other people saw when they looked at him. Unmasked, Yank sees his reflected image in the embrace of the gorilla and sees the zoo, ironically, as the cage in which he belongs.

The Emperor Jones even more emphatically demonstrates the action of unmasking as it tells the story of Brutus Jones, a former Pullman railroad porter in the United States escaped to an island in the South Seas, who has set up shop as a despotic ruler over the natives. In the course of only eight short scenes, Jones discovers that his time has run out and that he must escape from the island to avoid the murderous rebellion of the islanders. Confident at the outset about his ability to fool his adversaries, Jones loses his way on his exit route through the jungle and can't locate any of the landmarks that he had previously prepared. His labyrinthine trip in the night produces a series of hallucinogenic experiences that dramatize Jones's past, including the murder that first sent him to jail, abuse he suffered on a chain gang, the ancestral memories of a slave auction, a slave ship, and an African witch doctor. By the end, this emperor has nothing left to conceal, and the natives track and kill him with a silver bullet, the only kind that Jones said could pierce his skin. Stripped naked and thoroughly unmasked, Jones quakes before his personal demons and dies after having run around all night in circles.

The unmasking of Brutus Jones shares similarities with the action in *A Touch of the Poet* regarding Cornelius Melody. The tyrant of the first play wears a gaudy uniform with brass buttons, gold chevrons on the shoulders, gold braid, bright red pants, patent leather boots with brass spurs, and a pearl-handled revolver at his waist. With all that, however, O'Neill ends the description with a coda: "Yet there is something not altogether ridiculous about his grandeur. He has a way of carrying it off."[5] Jones, no doubt, was used to wearing a uniform, either as a prisoner or as a Pullman porter, but he never served as a military man of any kind. Yet he is able to wear the flamboyant attire because he has the skill and confidence to act the part, the mental sharpness to recognize his performance as a game, and the sense of dignity to be at ease in any mode of dress, whether it be at the top or bottom of the social, political, or economic order. Melody, on the other hand, who was an officer in the British army, needs his bright red uniform coat to assume a stature that he does not naturally possess. Even Sara, who routinely chastises her father for his many pretenses, wants her future mother-in-law, Deborah Harford, to catch sight of Con in his uniform. Like Jones, Melody can wear such a costume with great aplomb and never fail to impress his audience. Each comes to a similar end. Jones retreats through the forest and sheds his finery along the way until he is practically naked. Melody attacks the Yankees, but they shred his uniform and strip his pride in the ensuing street brawl.

The action unmasks both characters in their respective plays, but with one crucial difference: whereas the expressionistic framework of *The Emperor Jones* and the succession of scenes that review the hero's past reduce the man, the same pattern in a more realistic mode in *A Touch of the Poet* exposes Melody at the end of the play as the common, poor Irishman he had always pretended not to be. The dexterity with which Melody switches from proud major to crooked Ned Melody's son, however, raises questions about the authenticity of this new role. *The Emperor Jones* endeavors to show the *essence* of a man; *A Touch of the Poet* reveals a *version* of a man. The major is one aspect of Con Melody, but the Irishman lapsing into brogue at the end is another version of the same character. It is impossible to determine which one is more authentic than the other. In this sense, Melody does not unmask so much as don another mask at the end. Character, then, is not so much surface and depth, appearance and essence, but a choice of various surfaces in which one mask comes off to reveal only another mask. Melody's performance at the end resembles, oddly enough, Marcel Marceau's famous routine as Bip the Clown in his pantomime sketch "The Mask Maker." The rapid succession of masks that Bip takes on and off creates a different persona each time until one gets stuck. At the end of *A Touch of the Poet,* Melody elects to "stick" with a new version of himself as "friend av the common men," and the pathos of the conclusion stems from the fact that, like Bip, Melody must endure the mask of his own making that he can no longer remove (149).

Unmasking in *The Emperor Jones* or *The Hairy Ape,* two relentless dramas that transpire in about ninety minutes or less of playing time, touches the bottom or essence of character, as opposed to the spread of attributes in the lengthy Cycle plays. Sara, the best representative of plenitude, cannot rein in her greed; she craves more and more for fear of not having enough and not knowing how much is enough, or even when enough is enough. She cannot curb her materialism and desire to accumulate riches, and dreams of building bigger and bigger estates. She recognizes that her dreams are foolish, but cannot stop them. At the same time, though, she is a character who abundantly loves her husband, four children, and even her mother-in-law, and whose friendship with Deborah drives her husband to seek revenge and pit her against the other and older woman. Sara not only seeks the friendship of Deborah, but inherits her property. Later, she assumes ownership of Simon's business as well. Sara's boundless desires drive the action, highlighted by overt stylistic changes, experiments in nonrealistic acting and performance, and a conscious consideration of the audience and its role in the theater.

As a young woman in *A Touch of the Poet,* Sara brags about ambition, critiques her father, and vows to surpass him with her marriage to a rich husband whom she dearly loves. Four years later, in the first scene of *More Stately Mansions,* she returns home for the first time since her father's death. Pregnant with her fourth child and wildly happy with her new family, Sara is not yet rich but has more than enough to survive and seems content. The united couple that appears in act 1 at Melody's wake soon begins to fissure as fortunes ebb and flow. Simon's physical appearance directly reflects the financial rise and fall of his company as it grows from a single mill to an enormous corporation with interests in shipping, banking, and railroads. Sara maintains a "self-confident loving happiness and contentment" at the beginning of the second act four years later, but Simon has added a little weight from the mental strain and nervous tension of too much hard work (267). Another four years later, Sara, having moved into the Harford mansion and befriended her mother-in-law, appears more matronly, and her loving nature has matured into a "passive, satisfied contentedness" (324). Simon, though, has continued to age beyond his thirty-five years and added twenty pounds of flesh to his frame. Plans and possibilities for new and greater business conquests make him continually tense, and he resents the ways in which his mother and wife gang up on him at home and rob him of any influence except within his exclusive sphere of company business.

After Simon entices Sara to join him in the business as his mistress, they both show signs of degradation a year later in act 4. Stage directions describe Sara as a "hardened prostitute" who has become "strikingly voluptuous," with a "calculating feminine seductiveness" (446–47). At this point she has become more powerful than Simon, whose "countenance is ravaged and pale and haggard" (456). He continues down the slide of ill health through the play's epilogue, in which he appears "terribly emaciated" (556). Conversely, the last image of Sara, after the collapse of the company has robbed them of everything that they had owned, catches her in bare feet and a simple working dress, looking both younger and older than in the previous act. She seems younger in the sense that the lines in her face have disappeared due to the removal of financial stress, but older in the sense of having witnessed her husband's physical decline. She took the blame for his illness and assumed an obligation to nurse him back to health.

Sara displays multiple and dynamic aspects of her character as she pursues Simon, then gravitates to Deborah and sides with her against Simon, and ultimately assumes control of the mansion. Her reign expands when she leaves the safety of the home for the Harford Company and begins to relish both her sexual and business conquests. Convinced that she should drive her mother-in-law into madness to complete her takeover, Sara enters the garden in the final scene (4.2) fully intent on destroying her rival. Spying Deborah's vulnerable condition, however, softens Sara's stance and reminds her of former affections. Clearheaded now, Sara brokers a brief reconciliation. Moments later, after returning from the house, Sara sees Deborah and Simon near the summerhouse door and intuits that he intends to enter the world of dreams and madness and never return. Having pursued her greedy dreams for so long, Sara now gives them up in a flash—she gives up her hold on everything in her life, in order for Deborah to release Simon. The ambitious girl, the proud daughter, the sexy seductress, the loving wife, the fertile and doting mother, the matronly housewife, the salacious prostitute, the ruthless businesswoman, the fearful woman, the would-be murderess, the compassionate friend now becomes the repentant sinner who acknowledges all the harm she has done and renounces her former schemes in the name of love.

Sara's expansive and contradictory actions, both vile and sublime, reveal a multifaceted spirit. Simon, her lover and adversary, designed his divide-and-conquer strategy throughout the previous acts to shut her down and break her alliance with his mother. He prefers each woman for his exclusive relationship. While Sara seeks to inhabit every space, Simon tries to establish an arena in which he alone can enjoy the company of his wife, and another such space for the relationship between him and his mother to flourish. Alarmed by the growing intimacy between the two women,

Simon vacates the domestic space of the home interior and invites Sara to work with him at the company office. He reduces her role there to that of his mistress. He then cordons his mother from the house and grants her domain in the garden, where he proposes to be her lone visitor.

Despite Simon's best efforts, the women still come together in the parlor of the Harford house in act 3, scene 3, the most spectacularly theatrical scene in the play. The bonds among the three characters shift throughout the scene as Simon, Sara, and Deborah compete for dominance. The two women gang up on Simon once again, and he decides that he must choose one and dispatch the other. If Sara desires to control everything and to inhabit every space, Simon wants to limit her ubiquity. Within his own psyche, he does not know how to reconcile his aggressive business practices with his previous conviction that people are essentially good. In order to survive his own conflicts, he excises the poet from his soul. Regarding Sara and Deborah, whom he reductively defines as representing, respectively, physical and spiritual existence, he feels that he can only live with one or the other but certainly not integrate both. Simon's refusal to seek balance and to court nuance nearly leads to his death when he remembers his childhood dreams and mistakes the sepulcher of his mother's summerhouse for a sanctuary.

Simon is the only character who is not, in some way, an actor or performer in the sense of recognizing role playing as the essence of character. His mother, Deborah, is a consummate actress who frequently imagines herself as an "unscrupulous courtesan" in an eighteenth-century French memoir. At another time she imagines herself as Napoleon's Josephine. Such fantasies arise from the fact that Deborah married a man with whom she shared little in common and whose son, Simon, whom she doted upon as a little boy, abandoned her for marriage with Sara. Simon asks her directly in act 1, scene 2, at their first meeting in years: "Are you still as accomplished an actress as you used to be?" (222). She admits that she has trouble at times distinguishing between her own identity and that of a role, but she evades Simon's underlying queries: Did you love me as a child? Did you ever love me? Deborah withholds that answer. Later in the play she expresses the wish to him that he had never been born, and he interprets her vitriol as a true expression of regret. Deborah's strange aloofness and withdrawal from life's daily rituals are an act of self-protection. Deborah cannot admit how badly she misses Simon in her life and how much she loves him for fear of losing him. Her fight with Sara is at root a struggle to reclaim Simon as a little-boy companion. Simon never sees through his mother's façade and accepts her withdrawal at face value. Rejected, he taunts his mother in their meeting by laughing at her fantasies and hurting her so deeply that she can never fully recover.

In the throes of his spiritual and moral decay, Simon calls Sara "as unscrupulous and ruthless as a whore selling herself!" (323). If he had only known what she was, Simon laments in the third act, he would have slept with her but never married her. Perhaps she did entrap him originally, but Simon's narrative comes well after the fact and does not accord with previous accounts of their romance. Nevertheless, in the fourth act, after twelve years of marriage, Sara dresses the part of the whore and nearly seduces Simon's brother as a demonstration of her power over men. She is able to comment, though, on her brazen behavior: "Like a dirty whore smiling at men in the street and showing her leg!" (454). Sara plays the role of a prostitute for her husband at his office, but that performance does not make her one. Simon requires her to play a part that she never would have initiated on her own. Sara regards her performance as something that she does for love of him.

Con Melody is a con man, as accomplished an actor as Sara or Deborah. While Sara desires for him to face the truth about himself in *A Touch of the Poet*, it remains far from certain that Melody does not know the essential facts about his character and the world of illusion he creates. In act 3, Con hosts his annual celebratory dinner in honor of his great victory at Talavera and dons his brilliant uniform for the evening. With a patchwork of guests assembled, most of whom glory in the chance to sponge his liquor, Con holds court and recreates the battlefield with an array of cutlery, glasses, saltshakers, and condiments. One of the Irish rogues, O'Dowd, assumes that Con cannot hear him and comments: "Ain't he the lunatic, sittin' like a play-actor in his red coat, lyin' about his battles with the French!" (83). Con has the bearing of an actor, certainly, but Corporal Jamie Cregan, who has come to pay his former superior officer a visit, verifies the facts of Con's noble bravery on the battlefield twenty years earlier. Moreover, Con overhears O'Dowd's remarks and responds in a way that indicates his awareness of the theatrical double nature of the dramatic situation: "So you may go on fooling yourselves that I am fooled in you" (84). O'Dowd does not believe any part of Con's story; but Con knows that these Irish friends of his are not true friends. That realization tempers the end of the play when Con dispatches the major and chooses to imbibe with these same Irishmen in the barroom. He escapes to their realm with no illusions about what their toasts and raised glasses truly signify.

O'Neill expresses the plenitude of experience with several formal techniques in *More Stately Mansions,* the first of which is a succession of monologues by the three principal characters that function as soliloquies. Even when Joel, a supporting character, is present with Simon in act 3, scene 1 or with Sara in act 4, scene 1, he serves as a sounding board for the speaking subjects. Before he exits in the former scene, he replies to Simon's request for confidentiality: "I have not listened. I have no interest whatsoever in your private affairs. And I know you were simply using me to talk aloud to yourself" (320–21). Joel allows Simon to articulate his thoughts, but by extension, the theatrical device makes it possible for the speaking subjects to justify directly their actions to the audience.

Ivo van Hove shaped his 1997 production of *More Stately Mansions* at the New York Theatre Workshop around three monologues.[6] Having eliminated the first scene in the play as per the Gierow/Gallup version, van Hove's production began with Deborah's monologue (1.2 in the Bower edition of O'Neill's full text) in front of the cabin by the lake. Deborah worries whether Simon will come and meet her and wonders if she still holds any sway over him. The next big solo speech (3.1) featured Simon, who expresses his dissatisfaction with having to cope with both Deborah and Sara, mother and wife. Sara delivered the final monologue/soliloquy to begin the third and last act in van Hove's production (4.1). All the monologues feature strong assertions and counterstatements further supported by highly descriptive and detailed stage directions, but Sara's speech in the ultimate position reflects her central role in the Cycle.

In her speech, Sara comments on her own behavior and confides to the audience. She brags first about her ability to seduce Joel, then about her appeal to any man of her choosing. Next, she lambastes herself for such talk, and then blames her husband for transforming her into a dirty whore. Next she worries that she might lose her husband to Deborah, but comforts herself with the thought that she can reclaim him with a kiss. She dismisses her near seduction of Joel as something every woman dreams of and vows that she should make good on the threat if Simon continues to make her wait for him (he is late for their appointment). "Ah, you dirty whore, you!" she exclaims, and then blames Deborah again for trying to steal her husband, adding that she'll drive the old woman into the asylum if she does not cease and desist (454). Sara decides to pray about it and hopes not to resort to such extreme measures to get rid of Deborah. She will take the company's profits, build her estate elsewhere, and leave a pension for Deborah to remain in her garden. It won't take long, she reasons, but will Simon let her stop? Can she stop herself from wanting more and more? Now she worries that Deborah has kept Simon late in her garden and thinks she might ask Joel to return in order to pay Simon back for his rudeness. When at last Simon appears at the door, Sara throws her arms around him and exclaims: "Oh, Darling! I love you so!" (456).

The stage directions for Sara's long speech make the pattern of statement/counterstatement even more explicit. Here they are (with just a few exceptions) magnified in isolation for a closer look:

> *Looks after [Joel], smiling to herself with a cheap vanity.*
> *She stares in the mirror at herself admiringly — coquettishly in brogue.*
> *She suddenly shivers with repulsion and tears her eyes from the mirror. Strickenly —*
> *in a guilty whisper.*
> *She stares around her frightenedly.*
> *Then with angry defiance.*
> *Vindictively.*
> *She laughs spitefully — then suddenly tears her eyes from the mirror and shrinks into*
> *herself with horrified disgust.*
> *Then with increasing anger.*
> *With threatening hatred.*
> *Then hastily.*
> *Trying to reassure herself.*
> *She jumps from her stool and paces around in a nervous panic.*
> *In a fury.*
> *With a cry of hypocritical happy relief, rushes and throws her arms around [Simon]*
> *and hugs him passionately.* (453–56)[7]

The juxtaposition of oppositional statements, attitudes, and gestures, often in rapid succession, shows the mental processes of Sara as she evaluates her position and strategizes for her future. For her, and for Deborah and Simon earlier, O'Neill adapts a novelistic device, the psychological inner monologue, for theatrical purposes, and the stage directions serve as the physical and visible means to manifest the rolling tide of her thoughts and emotions.

O'Neill alternates dialogue with monologues among all three characters in the parlor of the Harford mansion in act 3, scene 3. The brief honeymoon period in which Sara, Simon, and Deborah get along has passed. Each now distrusts the others and looks for signs of weakness in his and her opponents. The needlepoint of Sara and the books of Deborah and Simon merely prop their preoccupied obsessions with each other. O'Neill used thought asides throughout *Strange Interlude* in order to contrast overt speech with underlying intent. Here, the effect works differently. There is no speech at first, only spoken thoughts. But, while these private thoughts must be spoken in order to be perceived, the effect is that the characters need to voice their thoughts for an audience in order to gain its favor over the other characters. By the end of the scene, Deborah and Sara realign as allies and drive Simon from the room, but initially all sit isolated from each other. The theatrical audience on the other side of the footlights is the only option for appeal. The accumulated egotism mounts throughout *More Stately Mansions* from the opening act and finally erupts at this juncture, the only scene that employs such asides. The stylistic variations in *More Stately Mansions*, not evident in *A Touch of the Poet*, result from the steadily increasing burden of greed and possessive desire. The monologues and spoken thoughts are more than theatrical means to express a novelistic technique—they manifest the sickness that rots within the souls of the three principals.

Characters directly address the audience in the examples above, but O'Neill also stages Deborah and Sara as members of an audience on other occasions. They witness events in which their commentary and spectatorship resolve the action. In her lone appearance in the first play, Deborah encounters Con Melody and the theatrical audience registers an appraisal of him through her eyes. Melody does not resist the opportunity to show off in front of her and approaches her seductively as a matter of old habit.

Deborah falls under the spell of his charisma and force of personality and thus verifies that Con's boasts about success with women through the years are not outright lies. Con goes too far, though, when he bends to kiss her and Deborah smells whiskey on his breath. She snubs him abruptly and condemns his elaborate and formal flirtation as an "absurd performance" (59). Deborah does not appear onstage again in the play, but she clinches Melody's abject humiliation outside the Harford mansion in act 4. Jamie Cregan describes her as looking down on the scene from her window with scorn as Con and his crew brawl in the street with Harford's servants and eventually the police. Con topped his outrageous flirtation with Deborah with a farcical parody of a soldier leading a charge or a gentleman seeking satisfaction in a duel. As Sara pointed out before he left, the days of duels have dwindled, yet Con, wearing a British officer's uniform, a relic from a battle fought years ago, storms the gates of a private citizen, raising Cain with his retinue of Irish drunks in the middle of the night. The disdain registered upon Deborah's face as she literally looks down on him from her perch on a window seat hurts him far worse than any of the blows he receives in the fight. After evaluating his crude behavior through her eyes, Con does not know how or why to continue as he was and elects to forfeit all pretense—or perhaps settle for another role upon which even he can frown.

While Deborah provides the eyes of judgment, Sara offers the face of compassion with which a theatrical audience may identify. Sara interrupts the exchange between her father and Deborah in *A Touch of the Poet* and hopes that her father can change into his uniform fast enough to catch Deborah again before she leaves—she wants her father to have a shot at redemption. At the end, she is the only character who wants him to retain his former Byronic stance as a lone soldier against the world, and when he begs her to let him go, she takes it upon herself to follow in his footsteps. In *More Stately Mansions,* Sara offers support to her rival, Deborah, after she witnesses Simon humiliate his mother in act 1, scene 2 in front of the cabin, and she allows her mother-in-law to take an active role in the lives of her four grandchildren. Twice in the final scene (4.2), she intervenes to prevent another's harm. While she planned to drive Deborah insane by encouraging her to pass through her summerhouse door, she refuses to idly stand by and allow Deborah to destroy herself. Moments later, she forgoes her claims upon Simon and relinquishes her dearest "possession" in order to let him live. She lets her father go in the first play; in the sequel she pulls her husband back to safety. Sara repents her many transgressions and redeems herself with her final actions. "The end of *Mansions*," in the analysis of Joel Pfister, "seeks to reinvest value in culture, social critique, and the soul, [. . .] even if humans persist in behaving [in Simon's world-view] like hogs."[8] If Sara's humility cannot last, if possessiveness creeps back into her relationships, then she is only all too human but not a hog, and the faults in her character only reveal more light by which an audience can trace the full trajectory of her condition.

Unfortunately, O'Neill and Carlotta were the only audience members to witness these plays during his lifetime. He wrote them in solitude at Tao House, 3,000 miles removed from the bright lights of Broadway. O'Neill earlier embraced loneliness in *Lazarus Laughed* (another almost unproduced play): "Tragic is the plight of the tragedian whose only audience is himself! Life is for each man a solitary cell whose walls are mirrors."[9] O'Neill's self-internment, though, came by choice. In his mansion on the hill in California, neither among the crowd nor of them, O'Neill wrote his very best plays for himself and Carlotta, and he delighted in the opportunity to play all the parts in the private study of his imagination. Regarding production plans, he repeatedly stalled Theresa Helburn and Lawrence Langner of the Theatre Guild to the extent that it is fair to question whether the playwright ever intended to produce the Cycle. Beyond his trail of written reticence, *A Touch of the Poet* was the only normal-length play of the Cycle that he finished. *More Stately Mansions* exceeded the combined length of *The Iceman Cometh* and *Long Day's Journey Into Night*.

O'Neill tried to pack everything into the Cycle in order to make it clear for a reading public. He felt certain that the play as written, not as performed, was the thing and wrote for posterity and not for the ephemeral applause of a theatrical production. The extensive dialogue, elaborate stage directions, and explanations and descriptions of scenes and characters, including the actual thoughts of characters in a pivotal scene, attempted to create a theatrical event for the reader that would surpass the experience in an actual theatrical space. The sheer amount of text that O'Neill produced in his desire to complete his theatrical vision in literary form belied the problem he attempted to solve in the Cycle. He endeavored to show

how thoughts and feelings reinforced and contradicted each other simultaneously and not sequentially, but the narrative form of writing, first one thing and then another, piled up word after word. Despite O'Neill's novelistic impulses, he needed a theatrical space to fulfill his vision.

While he was preparing for the Theatre Guild production of *Mourning Becomes Electra* in 1931 and still living in New York, O'Neill wrote a check for $1,000 to the Group Theatre, a young offshoot of the Guild, to help produce its first play, Paul Green's *The House of Connelly*. Harold Clurman, one of the directors of the Group, wrote an article in December for the *New York Times* in which he tabbed O'Neill, though not by name, as one of two donors supporting the new venture. O'Neill never saw the production; he usually didn't bother to see productions of his own plays either, but he wanted to support the young producers.[10] By May he was living in Georgia and did not return to New York until 1946, five years after the Group folded. The paths of O'Neill and the Group never crossed in what could be considered a missed opportunity for each party to take advantage of what the other had to offer. For O'Neill, the Group Theatre might have provided the talent, energy, dedication, and insight to interpret his massive Cycle. For the Group, O'Neill's Cycle would have offered the sort of important and topical work that they strived to produce, as well as prestige from America's foremost playwright at that time.

As an example of potential kismet that might have united the playwright with young theatrical artists, designer Mordecai Gorelik announced the Group's favorite theme as the one O'Neill identified with the Cycle: "What shall it profit a man if he gain the whole world and lose his own soul?" Harold Clurman credited Gorelik with that remark in *The Fervent Years*, Clurman's chronicle of the Group during the 1930s, and he agreed with the assessment. "It is true this theme was the oblique keynote of much of what I said in criticism not only of certain American ideals and customs but of everything that pertained to the practice of our profession. Though we had a combative air, we were lovers at heart."[11] Like O'Neill, the Group rebelled against the "Show Shop" of Broadway and sought plays that addressed modern problems and the challenges that Americans currently faced. The members dedicated themselves to the discovery of new methods and theatrical values in pursuit of truthful representations onstage. It was a true ensemble rather than a theatrical hierarchy with a few stars at the top. They refused the union timetable of only a few weeks to rehearse a play and often camped outside the city all summer in order to work on a play until it was ready for presentation. Acting techniques, derived from Stanislavsky and the Moscow Art Theatre, featured both improvisational and memory exercises, as well as ones to stoke the imagination.

The Group, with youth and boldness and courage on its side, but never any money, might have been a much better outfit to produce O'Neill than its original parent company, the Theatre Guild, tastemakers with a "collegiate stamp" according to Clurman: "They were admirers rather than makers. They were imitators rather than initiators, buyers and distributors rather than first settlers or pioneers." The Guild supported the Group somewhat in its early days but could not help but be taken aback by the self-confidence and brazenness of young people who had not had the opportunity to do much with their lives up to that point. "Do you think you would have anything to tell Eugene O'Neill?" Lawrence Langner grilled Clurman one day. "Certainly," the young man answered.[12] He did not elaborate at the time, but he could have responded years later with the advantage of history on his side. Then, he could have listed talented alumni of the Group who had gone on to invent, practically, the American school(s) of acting: Stella Adler, Lee Strasberg, Cheryl Crawford, Sanford Meisner, Bobby Lewis, and Elia Kazan. Surely such luminaries with such varied and intense approaches to the art of acting and the craft of theater would have had something to impart to Eugene O'Neill.

Clurman, who had a long career in theater as an author and critic, later directed the premiere production in the United States of *A Touch of the Poet* in 1958 with Eric Portman, Helen Hayes, and Kim Stanley (Fig. 10). In the lead of his review for the *New York Times*, Brooks Atkinson noted that O'Neill felt that his plays onstage rarely had the same force that he imagined when he wrote them. Atkinson then added: "If he could have seen the stunning performance that Harold Clurman has directed, it is possible that for once he might have been satisfied. For the performance fits the play exactly. And the performance includes the sort of inspired group acting that our theatre is seldom able to provide."

Passage of time affords a fresh perspective and reevaluation of theatrical legends. While the production that Atkinson loved so much did play for 284 performances, none of the principal actors got along, and each

FIGURE 10. Kim Stanley (standing) as Sara and Helen Hayes (sitting) as
Nora in *A Touch of the Poet*, directed by Harold Clurman at the Helen Hayes
Theatre, New York, 1958. (Photo by Fred Fehl/© Billy Rose Theatre
Division, The New York Public Library for the Performing Arts.)

created a mess backstage. Kim Stanley, after having missed a number of performances, left the show completely in the middle of the run.[13] In the end, this Broadway production, even though directed by Clurman, was perhaps not so very different in kind from the Theatre Guild productions of O'Neill that Clurman had criticized in the early 1930s. The Group Theatre collapsed in large part because it could not sustain the implementation of noncommercial means to produce plays in a highly commercial environment on Broadway. The success or failure of *A Touch of the Poet* in 1958, depending upon one's point of view, equally confronts the fact that the manner in which it was produced conflicted with the way it was conceived. While O'Neill desired each play of the Cycle to be independent and capable of standing alone, *A Touch of the Poet* does not make much sense without *More Stately Mansions*. What theatrical enterprise stands poised to take on that tandem in a single venue?

The Cycle, two plays as one event, still awaits its premiere production. Its demands pose a tremendous number of physical, financial, and creative challenges for one theater to undertake. But the Cycle is a challenge for an imaginative theater, not an imaginary one, and there must be individual talents today, reminiscent of those listed above from the Group Theatre, unknown talents at this point, young and vibrant talents, who might coalesce around O'Neill's opus and give it stage life.

CHAPTER EIGHT

THE *GLENCAIRN* TEMPLATE

A Touch of the Poet is a standard four-act play of 150 minutes or so, but the triple-length size of *More Stately Mansions* practically defies production. In a notable exception, Germinal Stage Denver garnered outstanding reviews for both plays in 2007, one of the few times they had ever been produced back to back in the same season. Using the same acting ensemble for both plays, the company staged the first play realistically and then stylized the sequel by incorporating a variety of plastic masks to highlight the contradictions between surface and depth among the characters.[1] Still, Germinal Stage produced the former play in October and the sequel the following month, so while they were produced consecutively in the production season, they were not produced together. Moreover, the director chose the shortened version of *More Stately Mansions* prepared by Karl Ragnar Gierow and Donald Gallup instead of the complete version edited by Martha Gilman Bower. While the theater could boast that it had produced the only two plays of the Cycle, it had presented much less than half of what O'Neill had actually written as *More Stately Mansions*. More important, the producers did not edit the second play to focus on Sara's story to match *A Touch of the Poet*. Gierow had removed the opening scene and the epilogue and cut many things in between to make the play stand on its own in Sweden in 1962. The challenge today remains to present both plays as a unified event that can still represent the whole Cycle.

Uncut, the Cycle might require as many as four separate performances for completion. The action of *A Touch of the Poet* takes place over the course of one day, 27 July 1828, and would fill the first performance slot in its entirety. Broken into three almost equal parts, *More Stately Mansions* would occupy the successive segments. Acts 1 and 2 take place in 1832 and 1836, respectively, and show Sara's increase in wealth and rise in society as she prepares to move as mistress into the Harford mansion. Act 3, the longest act, set in 1840, slots into the third position and presents the triangular tensions created by greed and possessiveness between Simon, Sara, and Deborah in three different spaces: Simon's office, Deborah's garden, and Sara's living room. The fourth act (1841) and epilogue (1842) dramatize Sara's degradation and rehabilitation, but also the repetition and resumption of her compulsive behavior. The prospect of production warrants the question: would the investment of time and money for such a project ever be worth the effort?

O'Neill announced time as part of his aesthetic with both *Strange Interlude* and *Mourning Becomes Electra,* but the two plays that he wrote immediately after putting down the Cycle serve as even better examples. A much-shortened version of *The Iceman Cometh* or *Long Day's Journey Into Night* does not make much sense. As the drunks in the former play need time to regain sobriety before desperately trying to get drunk again at the end, so members of the audience need time to absorb the many repetitive themes and motifs in the play in order to develop compassion for the characters and gain wisdom from their travails. Similarly, the action in *Long Day's Journey Into Night* occurs in a single day, and the audience follows the Tyrones as they try to discover the roots of their affliction. Initially, the audience might hope for a definitive answer, but the competing narratives of the four family members prove contradictory and complicate a definitive interpretation of what happened. Initial certainties become heavy doubts as the sunshine and clear skies of early morning give way to clouds, and then night and fog.

The two Cycle plays take place over not just a single day but fourteen years (1828–1842), and the audience certainly needs time to appreciate the transformation of Sara Melody. Normally, directors, designers, and actors fill out and expand the possibilities of a dramatic text with their creative and collaborative imaginations, talents, and interpretations. O'Neill insisted that the play as written was the real thing apart from any subsequent performance and that the drama in his mind always played better than on any actual stage.[2] He disparaged the "Show Shop" of Broadway and the toll of commerce upon the artist. By the time he wrote his final plays, he wrote to his own standard without regard for an actual production.[3] He filled the white space in his dramatic texts with lines of dialogue, but also with descriptions of how each character looks and what each one thinks and how each one feels at any moment, as if his extensive and elaborate stage directions and scene descriptions were attempts to play all the parts in the theater. The lengthy narrative of his novelistic dramas innovates, but it also intimidates possible producers and dodges the likelihood of theatrical performance. Ironically, posthumous productions of *The Iceman Cometh* and *Long Day's Journey Into Night* in 1956 revived interest in O'Neill and rescued his career. It remains to be seen if a revival of O'Neill's Cycle on the stage could add further luster to his enduring reputation.

While it would be uniquely fascinating to see *More Stately Mansions* in its uncut entirety, reason dictates that it could only happen on rare occasions. The play could be adapted, however, to fit with *A Touch of the Poet,* and the two plays could function as one event staged in successive performances. If the earlier play constitutes a full evening, *More Stately Mansions* fills the other half of a bill, but the shortened 1964 edition is no good for that purpose. It was never conceived to pair with the other Cycle play. That version, too, asserts Simon Harford's position at the apex of the triangular relationship that includes his wife (Sara) and his mother (Deborah). To alter that perspective and present a version of *More Stately Mansions* that compares in length to the shortened edition of the play, a new acting edition must be created that links with *A Touch of the Poet,* asserts Sara Melody as the protagonist, and highlights her struggle to reconcile love with the destructiveness of greed and materialism. Bower's unexpurgated version is the proper starting point for a new adaptation that can translate the narrative sequences of O'Neill's layered descriptions and directions into simultaneous actions for the stage, and effectively convert an overpowering and often overwhelming literary experience into an exciting and effective theatrical one.

A series of four sea plays by O'Neill, one-act dramas that form a cycle on a small scale at the start of his career, provides a model for new construction of the big Cycle. Although many of the same characters recur in two, three, or four of these sea plays, O'Neill wrote each one independently about the disparate lives of sailors. No master narrative connects one play to the next. *Bound East for Cardiff* (1914) chronicles the death of a sailor; the premiere performance at the Wharf Theater on the tip of Cape Cod marked O'Neill's debut with the Provincetown Players and launched a myth about the birth of the American theater.[4] O'Neill sold the second play, *In the Zone* (1917), to the Washington Square Players in New York (the organization that would later become the Theatre Guild), but he always regarded the lucrative success of the play as the triumph of melodrama. The next play, *The Long Voyage Home* (1917), heavily dramatized irony. Sailors might complain about the sea and long for the land they left behind, but, in the end, when the opportunity came to choose between worlds, they inevitably picked the familiar rhythms of the sea. O'Neill thickened the irony with his portrayal of a Swedish sailor who decided to return home to his mother after many years away only to be shanghaied by the crew of a rival ship and sent out to sea once again. The last of the plays, *The Moon of the Caribbees,* first produced by the Provincetown Players in Greenwich Village in 1918, contained almost no plot at all. Instead, the music from an offstage island and the idleness of the crew evoke a mood and atmosphere among the ensemble.

After O'Neill left the organization, the Provincetown Players produced all four plays together in a single bill in 1924 under the title *S.S. Glencairn*. In 1937, during the Depression, Canada Lee headed an African-American cast in a production sponsored by the Federal Theatre Project. The review of another production at the New York City Center the next decade referred to the plays as a "cycle" for the first time. By that time, news of O'Neill's massive Cycle plays had leaked in the *Times*, and it was easy to conflate the little with the big one. And, quite possibly, the reviewer had seen the recent film that linked all four of the plays.

John Ford's *The Long Voyage Home* (1940) updated the four plays and shifted the time period from World War I to the present day.[5] Dudley Nichols, a friend of O'Neill, developed a screenplay to connect the disparate plays into a cohesive whole. The film opens with the last play, *The Moon of the Caribbees,* and shows the *Glencairn* anchored near an island in the West Indies. As in O'Neill's play, the crew of merchant marines stirs restlessly in anticipation of welcoming native female islanders aboard the ship for a night of drinking and dancing. In the film, though, the captain's steward (Barry Fitzgerald) overhears the captain of the ship accept an assignment to transport explosives from the United States across the Atlantic and through the war zone to London. The party, then, is the crew's reward for what the captain knows will be a dangerous mission.

The rest of the first segment closely follows *The Moon of the Caribbees,* although it establishes the master through-line of the film as the last voyage of Ole Olsen (John Wayne), who vows to return home to his mother in Stockholm after he gets paid in London. Another character, Smitty, as in the play, hides painful memories of his wife and declares his desire to avoid London at all cost. Given that O'Neill wrote *The Moon of the Caribbees* last, Smitty's dialogue does not connect to any future events and only vaguely ties in with the previous plays. In the film, though, Nichols and Ford create a subplot for Smitty that develops in tandem with the main story of Ole Olsen. Finally, in O'Neill's play, a fight breaks out between shipmen as the natural and inevitable consequence for the supply and demand of native women and rum. In homage to another O'Neill play, the film interjects a confrontational line between shipmates in which one tells the other: "You look like a hairy ape!" The captain steps up, finally, to put an end to the festivities, send the women back to shore, and set course for the port at Baltimore.

The crew watches intently in the next segment as cranes raise and lower boxes labeled "explosives" down into the hold of the ship. True to his word from the previous segment, Smitty tries to jump ship and run away that night, but a patrol captures him and returns him to the *Glencairn* before it slips away from a Baltimore dock toward London. A violent storm at sea threatens the safety of the ship, and several of the crew venture out to stow the anchor and prevent further damage. One sailor falls and receives a serious injury. The film shows how Yank gets hurt, but *Bound East for Cardiff* picks up after his injury occurs. As in the play, Driscoll tends to Yank, and the stories they share in Yank's last moments come straight from O'Neill's text. The captain conveys the feeling of helplessness that nothing can be done to save Yank. If the ship were closer to one port or the other and not somewhere in between in the middle of the Atlantic, Yank could get needed medical attention. As it is, the *Glencairn* is bound for Cardiff (London in the film) and all hope is futile. To avoid the fate of Yank, Driscoll reminds Olsen, in the film version, of his obligation and promise to return home to his mother at the end of the current voyage. The film beautifully captures the loneliness and poignancy of Yank's life with his funeral at sea. The captain performs a brief eulogy before the crew releases the body overboard.

As the ship approaches its destination and enters the war zone, Smitty's behavior grows increasingly suspicious, and the crew suspects he might be a German spy. They begin to imagine that the small metal box that he hid from them in his bed is a bomb that could detonate and destroy them all. In the film, Smitty (who they think might really be a "Schmidt") checks navigational charts in the wheelhouse, picks up the international code book in the captain's quarters, and opens a porthole window in the forecastle that should have been blacked out. Sailors recall seeing Smitty in each locale, and collectively they build a circumstantial case against him. The camera zooms in on Smitty's tortured face after the crew ties him up and breaks into his private and locked box, only to discover a pack of letters from Smitty's wife. Still not convinced that the notes are not somehow coded instructions for seditious acts, Driscoll reads the last one aloud, only to learn that Smitty's alcoholism and refusal to come home have caused his family to sever all future relations with him. *In the Zone* concludes with the crew's silent withdrawal and return to work, but the film adds a transitional scene before the *Glencairn* gets to London. A day or so later, the crew languishes on deck with all its work done. Suddenly, the distant whine of engines indicates incoming aircraft, and the crew quickly takes cover to avoid the bombs and strafing of machine guns from German fighter planes. The last pass takes the life of Smitty, who, sadly, never wanted to reach London in the first place.

The last segment of *The Long Voyage Home* comes from O'Neill's play of the same name but begins with new material that is not in the play at all. The scene begins on a dour note as the *Glencairn*, having just reached port in London, welcomes the funeral procession of Smitty's wife and children as they arrive by black car to accept the captain's condolences and Smitty's meager possessions. After their departure, the next scene features the captain distributing pay to the crew before it disembarks from the ship and disappears in the dark city. Despite every man's statement to the contrary, the captain claims that almost all of them will return to the ship and sign for another tour. O'Neill's play takes place in a waterfront dive, but the film takes its time to show the maritime cohort on its way to ruin along wet and rainy cobblestone streets. Once at the bar, as in the play, the sailors get drunk and forget about their naïve shipmate Olsen, who has a ticket to sail home to Sweden. The unscrupulous proprietor and his henchmen drug Olsen and take their cut from the crew of a rival ship, *Amindra,* who drag the unsuspecting Swede aboard their notorious vessel for a dangerous voyage around Cape Horn. The play ends at this point with the ironic prospect of another long voyage for Olsen that never leads home.

In the film, however, the rest of the shipmates, headed by Driscoll, realize that misfortune has befallen their friend and retrace his path along the streets of London until they reach the *Amindra.* They climb aboard, engage the crew of that ship in a fistfight, and rescue Olsen. Before they get away, a member of the opposing crew knocks Driscoll out and takes him in Olsen's place. The ship sets sail before Driscoll's mates realize their new loss. The film ends the following morning with the return, one by one, of the crew to the *Glencairn,* reminiscent of the return of all the drunks to Harry Hope's bar after their pipe dreams have been exposed and crushed, in fulfillment of the captain's prophesy that they would all re-up for yet another voyage. The final shot, as the *Glencairn* departs, focuses on a newspaper floating in the water with a banner headline proclaiming that the Germans have torpedoed the *Amindra.*

Made in 1940, after the war in Europe had started, Ford's film urges the United States to drop its isolationist policy and enter the conflict. *The Long Voyage Home* champions the common sailor and ordinary citizen whose uncommon valor under threat of imminent danger assists in "forging the life-lines of Nations," as the opening reel attests. Yank dies at sea, but so do Smitty and Driscoll, the latter played by the charismatic Thomas Mitchell. The variety of dialects and ethnicities among the crew suggests that it will take the whole world to defeat the Nazis. Lest the audience not catch the film's drift, an unnamed citizen walks the streets of London in the final segment wearing a sandwich board that reads: "Nazis attack Norway." Gregg Toland's cinematography, which would reach its height of fame the next year with Orson Welles's *Citizen Kane*, creates the somber mood of the world with chiaroscuro effects. The only scene not set at night features John Wayne as Olsen lying on his back and looking up at the sky, but the camera never takes its eye off him and the other men on deck as they relax and enjoy a moment's rest. The German attack quickly follows and ends with the death of Smitty, as if to say that the light of the world will soon go out and not return until the United States commits to end the Nazi reign of terror. Ford does not pretend that winning the war will be easy or that victory is a foregone conclusion. The scrolled text at the end of the film, mirroring that from the beginning, pays tribute once again to the noble sacrifice of the merchant marines, but allows that some men, like Olsen, do get a chance to return home, though "for others the long voyage never ends."

Despite all the changes and interpolations that Nichols and Ford imposed upon his plays, O'Neill unequivocally loved the film and did not hesitate to congratulate the director and the screenwriter for their great accomplishments. He dismissed most film versions of his plays as cheap derivatives and did not even bother to attend, for example, the film version of *The Hairy Ape* in 1944.[6] He did not see theatrical productions of his own plays, either, though he frowned upon any would-be producer or director who planned on taking liberties with his texts. Ford's film proved to be a spectacular exception. First of all, O'Neill appreciated the fact that the filmmaker did not pay slavish attention to the text and emphasize the essence of each little play, but sublimated the individual plays to a master narrative and theme that perfectly matched the times in which the film was produced. O'Neill appreciated, too, how the film exploited its medium to convey meanings and do things that he could not do onstage.[7] The film uses close-ups, for example, to gauge the emotions and tensions among the various characters; the camera cuts from scene to scene to show different sections of the ship; the camera pulls back to frame the entire *Glencairn* for context as it sets sail for London; the transitions between the segments are quick and effortless and require no theatrical technology. Toland's camera establishes rhythm and mood with its varieties of filters, angles, and distance from the subjects.

The film also shows things that would be impossible to stage in a theater: the loading of cargo; the storm at sea as the ship rocks and the waves roll over the rails; sailors at work performing their daily tasks; the wheelhouse of the ship and a variety of shots on board outside the forecastle (the single setting of *Bound East for Cardiff* and *In the Zone*). O'Neill regarded *The Long Voyage Home* as the finest adaptation of his work to date and a great film in its own right. Donald Gallup had dubiously commented that the shortened version of *More Stately Mansions* in 1964 might have been one that O'Neill would have approved, and even done himself if he had had the time.[8] Suffice it to say that O'Neill never would have imagined his four one-acts as *The Long Voyage Home* in the fashion that Nichols and Ford conceived it for their film. The film takes liberties with O'Neill's plays to fulfill a theme that could not have been O'Neill's (a patriotic call to arms and an endorsement to declare war on Germany). It is not necessary to ask whether O'Neill would or would not approve of a new version of his play. But it is heartening to point out that O'Neill admired and respected the filmmakers. Their conviction and integrity matched the playwright's and persuaded him that their film was worthy.

As far as the contemporary theater is concerned, Michael Kahn has proven to be one of the most sensitive and innovative interpreters of O'Neill. The former head of the American Shakespeare Theatre in Stratford, Connecticut, the McCarter Theatre in Princeton, New Jersey, and the Acting Company in New York City, as well as a long-time acting teacher at Julliard, Kahn retired in 2019 from the Shakespeare Theatre Company (STC) in Washington, D.C., after almost thirty-five years as artistic director. While he is lauded for his productions of epic works (he scheduled a new version of the *Oresteia* as his final production at STC), Kahn never attempted to tackle *More Stately Mansions*. He did produce *A Touch of the Poet* and *Long Day's Journey Into Night* at Stratford. He also directed *Mourning Becomes Electra* on two occasions, first with Jane Alexander at Stratford, later with Kelly McGillis in Washington. He received permission from the O'Neill estate on both occasions to edit the text in order to reduce the play's running time to suit a contemporary audience.[9] More recently, he directed a stunning production of *Strange Interlude* at STC in 2012 for which he once again sought and received permission to edit the text and cut the nine-act drama to a running time of three hours and forty-five minutes, with two intermissions. For the STC productions of *Mourning Becomes Electra* and *Strange Interlude*, Kahn exploited modern theater technology to establish and maintain a brisk pace and tempo. The design of the former featured a revolve that rhythmically transitioned interior scenes in the Mannon house to exterior ones. The latter production used film projections to bridge the intervals of time and space between scenes. Kahn's work history inspires confidence that O'Neill's plays can be adapted and trimmed to meet the demands of a modern audience.

Following Kahn's lead, the rest of this final chapter outlines how a director might cut *More Stately Mansions* to fit with *A Touch of the Poet,* tell the whole story of the Cycle, and yet remain within a playing time acceptable to both audiences and theaters. Although the overall length of this adaptation must necessarily compare reasonably with the length of the 1964 shortened version, a new edition must differ from its predecessor in several important ways. First, *A Touch of the Poet* stands as the first half of the event, *A Tale of Possessors Self-Dispossessed,* and not as a single play on its own. The Cycle is Sara's story, and cuts in *More Stately Mansions* reflect her role as the protagonist of both plays when placed in tandem. The arc of the Cycle follows her development and rise in society, her insatiable acquisitive instinct, and the consequences of her greedy desires that culminate with her repentance and further regressions. The triangular relationship between her, Simon, and Deborah remains intact, but the scenes between Simon and Deborah receive much less emphasis than even in the shortened edition of the play. Finally, the end of *More Stately Mansions* must allude to future events, just as *A Touch of the Poet* chronicles the history of the Harfords, in order to fill in what O'Neill left undone with respect to the other plays of the Cycle. Fortunately, there is an economical way to craft a fitting conclusion that also describes perfectly the compulsive behavior that spins the Cycle.

The opening scene of *More Stately Mansions* eases the transition from *A Touch of the Poet* with the wake of Cornelius Melody. He and his daughter were the only ones to regard the killing of his mare as a kind of suicide. Con's death four years later confirmed their insight. He never recovered from the injury to his pride. The initial dialogue in act 1 between Jamie Cregan and Mickey Maloy restates the same information and could therefore be removed in favor of a new opening with Sara's entrance. Her return home for her father's funeral marks her first visit since the night of her father's fateful demise and her decision to seduce Simon Harford. Now she is with her husband and visibly pregnant. Simon holds another child, and they mention that they left two more at their home. Sara and Simon interact happily and lovingly, the only instance in the play in which their relationship seems uncomplicated, and thus establish a baseline for their marriage from which each will drift in future scenes.

Scenically, Melody Tavern represents the point of origin from which Sara departs on her quest to rise in the world. Subsequent scenes show her in the living room of her own home, then at the Harford mansion after she has taken possession, and finally at Simon's office with plans and drawings for an even more extravagant estate tacked upon the wall. Sara becomes more expansive, too, with each scene change: physically provocative and emotionally desperate with her accumulation of vast fineries. The increase in wealth degrades her spirit.

Inclusion of the opening scene necessitates extensive cuts elsewhere in the text in order to maintain a comparable playing length with the Gierow/Gallup version. Reduction of Deborah's monologue in the second scene at the cabin, the first scene in the Gierow/Gallup version, helps, but elimination of the following scene (2.1, or 1.2 in Gierow/Gallup), the first of three scenes set in Deborah's garden, offers an elegant solution. The scene adds more exposition (four years have passed since the end of the previous scene) with the news of the death of Simon's father/Deborah's husband, Henry Harford, and reveals his reckless speculations in land that nearly destroyed his shipping company. Nicholas Gadsby, the family attorney from the previous play, and Joel Harford, Simon's brother, discuss the catastrophe before they urge Deborah to approach Simon and beg him to save the company from financial ruin. The latter half of the scene displays the eccentricities of Deborah and her reluctance to visit her son after their previous meeting at the cabin.

Cutting the garden scene in its entirety does not detract from the narrative of the play in any way. Deborah and Joel visit Simon and Sara in the next scene (2.2) and make the enticing offer to run the company and inherit the mansion. It is clear that they do so because of the poor shape in which Harford, Sr., left the business. Simon and Sara discuss Harford's death and the rumors of demise circling about the company even before Deborah and Joel arrive. Excision of act 2, scene 1 would eliminate a character (Gadsby) who only appears in one other scene and also remove repetitive evidence that Deborah behaves oddly. She firmly established her fantastical life in eighteenth-century French memoirs in the preceding scene with her son. Simon humiliated her in that encounter and motivated the grudge she bears against him throughout the rest of the play.

Additional cuts in the later garden scenes between Deborah and Simon further reduce the role and influence of Deborah in the play and tighten the focus upon Sara and the themes of greed and materialism. Sara must curb her habits and sacrifice what she wants in order to save Simon. The entire production leads to that moment of decision. Exchanges between Simon and Deborah threaten to dilute and derail the main action. As noted in Chapter 1, O'Neill observed early in his writing process that *More Stately Mansions* was beginning to develop around Deborah, and his obsession with that character undoubtedly led to the creation of "Greed of the Meek," with Deborah as a young woman prior to her marriage to Henry Harford. Martha Gilman Bower claimed that O'Neill's suppressed feelings about his mother provided a rich subtext for *More Stately Mansions,* and she sees the fractious relationship between Simon and Deborah as a forerunner of the mother-son dynamic portrayed just a few years later in *Long Day's Journey Into Night.* In that play, Mary catches herself saying it might have been better if Edmund had not been born. In the Cycle play, Deborah viciously tells Simon that his birth enslaved her and ruined her life.[10] What remains a choked subject in the later play is verbal abuse in the earlier one. Simon blames his mother for abandoning him emotionally and physically as a child and longs for his mother to reclaim him. Deborah cannot forgive Simon for growing up, marrying a woman (Sara) who is quite different from her, and leaving her with a husband with whom she shares no common interests. That Simon takes over her husband's business and abandons his literary and political dreams for creating a new society strikes Deborah as horribly ironic and further alienates her. She retreats behind her garden wall, never ventures outside, and creates dream fantasies of herself as King Louis' favorite courtesan. Excessive attention to Deborah and the conflict between mother and son in *More Stately Mansions* threaten to detract from the central story as O'Neill, in Bower's words, "empties his own sicknesses into the minds of his characters."[11]

Two other scenes in Deborah's garden, act 3, scene 2 and act 4, scene 2 (2.2 and 3.2 in Gierow/Gallup), remain vital to the action but require pruning to maintain primary focus upon Sara. As in the shortened version, the first of the two remaining garden scenes can do away with the children's parts. The young boys, Jonathan, Ethan, Wolfe, and Honey, all gather around Deborah as she reads Byron's poetry to them and encourages each one of them to pursue his own independent dreams. Simon and Sara discuss her influence over them earlier in act 3, scene 1, so there is no need to repeat the same information with four child actors. O'Neill's portrayal of little Mary in *Beyond the Horizon* is painful to witness, and the adolescents in *More Stately Mansions* receive no better treatment. O'Neill has no feel for how to dramatize children, and their dialogue is woodenly awkward. Act 3, scene 2 could easily begin with Simon's interruption of Deborah reading poetry aloud. After that, however, more than thirty pages of dialogue can be cut in half by eliminating many of the opening salvos between them and forwarding to Simon's childhood memories of his mother outside her summerhouse and the magical story of the prince who stood forever outside a door (372–406). Similarly, a large section of the final scene (4.2, pp. 511–33), depicting their second meeting in Deborah's garden, can be halved. Extensive cuts of repetitive dialogue from their previous encounter sharpen the line of attack here in which Simon successfully pleads for his mother to open the summerhouse door and lead him across the threshold.

Sara's intervention precipitates the end of the play, but several edits could tighten the transition, focus properly on Sara, and forecast the future. After Deborah finally pushes Simon away, enters her summerhouse, and closes the door behind her, she does not come out again. In Bower's unexpurgated version, she comes back as utterly mad, but there is no dramatic payoff for the confirmation of what that entrance into the summerhouse has always implied. Moreover, just as Con's exit through the barroom door at the end of *A Touch of the Poet* signified a kind of death, so does Deborah's decision to leave by herself in *More Stately Mansions*. Sara is left onstage to cradle Simon, lament what she has done, and make promises for what she will do to make amends in the future. The play is over at this moment (544–45).

As a whole, the epilogue is a tedious affair that once again brings the four sons of Sara and Simon onstage to present a great deal of exposition even as time is running out for an audience undoubtedly looking forward to going home: Simon got brain fever after his fall and remembers nothing;

Deborah never recovered her wits and died recently; the company imploded; and Simon and Sara are now as poor as Job's turkey. In her big speech in act 4, Sara suggested that the company would face bankruptcy, and Deborah died for all intents when she went into her summerhouse. As for Simon, brain fever is an awful contrivance to contract as an excuse for Sara and sons to tell him what he missed. A simple solution would be to splice just the final page of the epilogue, hopes for the future of her four sons, onto Sara's long speech in act 4, scene 2 that finishes with her promise to let Simon plan his book "that will save the world and free men from the curse of greed" (544–45). At the same time, Sara wants each son to fulfill the dreams that her husband held for them in shipping, banking, politics, and railroads—all subsidiary businesses and pursuits that could have supported and uplifted Simon's business. Simon's company no longer exists, but Sara's compulsion thrives. The poignancy of this conclusion compounds the sense that the cycle of greed is far from done.

A number of theatrical possibilities could further help to shorten the play. O'Neill always sketched designs and groundplans for his plays. One drawing for *A Touch of the Poet* in 1942 shows the interior of Melody Tavern as though it were the section of a dollhouse (Fig. 11). The bottom floor shows the doors, tables, and chairs of the dining room; the top floor exposes the bed where Simon convalesces. O'Neill conceived the same device in 1924 with the dollhouse staging of *Desire Under the Elms*. O'Neill's plan and Robert Edmund Jones's design produced exterior walls that could be removed to show the kitchen or the parlor room downstairs, or the two bedrooms upstairs. In the sketch for *A Touch of the Poet*, O'Neill later crossed out the upstairs space with two intersecting lines as though he changed his mind about the idea of having all spaces visible. He probably made that decision during the final draft of the play after he had decided to make Simon an offstage character.

O'Neill's scheme of two visible spaces could work quite effectively at the start of *More Stately Mansions*. He specifies that mourners keen over Melody's corpse in an upstairs and offstage bedroom. If Con's body, laid out in his bright red British officer's uniform, were visible, the audience could deduce what had happened in the four prior years and forgo the need for expository dialogue. Nora could perform the highly theatrical keen in the upstairs bedroom and therefore be in no position to hear Simon and Sara

FIGURE 11. O'Neill's drawing for *A Touch of the Poet* in February 1942, the year in which he completed a fourth and final draft of the play. Although he decided not to expose the upstairs bedroom to view, his design concept might work very well for the opening act of *More Stately Mansions* at Melody Tavern. (Courtesy of Eugene O'Neill Papers, Yale Collection of American Literature, Beinecke Rare Book and Manuscript Library. Copyright © Yale University. All rights reserved.)

knock at the door to begin the play. Sara comments about the primitive nature of keening, and she does not appreciate that it is an Irish ritual from bygone days that seems quite foreign and antiquated in America. Happily married to a Yankee from a wealthy family, Sara does not welcome any reminder of her Irish heritage. Tellingly, though, Sara's speech reverts to brogue in moments of high stress and anxiety, and, try as she might, she cannot completely eradicate her cultural and ethnic background. She hates the ignorant Irish, much as her father did, but she loves her mother dearly. While she holds a grudge against her father, she wants badly to avenge what happened to him at the hands of the Yankees. Sara may complain about the Irish and their primitive customs, but at the same time she never drops the pride of being not only her mother's daughter, but also her father's.

Melody's body, laid out and mourned, provides more than a transition from one play to the next. It also makes a strong visual statement about the nature of human endeavor. His uniform insults the regular Irish who lounge at his tavern, but it is an equal affront to the Yankees in his new country. The British tossed Con out of the army, but Con's triumph in his life came at the battle of Talavera against Napoleon's forces during the Peninsular War. Combined, *A Touch of the Poet* and *More Stately Mansions* refer to Napoleon almost fifty times. Deborah mocks Simon at times by teasing him as a "Napoleon of finance," but Simon and Sara take the title seriously. Simon embarks on his mission to separate his wife from the thrall of his mother as if it were a Napoleonic campaign. He congratulates himself on his own cunning strategy as though he were the Little Emperor. Yet, from *A Touch of the Poet* to *More Stately Mansions*, Con's bright red uniform provides an iconic image for the victorious side. The "Napoleon of business" collapses by the end of the Cycle. The sneer that Sara thinks she still sees on her father's dead lips persists as an indelible "I told you so."

Pantomimic action could replace Deborah's histrionic monologues and further reduce the running time of the play. Deborah makes her initial entrance outside Simon's cabin by the lake near Melody Tavern and waits for her son to meet her there. A very long monologue recounts her fantasies and obsessions with eighteenth-century French memoirs. By the end, O'Neill directs that "she dreams aloud to herself" (208). It would be theatrically effective and economical if she were to perform the entire introductory scene as an elaborate ballet in which she plays the part of her imaginary king's lover. Simon regards her as a consummate actress, and this opportunity would foreground that aspect of her character. At the end of the exchange with her son, Simon expresses disgust for his mother's fantasies. Deborah could resume her pantomime after he leaves, but cut herself short with her final resolution: "I will never dream again! Never! Not if I have to pluck my idiot brain from my skull! [. . .] After all, what else can you do now, Deborah? You would always hear his laughter" (239).

The juxtaposition of Deborah's silent action with Simon's pointed insult highlights the injury to her pride that Deborah never forgives. Her long monologue that begins the final scene of act 4 could be handled similarly. Initial stage directions describe "a pitiful aspect about her of an old portrait of a bygone age come back to haunt the scene of long-past assignation" (485). As in the earlier scene, she waits for Simon to arrive, but there is no need for her to retain all the lines that voice her outrage and anxiety over a perceived affront. By the end of her speech she lapses into a dream state again and attempts to recall her fantasies, but if she were to panto-mime these visions it could effectively and economically show the ravages of time upon her body and mind.

In both of the above scenes, Sara spies upon Deborah from a distance and then makes her presence known to her adversary. In the first example, Sara hides inside the cabin and comes out to threaten her with physical violence. At the same time, Deborah does not know the depth of Sara's love for Simon. In the final scene, encouraged by Simon, Sara watches Deborah in her garden and waits for a chance to destroy her fragile rival. Sara realizes that she is wrong to flaunt her superior strength against a weak opponent. In O'Neill's text, Sara is upstage of Deborah and faces the audience. It would strengthen Sara's role as a witness, however, if she were downstage of Deborah and enabled the theatrical audience to see the ac-tion from her point of view. The reversal of perspective would render the cabin no longer as a façade behind which Sara listens to the private con-versation between Simon and Deborah. Instead, Sara joins the audience and the upstage area becomes a vast panorama, perhaps, of the lake and surrounding woods. In another style of production, an open area upstage might reveal the theatrical trappings of the space.

While *A Touch of the Poet* adheres to a realistic style of presentation, *More Stately Mansions* embraces many of the theatrical motifs with which O'Neill had experimented years earlier, particularly the thought asides of *Strange Interlude*. In that play, O'Neill juxtaposed dialogue with other speeches de-signed to reflect private or inner thoughts and thus offset public speech to show the differences and further create the illusion of surface and depth. Thought asides in *More Stately Mansions* appear only in act 3, scene 3 to disclose the inner thoughts and feelings of characters that would normally remain hidden. More theatrically, they show the deleterious effects of greed and possessiveness as they metastasize in the principal characters. They begin to transform into monsters. Travis Bogard complained that the differences in style between the two adjacent Cycle plays represented flaws in construction.[12] The alterations exist on a continuum, however, and increase in kind and number from *A Touch of the Poet* to *More Stately*

Mansions as the sickness of greed and materialism spreads. They do not begin until Deborah lures Simon back to her by offering him her dead husband's company, and she appeals to Sara's greed by deeding the Harford mansion to her. These enticements breed distrust and exact a severe physical and emotional toll upon all three of them. The strain is evident when they come together in the living room of the Harford mansion for the last scene of act 3, the last time prior to the final scene in which they all appear together.

Each character sits in a separate area and attempts to concentrate on a private activity and block awareness of the room's other inhabitants. Sara pretends to work on a needlepoint; Simon and Deborah both feign to read a book. Most of the scene is a series of inner monologues or thought asides as each one tries to plot an advantage over the others. Simon vents his displeasure that his wife and mother have joined forces, taken over the children, almost forced him out of his happy home, and consigned him to his office at the company. He considers strategies to strengthen his position and get the women back on his side. Deborah and Sara gloat over their conquest of Simon, but, at the same time, they do not trust the new alliance that they have forged. They make up in the scene but still eye each other suspiciously and look for signs of weakness that they can exploit to win Simon back without having to share him.

Visually, the scene follows a choreographed pattern. First, the three are separate, and then the women come together and sit. Simon complains that he cannot distinguish between the two of them, and they next approach him and surround him on both sides and threaten to suffocate him emotionally. Defeated by the two women, Simon retreats from the battlefield of the living room to the privacy of his study to draw up a new counterattack to recoup his loss. Meanwhile, Deborah and Sara break apart with mutual distrust and a resolve to vanquish each other in the future.

The clarity of the physical relationships makes the full articulation of each thought aside unnecessary. Rather than present the text as a succession of discrete speeches, it would be highly theatrical and emotionally compelling to overlap the competing monologues to achieve a choral effect. Each character would not so much speak private thoughts aloud as appeal to the theatrical audience for sympathy and support for righteous supremacy. Obviously, an audience might lose its capacity to understand each claim in its entirety through the din of up to three simultaneous speeches. It could not fail to get the point of each plea, though, and the compression from narrative sequence to theatrical simultaneity would reduce the playing time even as it amplified the dramatic impact.

The following scene, the first of two in the last act, presents Sara's hollow victory. She has now colonized Simon's office to look as though it were a brothel. Sara dresses, not in business attire, but as a prostitute, and the purpose and function of the gaudy couch, not present in the prior office scene of act 3, scene 1, leaves little room to the imagination or to the possibility for misinterpretation. Once again, the lengthy monologue that opens the scene, this time by Sara, can be significantly trimmed because of the dynamic sequence of images that follow: the degraded relationship of husband and wife; the hard analogy between the trade of business and that of prostitution; Sara's interrogation of the banker Tenard, which affirms her affinity for business surpassing that of her husband; and a quick reversal of thought with Sara's desperate plea to stop work and the protest that she has finally earned enough.

The dizzying pace of the action complements the image that hangs over the scene—Sara's plans for her impossibly ornate Irish-castle-in-Spain. Even as she tries to reify her illusions of grandeur, she begins to see the empty folly in vain and greedy exploits. But Simon is just as determined to make her continue as she is to stop. By the end of the scene they appear to be driving each other into a kind of madness, and it is clear that there will never be a point at which they can rest and say that enough is enough. Simon will keep going until he breaks down completely in an effort to transfer all of the risks and debts and wild profligacy of the company to his wife. The moral and spiritual bankruptcy of the two Harfords is most evident in this penultimate scene, which displays their greatest signs and prospects of material and financial success. The images and plans for the enormous estate are enough to make Simon's reading of the poem by Oliver Wendell Holmes, from which the title comes, redundant.

Sara nearly collapses under the weight of the mansion that she imagines in her mind. By the time the final scene (4.2) starts, O'Neill's stage directions describe her as "worn out and dissipated, with dark circles under her eyes, her hair disheveled, her dress wrinkled and awry, like a prostitute the morning after a debauch" (469–70). At the end of *A Touch of the*

Poet, Sara tries to prevent her father from entering the barroom to join his rowdy countrymen. Con admonishes his daughter to let him go, and she finally relents. In truth, though, she never really let him go in her mind, and Sara carried the image of her father with her for years, along with the desire to avenge his humiliation at the hands of the Harfords. If she could accumulate enough money, if she could live in a big enough house, then the slights against her father that rubbed off onto her would fade away. She remembered the insults against him as though they had been levied against her. But by the end of *More Stately Mansions* she learns a lesson that she must let go in order to possess herself and not grasp for that which lies beyond her. Despite her advantage of physical strength versus Deborah, Sara relinquishes her hold on Simon and surrenders to his mother in a fleeting gesture of genuine humility.

The six hours, more or less, that it would take to perform *A Touch of the Poet* and a re-edited version of *More Stately Mansions* qualify as, in a term phrased by Jonathan Kalb, "marathon theater." Kalb mentions *Strange Interlude* in his book as one example and discusses a number of other works that resist the normal reductionism that comes with the hectic pace of contemporary life today.[13] The boredom that might creep into a long performance that features repetition and a tortoise-like pace is a necessary part of the experience. Kalb does not discuss any other O'Neill play, but he does devote significant space to Tony Kushner's *Angels in America.* Like O'Neill's extant Cycle plays, the first part of Kushner's epic, *Millennium Approaches,* is much better known and more often produced than the second part, *Perestroika.* It is often anthologized or staged independently, as if to suggest that a touch of *Angels* were enough to get the full effect. But surely an audience deserves to see the other half of the story about the refusal to stand still and halt human progress. Just so, an audience for *A Touch of the Poet* ought to stick around to see how Sara responds to the death of her father, a marriage proposal, and a jealous prospective mother-in-law. Kushner, an unadulterated O'Neill fan, once wrote that *More Stately Mansions* "reveals the cycle's true nature; it is an illimitable, encyclopedic work, a monstrous invention."[14] Now, with a revised focus on Sara Melody, a theater could stage the extant Cycle in repertory, either as two successive plays or as part of a single marathon performance.

Contemporary audiences might see their own daily struggles played out in an epic production of *A Tale of Possessors Self-Dispossessed—A Touch of the Poet* followed by *More Stately Mansions.* In the greedy times of today, the divide in the United States between citizens appears vividly represented in geographic terms: red states versus blue states. The one has nothing to do with the other, according to news pundits, and the inhabitants of each region might as well speak different languages. The action of O'Neill's Cycle plays can remind an audience that the deepest divides are not between people but within themselves. Deborah willfully decides to dwell in the past rather than embrace come what may in the future. Simon kills the best parts of himself to triumph in business. And, at the apex of this triangular relationship, Sara Melody Harford tries to balance her desire to accumulate great wealth and build a lavish estate with devoted love for her husband and children. She chooses love over money, though she stumbles and cannot completely commit to one course of action. She gives up materialism for herself and for Simon, but she struggles to let go of dreams for her sons to carve profits from the country. Still, Sara goes a long way to make amends for the harm she has done. Time draws nigh for the great work of the Cycle to begin.

THE ELEVEN-PLAY LINEUP: "A TALE OF POSSESSORS SELF-DISPOSSESSED"

"Lament for Possessors Self-Dispossessed" (9-play Cycle)
"A Touch of the Poet" (5- and 7-play Cycle)

1. "Give Me Liberty and—"
    "The Poor in Spirit"
    "The Pride of the Meek"
2. "The Rebellion of the Humble"
    "The Rights of Man"
    "The Patience of the Meek"
3. "Greed of the Meek"
    "Greed of the Meek" (9-play Cycle, destroyed 1944)
    "And Give Me Death" (9-play Cycle)
4. "And Give Me Death"
    "And Give Me Death" (9-play Cycle, destroyed 1944)
    "Greed of the Meek" (8-play Cycle)
5. *A Touch of the Poet*
    "The Hair of the Dog" (5- and 7-play Cycle)
6. *More Stately Mansions*
    "Brahma or Nothing" (1941, considered)
    "Oh, Sour-Apple Tree"

7. *The Calms of Capricorn* (scenario)
8. "The Earth Is the Limit"
9. "Nothing Is Lost but Honor"
10. "The Man on Iron Horseback"
    "Hail, My Columbia!"
    "My Gem of the Sea"
11. "The Hair of the Dog"
    "Twilight of Possessors Self-Dispossessed" (7-play Cycle)
    "Bessie Bowen" (various iterations)
    "On to Betelgeuse"
    "It Cannot Be Mad?"

CHRONOLOGY OF THE CYCLE

1927	Bermuda (Spithead)	Outlines "Billionaire"/ "It Cannot Be Mad?" (Aug.)
1928	Guéthary, France	Begins scenario, "It Cannot Be Mad?" (Oct.)
1929	Cap d'Ail (French Riviera)	Changes title to "On to Betelgeuse" (Feb.)
	Saint-Antoine-du-Rocher (Château du Plessis)	Sets aside to write *Mourning Becomes Electra* (May)
1931	Northport, Long Island	Idea for "clipper-ship play" (June) Notes for "Betelgeuse" (July)
1933	Sea Island, GA (Casa Genotta)	Notes for "The Life of Bessie Bowen" (formerly "On to Betelgeuse") (Jan.) Clipper-ship title: *The Calms of Capricorn* (March)
1934		Notes for "Career of Bessie Bowen" (Nov.)
1935		1st mention of "Cycle" in *Work Diary*—outlines plays about 4 brothers: *The Calms of Capricorn*, "The

		Earth Is the Limit," "Nothing Is Lost but Honor," and "The Man on Iron Horseback" (Jan.)
		Expands Cycle to 5 plays, writes scenario for new first play about how their parents met, "The Hair of the Dog" (later renamed *A Touch of the Poet*) (Feb.)
		Expands Cycle, writes scenario for 2nd play of 6, *More Stately Mansions*, about the lives of their parents (March)
		Scenario for *The Calms of Capricorn* (May)
		Outlines other 3 plays about the brothers (June–Aug.)
		Expands Cycle, decides to add "Bessie Bowen" material as 7th and final play, "Twilight of Possessors Self-Dispossessed" (Aug.)
		Expands Cycle to 8 plays with new first play about the boys' grandmother, "Greed of the Meek" (Sept.)
1935–1936		1st draft, "The Hair of the Dog" (Nov.–March)
1936		Begins 1st draft, "Greed of the Meek" (March–June)
		Notes and outline for "And Give Me Death," new 1st play in expanded 9-play Cycle (June)
		2nd draft, "The Hair of the Dog" (June–Aug.)
		Finishes 1st draft, "Greed of the Meek" (Aug.)
		1st draft, *More Stately Mansions* (act 1) (Sept.)
	Seattle, WA	Receives news of Nobel Prize (Nov.)
1936–1937	Oakland, CA (Merritt Hospital)	Appendicitis, then near-fatal infection (Dec.–March)
1937	Berkeley, CA	Resumes work on Cycle (May)
	Lafayette, CA (Woods House)	Drafts Harford family tree (July)

		Rearranges titles of plays in 9-play Cycle (Aug.)
		1st draft, "Greed of the Meek" (formerly "And Give Me Death") (Aug.–Dec.)
1938	Danville, CA (Tao House)	1st draft, *More Stately Mansions* (April–Sept.)
1938–1939		2nd draft, *More Stately Mansions* (Sept.–Jan.)
1939		3rd draft, *More Stately Mansions* (Jan.)
		3rd draft, *A Touch of the Poet* (formerly "The Hair of the Dog") (Jan.–May)
		Prologue, *The Calms of Capricorn* (May)
		Destroys prologue (June)
1940		Cycle expands to 11 plays with decision to split "Greed of the Meek" and "And Give Me Death" into 4 normal-size plays: outlines "Give Me Liberty and—," "The Rebellion of the Humble," "Greed of the Meek" (new), "And Give Me Death" (new) (Oct.–Nov.)
1941		Discards idea of working Three Sisters into *A Touch of the Poet* and *More Stately Mansions;* considers "Brahma or Nothing" as new title for the latter play (Sept.–Oct.)
1942		4th draft, *A Touch of the Poet* (Feb.–Nov.)
1944		Destroys 1st drafts of "Greed of the Meek" and "And Give Me Death" from 9-play version of Cycle (Feb.)
1951	Marblehead Neck, MA	O'Neills send to Yale University typescripts of *A Touch of the Poet, More Stately Mansions, Long Day's Journey Into Night, Hughie, The Calms of Capricorn* (scenario), and other Cycle papers
1953	Boston (Shelton Hotel)	O'Neill dies (Nov.)

1956	New York	Donald Gallup returns typescript of *More Stately Mansions* to Carlotta Monterey O'Neill at her request (May)
1957	Stockholm	Premiere of *A Touch of the Poet* at Swedish Royal Dramatic Theatre (March)
	New York	Carlotta O'Neill gives permission to Karl Ragnar Gierow to produce shortened version of *More Stately Mansions* in Sweden
1958	New York	U.S. premiere of *A Touch of the Poet*, directed by Harold Clurman, with Eric Portman, Helen Hayes, and Kim Stanley, at Helen Hayes Theatre (Oct.)
1959	New Haven, CT	Carlotta returns original typescript of *More Stately Mansions* to Yale University (April)
1962	Stockholm	Premiere of *More Stately Mansions* at Swedish Royal Dramatic Theatre (Sept.)
1964	New Haven, CT	Publication of *More Stately Mansions*, shortened by Karl Ragnar Gierow and edited by Donald Gallup, by Yale University Press
1967	Los Angeles	U.S. premiere of *More Stately Mansions*, directed by José Quintero, with Ingrid Bergman, Arthur Hill, and Colleen Dewhurst, at Ahmanson Theatre (Sept.)
1981	New Haven, CT	Scenario of *The Calms of Capricorn*, transcribed by Donald Gallup, published by Yale University Library
1988	New York	"Unexpurgated" version of *More Stately Mansions*, edited by Martha Gilman Bower, published by Oxford University Press (Sept.)
		Bower's edited version of *More Stately Mansions* appears in *Complete Plays: 1931–1943*, 3rd volume of a three-

		volume set published by Library of America, edited by Travis Bogard (Oct.)
1997	New York	Avant-garde production of *More Stately Mansions,* using Gierow/Gallup script, directed by Ivo van Hove, with Joan MacIntosh, Tim Hopper, and Jenny Bacon, at New York Theatre Workshop
1998	New Haven, CT	Transcriptions of the Cycle papers done in the late 1960s are published for the first time by Yale University Press in Donald Gallup's *Eugene O'Neill and His Eleven-Play Cycle*
2004	New Haven, CT	*A Touch of the Poet* and the complete version of *More Stately Mansions* published together in one volume, edited by Martha Gilman Bower, by Yale University Press

NOTES

Complete citations for the works referenced below may be found in the Bibliography.

Introduction

1. O'Neill, *"A Touch of the Poet" and "More Stately Mansions,"* 463–64.

2. Mark: 8:36 (King James Version).

3. Dates for Wilson's plays indicate first copyright notice, or, in the case of *Joe Turner* and *Radio Golf,* first performance.

4. Lee, "Meaning of What You Mean Now," 2.

5. The original volumes, "1924–28," "1929–33," "1934–38," and "1939–43," referred to throughout this study are part of the Eugene O'Neill Papers, Yale Collection of American Literature (YCAL), Beinecke Rare Book and Manuscript Library, New Haven, CT (hereafter cited as WD). They were published in a limited print run as Eugene O'Neill, *Work Diary, 1924–1943,* transcribed by Donald Gallup, 2 vols. (New Haven, CT: Yale University Library, 1981).

6. WD; see entries for 2, 10, 14, 26 June 1936; 6, 7, 17 September 1936; 4 April, 12 July, 23 December 1937.

7. These figures/numbers derive from "A Chronology of Composition" (265–67), the appendix of Donald Gallup's book *Eugene O'Neill and His Eleven-Play Cycle.*

8. (*Poet* [225] + *Mansions* [350]) = 575 / total working days (575 + 445 = 1,020) = 56%.

9. 150 / (150 + 60 + 14 = 224) = 67%.

10. Simon is a principal character in the scenario and first draft of "The Hair of the Dog," later renamed *A Touch of the Poet*. See Gallup, *Eleven-Play Cycle*, 40–50.

11. Quoted in ibid., 244.

12. Williams, *Plays*, 908.

13. Williams initially published two endings, the one he first wrote and the one that Elia Kazan directed on Broadway. He later wrote and published a third version, a combination of the first two, for a production directed by Michael Kahn at the American Shakespeare Theatre in 1974.

14. Alexander Pettit observes that Ruth is much more complex and vital in the first edition of the play, which has not been reprinted since 1922. The theatrical producer and the male star made cuts for the 1920 production that reduced Ruth's role. This version was published in O'Neill's *Complete Works* in 1924 and became the basis for all subsequent editions. See Pettit, "Texts," 16–28.

15. Barlow, "O'Neill's Female Characters," 174; see also William Davies King's reviews of *A Touch of the Poet* and Synge's *The Playboy of the Western World* for apt comparisons between Sara Melody and Pegeen Mike.

16. WD, 12 January 1937.

17. Travis Bogard and Jackson Bryer, eds., *Selected Letters of Eugene O'Neill* (New Haven: Yale University Press, 1988; New York: Limelight Editions, 1994), 467 (hereafter cited as SL).

18. Carlotta Monterey O'Neill Diary, Eugene O'Neill Papers.

19. Bogard, *"From the Silence of Tao House,"* 150; Gelb and Gelb, "O'Neill's Elephant Opus," 111–12; Floyd, *Plays of Eugene O'Neill*, 380; Berlin, "Late Plays," 83; Gallup, *Eleven-Play Cycle*, 3; Bower, *O'Neill's Unfinished Threnody*, 7.

20. O'Neill received the Nobel Prize for Literature in 1936. As of this writing, he remains the only American playwright to win the prestigious award.

21. Gallup, Prefatory Note, x.

22. Bower, Introduction to *More Stately Mansions*, 17; Black, *O'Neill*, 407.

23. Bower, *"More Stately Mansions* Redux," 241.

24. Bogard, *Contour* (1988), 461.

25. Gallup, *Eleven-Play Cycle*, xi.

26. Brustein, *Theatre of Revolt*, viii.

27. "A Brief History of Yale University Press," https://yalebooks.yale.edu/brief-history-yale-university-press#III (accessed 15 April 2020).

28. Brustein, *Theatre of Revolt*, 359.

29. Ibid.

30. Sheaffer, *O'Neill*, 482–83.

Chapter 1. From Spithead to Tao House

1. WD, 20 January 1935.

2. *Mourning Becomes Electra*, in Eugene O'Neill, *Complete Plays*, ed. Travis Bogard (New York: Library of America, 1988), vol. 2 (hereafter cited as CP2), 903.

3. Ibid., 907.

4. Ibid., 990.

5. Robert M. Dowling observed that Robert Edmond Jones's design evoked an image of the four chambers of the human heart. See *Eugene O'Neill,* 293. Special thanks to Patrick Midgley for bringing this to my attention.

6. SL, 433–34.

7. *Mourning Becomes Electra,* CP2, 987.

8. *The Hairy Ape,* CP2, 126–27.

9. *Mourning Becomes Electra,* CP2, 993.

10. Ibid., 909–10.

11. Ibid.

12. Ibid., 972.

13. Ibid., 1023.

14. Ibid., 1024.

15. WD, 20 June 1931.

16. *Desire Under the Elms,* CP2, 321.

17. Donald Gallup noted the anachronism of Simon reading the poem to Sara in act 4, scene 1 (3.1 in the Gierow/Gallup version), set in 1841. Holmes did not write "The Chambered Nautilus" until 1858. See Gallup, Prefatory Note, vii fn.

18. Floyd, *O'Neill at Work,* 168.

19. Ibid., 169.

20. Sheaffer, *O'Neill,* 441.

21. *Days Without End,* in Eugene O'Neill, *Complete Plays,* ed. Travis Bogard (New York: Library of America, 1988), vol. 3 (hereafter cited as CP3), 158.

22. Ibid., 161.

23. WD, 9 March 1935.

24. SL, 423.

25. Ibid., 454.

26. Ibid., 472–73. Shane O'Neill did not matriculate at Duke University.

27. Ibid., 452.

28. *New York Times,* 22 November 1936.

29. SL, 467.

30. Ibid., 468.

31. Ibid., 488.

32. Ibid., 507.

33. Ibid., 508.

34. Ibid., 517.

35. Ibid., 550.

36. Ibid., 551.

37. Ibid., 552.

38. Crichton, "O'Neill and the Iceman," 188.

39. Wilson, "O'Neill on the World," 164–65.

40. Basso, "Profiles," 231.

41. Ibid., 236.

42. Dowling, *O'Neill*, 474.

43. Peck, "Talk"; Gelb and Gelb, *O'Neill*, 938.

44. Sheaffer, *O'Neill*, 667; Dowling, *O'Neill*, 471; Gelb and Gelb, *By Women Possessed*, 730; Gelb and Gelb, *O'Neill*, 938.

45. Quoted in Bogard, *Contour* (1972), 369.

Chapter 2. Løvborg's Lost Manuscript

1. Ibsen, *Hedda Gabler*, 286.

2. Ibid., 288.

3. SL, 477.

4. Gelb and Gelb, *By Women Possessed*, 729; *O'Neill*, 938.

5. Gage, *A Place for Us*, 320.

6. Gage earned a master's degree in journalism from Columbia University and later worked as an investigative reporter for the *Wall Street Journal* and the *New York Times*.

7. Gage, *A Place for Us*, 320.

8. Black, *O'Neill*, 504; Pfister, *Staging Depth*, xxiv; CP3, 990.

9. Bogard, *Contour* (1972), 369.

10. Chekhov, *Uncle Vanya*, 243.

11. SL, 449.

12. Ibid., 447.

13. Ibid., 486–87.

14. Ibid., 488.

15. Bergman, "Ingrid Bergman," 212–14. Bergman's recollection of meeting O'Neill originally appeared in Virginia Floyd, "A Meeting with O'Neill," *Eugene O'Neill: A World View* (New York: Frederick Ungar, 1979), 293–96.

16. Nathan, "O'Neill after Twelve Years," 176.

17. Gallup, "A tale," 189.

18. SL, 311.

19. Ibid., 312.

20. O'Neill, *"As Ever, Gene,"* 87 fn4.

21. SL, 317.

22. Performance review, *New York Times*, 9 January 1934.

23. See *New York Times*, 13 September 1935; 11 August 1936; 30 May 1937; 25 July 1940; 5 September 1940.

24. WD, 21 May 1941.

25. Gallup, *Eleven-Play Cycle*, 9.

26. Ibsen, *Hedda Gabler*, 260.

27. Floyd, *O'Neill at Work*, xiii–xiv.

28. Manheim, *O'Neill's New Language*, 226, n8.

29. Bower, *"More Stately Mansions* Redux," 239–40.

30. Wilde, *Importance of Being Earnest*, 315.

Chapter 3. The Remainder in the Middle

1. Diggins, *O'Neill's America*, 111.

2. Gallup, Prefatory Note, x; "A tale," 180; *Eleven-Play Cycle*, 262–63; Dowling, *O'Neill*, 434; Sheaffer, *O'Neill*, 667.

3. Gelb and Gelb, "Behind the Scenes," 111–12.

4. Brietzke, *Aesthetics of Failure*, 232.

5. Dowling, *O'Neill*, 462; he settled for "Rest in Peace," 474.

6. Gelb and Gelb, *By Women Possessed*, 729.

7. Bergman, "Ingrid Bergman," 213.

8. SL, 570.

9. Commins, *"Love and Admiration,"* 218.

10. Gelb and Gelb, *By Women Possessed*, 748.

11. Gallup, Prefatory Note, x.

12. See "Strindberg and Our Theatre" and "The Nobel Prize Acceptance Letter" in O'Neill, *Unknown O'Neill*, 386–88, 426–28.

13. Peck, "Talk with Mrs. O'Neill." This was the same interview in which Carlotta described burning the Cycle manuscripts at the Shelton Hotel.

14. Gelb, "Drama by O'Neill."

15. Gallup, Prefatory Note, xi.

16. Ibid., xii.

17. Barnes, Performance review, *More Stately Mansions*.

18. This audio version is accessible through the excellent website of Dr. Harley Hammerman. The Hammerman Collection and the Oneill.com website are now part of the Modern Literature Collection at Washington University in St. Louis. A copy of the Los Angeles / Broadway production script is part of the Hammerman Collection and is also available at the New York Library for the Performing Arts, Billy Rose Theatre Division.

19. Gallup, *Pigeons*, 305.

20. O'Neill, "More Stately Mansions," LA / Broadway typescript, act 4, scene 2, page 15.

21. Gelb, "New O'Neill Drama"; "Drama by O'Neill."

22. *Amadeus*, directed by Milos Forman, screenplay by Peter Shaffer from his play.

23. Bower, Introduction to *More Stately Mansions: The Unexpurgated Edition*, 17.

24. O'Neill, *More Stately Mansions: The Unexpurgated Edition*, 49 fn6.

25. WD, 21 December 1937.

26. Elizabeth Shepley Sergeant Papers.

27. Bogard, *"From the Silence of Tao House,"* 141.

28. Maufort, Review, 850.

29. Rothstein, "O'Neill Centenary."

30. Bogard, *Contour* (1988), 379 fn. In his later discussion of *More Stately Mansions* (400–412), Bogard once references the "unpublished first scene" (406), but exclusively quotes from the shortened Gierow/Gallup version of 1964.

31. For Bower's story, see her 2004 article in the *Eugene O'Neill Review*, "*More Stately Mansions* Redux." Also, see Gelb and Gelb, "Twisted Path" and "Behind the Scenes"; Gallup, *Eleven-Play Cycle*, 7.

32. Brustein, "Ruined Colossus."

33. Drukman, "Off the Spike."

34. Ibid.

Chapter 4. Sara Melody and the American Dream

1. Bowen, "Black Irishman," 204.

2. Clark, *Eugene O'Neill*, 142.

3. Shaughnessy, *Down the Nights*, 49.

4. Michael Manheim termed these oppositions the "rhythm of kinship" in *Eugene O'Neill's New Language of Kinship*.

5. O'Neill, *"A Touch of the Poet" and "More Stately Mansions,"* 393. Citations to the two extant Cycle plays refer to this combined volume, edited by Martha Gilman Bower, and all further references to these two plays will be placed parenthetically in the text.

6. Shaughnessy, *Down the Nights*, 171.

7. Porter, "Banished Prince Revisited," 13.

8. Quoted in Gallup, *Eleven-Play Cycle*, 244.

9. Floyd, *Plays of Eugene O'Neill*, 378, 456; Porter, "Banished Prince Revisited," 16; Bogard, *Contour* (1988), 412.

10. *Long Day's Journey Into Night*, CP3, 738.

11. Sheaffer, *O'Neill*, 470.

12. SL, 530.

13. Bower, *O'Neill's Unfinished Threnody*, 12.

14. Diggins, *Eugene O'Neill's America*, 131.

15. Shaughnessy, *Down the Nights*, 178.

16. O'Neill, *Calms of Capricorn*, 14–15.

17. Ibid.

18. Quoted in Gallup, *Eleven-Play Cycle*, 248.

19. Ibid.

Chapter 5. Climbing the Harford Family Tree

1. The other paired opposites are Land/Sea, Hate/Love, Possession/Detachment, World/Oneself, and Fear/Security. See Eugene O'Neill Papers, Box 141, Folder 2513.

2. Reaver, *O'Neill Concordance* records seven references to "slave" in *A Touch of the Poet* and fifteen more in *More Stately Mansions*. Other forms of the word, either as a noun or a verb, including plurals and past tenses, crop up eight times apiece in each play. Words that denote freedom, by contrast, including the various forms of "escape," appear even more frequently: twenty-six times in *A Touch of the Poet* and forty-nine in *More Stately Mansions*. The number of references is even more significant, however, with the realization that the *Concordance*, published in 1969, is keyed to the shortened version of *More Stately Mansions*. In Bower's complete version, the number of references to "slave" jumps from fifteen to forty-two; other forms of "slave" increase from eight to forty-two; and the mentions of free/freedom/escape more than double, from forty-nine to 108.

3. SL, 493.

4. *Desire Under the Elms*, CP2, 318.

5. Quoted in Gallup, *Eleven-Play Cycle*, 204.

6. O'Neill, *Calms of Capricorn*, 8–9.

7. Quoted in Gallup, *Eleven-Play Cycle*, 142.

8. Ibid., 36.

9. The text mistakenly refers to Jonathan's stepdaughters as daughters-in-law (69).

10. Elizabeth Shepley Sergeant Papers.

11. Quoted in Gallup, *Eleven-Play Cycle*, 153.

12. See Sara's monologue near the beginning of act 4 (454–55).

13. Pfister, *Surveyors of Customs*, 115.

14. Quoted in Gallup, *Eleven-Play Cycle*, 190.

Chapter 6. Stripped Stark Naked

1. SL, 511.

2. See Shaughnessy, *Down the Nights*, 49–50.

3. Floyd, *Plays of Eugene O'Neill*, 380; Bower, *O'Neill's Unfinished Threnody*, 7.

4. Bower, Introduction to *"A Touch of the Poet" and "More Stately Mansions,"* ix.

5. Berlin, "Late Plays," 83.

6. Bogard, *"From the Silence of Tao House,"* 143, 143–44.

7. O'Neill, *Long Day's Journey Into Night*, CP3, 783.

8. Bogard, *"From the Silence of Tao House,"* 149.

9. Ibid., 150.

10. *Long Day's Journey Into Night*, CP3, 812; *A Moon for the Misbegotten*, CP3, 874, 937.

11. Bogard, *Contour* (1988), 475.

12. Gallup, *Eleven-Play Cycle*, 3.

13. Alexander argues, for example, that O'Neill was actually thinking of Carlotta and a picture of her in a dress in her youth rather than that of his mother's actual wedding dress (*O'Neill's Last Plays*, 81).

14. Bogard, *Contour* (1988), 471–77.

15. Nathan, "Discourses on Dramatic Art," 162.

16. *Iceman Cometh*, CP3, 609, 629.

17. Ibid., 649.

18. Ibid., 570.

19. Ibid., 581.

20. *Chris Christophersen*, in Eugene O'Neill, *Complete Plays*, ed. Travis Bogard (Library of America, 1988), vol. 1 (hereafter cited as CP1), 881, 858.

21. *Iceman Cometh*, CP3, 578.

22. Ibid., 704, 635, 700.

Chapter 7. Beyond the Threshold

1. The first two plays, "Greed of the Meek" and "And Give Me Death," both double-length, existed only as handwritten first drafts. O'Neill was never satisfied with them and eventually destroyed them in 1944.

2. SL, 488.

3. *Great God Brown*, CP2, 528.

4. O'Neill, *Unknown O'Neill*, 406.

5. *Emperor Jones*, CP1, 1033.

6. In addition to the video of the performance at the New York Library for the Performing Arts, see Ryder Thornton's interviews in 2017 with the two female leads for van Hove's New York Theatre Workshop production, Joan MacIntosh and Jenny Bacon.

7. The New York Neo-Futurists, a contemporary avant-garde performance troupe, acted only O'Neill's stage directions in its hilarious production *The Complete and Condensed Stage Directions of Eugene O'Neill, Vol. 1, Early Plays / Lost Plays*, at the Kraine Theatre in the East Village, New York City, in 2011. See my article "Condensed Comedy" for analysis of that production. For a more recent take on O'Neill's varied use of stage directions, see Rowen, "Crushing Her with the Weight of His Eloquence."

8. Pfister, *Surveyors of Customs*, 117.

9. *Lazarus Laughed*, CP2, 572.

10. Crawford, *One Naked Individual*, 55; Clurman, "Group Theatre Speaks for Itself"; Clurman, *Fervent Years*, 56.

11. Clurman, *Fervent Years*, 35.

12. Ibid., 25, 69.

13. For a complete account of this production, see Shea, "Give my regards," 89–107.

Chapter 8. The *Glencairn* Template

1. Bows, Performance review, *More Stately Mansions*.

2. Cargill, *O'Neill and His Plays*, 112.

3. See SL, 338, 488, 501.

4. See Glaspell, *Road to the Temple*, 204.

5. For more on the Ford film, see my "A Vicious Cycle at Sea."

6. SL, 557–58.

7. Ibid., 503, 508, 513.

8. Gallup, Prefatory Note, xii.

9. Kahn, Blog.

10. Cf. *Long Day's Journey Into Night*, CP3, 769, 786, 790; and *More Stately Mansions*, CP3, 384, 530.

11. Bower, *O'Neill's Unfinished Threnody*, 86.

12. Bogard, *Contour* (1988), 393.

13. Kalb, *Great Lengths*, 2.

14. Kushner, "Genius of O'Neill," 252.

BIBLIOGRAPHY

Alexander, Doris. *Eugene O'Neill's Last Plays: Separating Art from Autobiography*. Athens, GA: University of Georgia Press, 2005.

Amadeus. Directed by Milos Forman. Screenplay by Peter Shaffer from his original play. Performances by Tom Hulce, F. Murray Abraham, and Jeffrey Jones. Warner Brothers, 1984. Streaming. Amazon Video, 2002.

Atkinson, Brooks. Performance review. *Days Without End. New York Times*, 9 January 1934.

———. Performance review. *A Touch of the Poet. New York Times*, 3 October 1958.

Barlow, Judith E. "O'Neill's Female Characters." In Manheim 1998, 164–77.

Barnes, Clive. Performance review. *More Stately Mansions. New York Times*, 1 November 1967.

Basso, Hamilton. "Profiles: The Tragic Sense." In Estrin 1990, 224–36.

Bergman, Ingrid. "Ingrid Bergman." In *Eugene O'Neill Remembered*. Ed. Brenda Murphy and George Monteiro. Tuscaloosa, AL: University of Alabama Press, 2017. 212–14.

Berlin, Normand. "The Late Plays." In Manheim 1988, 82–85.

Black, Stephen A. *Eugene O'Neill: Beyond Mourning and Tragedy*. New Haven, CT: Yale University Press, 1999.

Bogard, Travis. *Contour in Time: The Plays of Eugene O'Neill.* New York: Oxford University Press, 1972; rev. ed., 1988.

———. *"From the Silence of Tao House": Essays About Eugene and Carlotta O'Neill and the Tao House Plays.* Danville, CA: Eugene O'Neill Foundation, 1993.

Bowen, Croswell. "The Black Irishman." In Estrin 1990, 203–23.

Bower, Martha Gilman. *Eugene O'Neill's Unfinished Threnody and Process of Invention in Four Cycle Plays.* Lewiston, NY: Edwin Mellen Press, 1992.

———. Introduction. *More Stately Mansions: The Unexpurgated Version.* In O'Neill 1988, 3–17.

———. Introduction. *"A Touch of the Poet" and "More Stately Mansions."* In O'Neill 2004, vii–xiv.

———. *"More Stately Mansions* Redux: Straightening Out the 'Twisted Path.'" *Eugene O'Neill Review* 26 (2004): 239–47.

Bows, Bob. *More Stately Mansions.* Performance review. *Denver Post,* 21 November 2007. https://www.denverpost.com/2007/11/21/review-more-stately-mansions/. Accessed 25 August 2018.

Brietzke, Zander. *The Aesthetics of Failure: Dynamic Structure in the Plays of Eugene O'Neill.* Jefferson, NC: McFarland, 2001.

———. "Condensed Comedy: The Neo-Futurists Perform O'Neill's Stage Directions." In *Eugene O'Neill's One-Act Plays: New Critical Perspectives.* Ed. Michael Y. Bennett and Benjamin D. Carlson. New York: Palgrave Macmillan, 2012. 193–201.

———. "A Vicious Cycle at Sea." In Zander Brietzke. *American Drama in the Age of Film.* Tuscaloosa, AL: University of Alabama Press, 2007. 35–50.

Brustein, Robert. "Reclaiming a Ruined Colossus." *New Republic* 217, no. 24 (1997): 30–32.

———. *The Theatre of Revolt.* 1964. Chicago: Elephant Paperbacks, 1991.

Cargill, Oscar, N. Bryllion Fagin, and William J. Fisher, eds. *O'Neill and His Plays: Four Decades of Criticism.* New York: New York University Press, 1961.

Chekhov, Anton. *Uncle Vanya.* In *The Plays of Anton Chekhov.* Trans. Paul Schmidt. New York: HarperPerennial Modern Classics, 1998.

Clark, Barrett H. *Eugene O'Neill: The Man and His Plays.* 1926. Rev. ed. New York: Dover, 1947.

Clurman, Harold. *The Fervent Years: The Group Theatre and the Thirties.* 1945. New York: Da Capo, 1983.

———. "The Group Theatre Speaks for Itself." *New York Times,* 13 December 1931.

Commins, Dorothy, ed. *"Love and Admiration and Respect": The O'Neill–Commins Correspondence.* Durham, NC: Duke University Press, 1986.

Crawford, Cheryl. *One Naked Individual: My Fifty Years in the Theatre.* Indianapolis: Bobbs-Merrill, 1977.

Crichton, Kyle. "Mr. O'Neill and the Iceman." In Estrin 1990, 188–202.

Diggins, John Patrick. *Eugene O'Neill's America: Desire Under Democracy.* Chicago: University of Chicago Press, 2007.

Dowling, Robert M. *Eugene O'Neill: A Life in Four Acts.* New Haven, CT: Yale University Press, 2014.

Drukman, Steven. "Off the Spike and onto the Stage: An O'Neill Reject." *New York Times,* 5 October 1997.

Eisen, Kurt. *The Inner Strength of Opposites: O'Neill's Novelistic Drama and the Melodramatic Imagination.* Athens, GA: University of Georgia Press, 1994.

Estrin, Mark W., ed. *Conversations with Eugene O'Neill.* Jackson, MS: University Press of Mississippi, 1990.

Floyd, Virginia, ed. *Eugene O'Neill at Work: Newly Released Ideas for Plays.* New York: Frederick Ungar, 1981.

———. *The Plays of Eugene O'Neill: A New Assessment.* New York: Frederick Ungar, 1985.

Gage, Nicholas. *A Place for Us.* Boston: Houghton Mifflin, 1989.

Gallup, Donald. *Eugene O'Neill and His Eleven-Play Cycle.* New Haven, CT: Yale University Press, 1998.

———. Introductory Note. *The Calms of Capricorn.* In O'Neill 1981, v–xiii.

———. *Pigeons on the Granite.* New Haven, CT: Beinecke Rare Book and Manuscript Library, Yale University, 1988.

———. Prefatory Note. *More Stately Mansions.* In O'Neill 1964, i–xii.

———. "A tale of possessors self-dispossessed." In Manheim 1998, 178–91.

Gelb, Arthur. "Drama by O'Neill Slated in Sweden." *New York Times,* 27 April 1959.

———. "New O'Neill Drama Is Found by Swede." *New York Times,* 18 March 1957.

Gelb, Arthur, and Barbara Gelb. "Behind the Scenes of O'Neill's Elephant Opus." *Eugene O'Neill Review* 28 (2006): 101–12.

———. *By Women Possessed: A Life of Eugene O'Neill.* New York: Putnam, 2016.

———. *O'Neill.* 1962. Rev. ed. with new epilogue. New York: Harper and Row, 1973.

———. "The Twisted Path to *More Stately Mansions.*" *Eugene O'Neill Review* 22, nos. 1–2 (Spring/Fall 1998): 105–9.

Gilman, Richard. *The Making of Modern Drama.* 1972. New Haven, CT: Yale University Press, 1999.

Glaspell, Susan. *The Road to the Temple.* 1926. Edited and with an introduction by Linda Ben-Zvi. Jefferson, NC: McFarland, 2005.

Ibsen, Henrik. *Hedda Gabler.* In *Four Major Plays.* Vol. 1. Trans. Rolf Fjelde. New York: Signet Classics, 2006.

Kahn, Michael. Blog: "Stage Interludes from Michael Kahn." 15 February 2012. https://dctheatrescene.com/michael-kahn-on-strange-interlude/. Accessed 25 August 2018.

Kalb, Jonathan. *Great Lengths: Seven Works of Marathon Theater.* Ann Arbor, MI: University of Michigan Press, 2011.

King, William Davies. Performance review. *A Touch of the Poet* and *The Playboy of the Western World.* Eugene O'Neill Review 39, no. 1 (2018): 190–95.

Kushner, Tony. "The Genius of O'Neill." *Eugene O'Neill Review* 26 (2004): 248–56.

Lee, E. Andrew. "The Image of the Irish in the Life and Work of Eugene O'Neill." *Eugene O'Neill Review* 35, no. 2 (2014): 137–60.

———. "'The Meaning of What You Mean Now': Domestic and Psychological Spaces in *More Stately Mansions.*" *Eugene O'Neill Review* 37, no. 1 (2016): 1–20.

Manheim, Michael, ed. *The Cambridge Companion to Eugene O'Neill.* New York: Cambridge University Press, 1998.

———. *Eugene O'Neill's New Language of Kinship.* Syracuse, NY: Syracuse University Press, 1982.

Maufort, Marc. Review. *More Stately Mansions: The Unexpurgated Edition.* Ed. Martha Gilman Bower. *Belgian Review of Philology and History* 70, no. 3 (1992): 849–51.

Nathan, George Jean. "Eugene O'Neill after Twelve Years." In Estrin 1990, 174–79.

———. "Eugene O'Neill Discourses on Dramatic Art." In Estrin 1990, 161–66.

Neuberger, Richard L. "O'Neill Turns West to New Horizons." *New York Times,* 22 November 1936.

O'Neill, Eugene. *"As Ever, Gene": The Letters of Eugene O'Neill to George Jean Nathan.* Transcribed and edited by Nancy L. Roberts and Arthur W. Roberts. Rutherford, NJ: Fairleigh Dickinson University Press, 1987.

———. *The Calms of Capricorn.* The Scenario. Transcribed by Donald Gallup. New Haven, CT: Yale University Library, 1981.

———. *Complete Plays.* Ed. Travis Bogard. 3 vols. New York: Library of America, 1988.

———. *More Stately Mansions.* Shortened from the author's partly revised script by Karl Ragnar Gierow and edited by Donald Gallup. Prefatory Note by Donald Gallup. New Haven, CT: Yale University Press, 1964.

———. *More Stately Mansions.* Sound recording of 1967 Broadway production with Ingrid Bergman, Colleen Dewhurst, and Arthur Hill. New York: Caedmon, 1968. Audio Archive at http://www.eoneill.com /artifacts/flash/msm1/ msm1.htm.

———. "More Stately Mansions." Typescript. Eugene O'Neill Papers. Yale Collection of American Literature, Beinecke Rare Book and Manuscript Library, Yale University.

———. "More Stately Mansions." Typescript of Los Angeles/Broadway production script of 1967. Billy Rose Theatre Division, New York Library for the Performing Arts, Lewis B. Cullman Center.

———. *More Stately Mansions: The Unexpurgated Version.* Edited and with an introduction by Martha Gilman Bower. New York: Oxford University Press, 1988.

———. *More Stately Mansions.* Video recording. Directed by Ivo van Hove. Performances by Tim Hopper, Jenny Bacon, and Joan MacIntosh. New York Theatre Workshop: New York Public Library Theatre on Film and Tape Archive, 22 October 1997. Billy Rose Theatre Division, New York Library for the Performing Arts, Lewis B. Cullman Center.

———. *Selected Letters.* Ed. Travis Bogard and Jackson R. Bryer. New Haven, CT: Yale University Press, 1988; New York: Limelight Editions, 1994.

———. *"A Touch of the Poet" and "More Stately Mansions."* Edited and introduced by Martha Gilman Bower. New Haven, CT: Yale University Press, 2004.

———. *The Unknown O'Neill: Unpublished or Unfamiliar Writings of Eugene O'Neill.* Ed. Travis Bogard. New Haven, CT: Yale University Press, 1988.

Peck, Seymour. "Talk with Mrs. O'Neill." *New York Times,* 4 November 1956.

Pettit, Alexander. "The Texts of O'Neill's *Beyond the Horizon.*" *Eugene O'Neill Review* 35, no. 1 (2014): 15–40.

Pfister, Joel. *Staging Depth: Eugene O'Neill and the Politics of Psychological Discourse.* Chapel Hill, NC: University of North Carolina Press, 1995.

———. *Surveyors of Customs: American Literature as Cultural Analysis.* New York: Oxford University Press, 2015.

Porter, Laurin R. "The Banished Prince Revisited: A Feminist Reading of *More Stately Mansions.*" *Eugene O'Neill Review* 19, nos. 1 and 2 (1995): 7–27.

Reaver, J. Russell, ed. *An O'Neill Concordance.* 3 vols. Detroit, MI: Gale Research, 1969.

Rothstein, Mervyn. "O'Neill Centenary: Celebrating the Master." *New York Times,* 13 October 1988.

Rowen, Sarah Bess. "Crushing Her with the Weight of His Eloquence: Reconsidering the Theatricality of Eugene O'Neill's Stage Directions." *Eugene O'Neill Review* 39, no. 2 (2018): 294–312.

Sergeant, Elizabeth Shepley. Papers. Yale Collection of American Literature. Beinecke Rare Book and Manuscript Library, Yale University.

Shaughnessy, Edward L. *Down the Nights and Down the Days*. Notre Dame, IN: University of Notre Dame Press, 2000.

———. *Eugene O'Neill in Ireland: The Critical Reception*. Westport, CT: Greenwood Press, 1988.

Shea, Laura. "'Give my regards . . .': *A Touch of the Poet* on Broadway." *Eugene O'Neill Review* 37, no. 1 (2016): 89–107.

Sheaffer, Louis. *O'Neill: Son and Artist*. Vol. 2. 1973. New York: Cooper Square Press, 2002.

Skinner, Richard Dana. *Eugene O'Neill: A Poet's Quest*. 1935. New York: Russell and Russell, 1964.

Thornton, Ryder. "Stately Women in Retrospect: Actresses Jenny Bacon and Joan MacIntosh Recall Their Roles as Sara and Deborah Harford in Ivo van Hove's *More Stately Mansions*." *Eugene O'Neill Review* 38, nos. 1–2 (2017): 122–36.

Wilde, Oscar. *The Importance of Being Earnest*. In *The Norton Anthology of Drama*. Ed. J. Ellen Gainor, Stanton B. Garner, Jr., and Martin Puchner. 2nd ed. Vol. 2. New York: Norton, 2014. 307–50.

Williams, Tennessee. *Plays, 1937–1955*. New York: Library of America, 2000.

Wilson, John S. "O'Neill on the World and *The Iceman*." In Estrin 1990, 164–66.

Winther, Sophus Keith. *Eugene O'Neill: A Critical Study*. 1934. New York: Russell and Russell, 1961.

INDEX